Against Theory

Against Theory

Continental and Analytic Challenges in Moral Philosophy

Dwight Furrow

Routledge   New York and London

Published in 1995 by
Routledge
29 West 35th Street
New York, NY 10001

Published in Great Britain by
Routledge
11 New Fetter Lane
London EC4P 4EE

Library of Congress Cataloging-in-Publication Data
Furrow, Dwight.
    Against theory : continental and analytic challenges in moral philosophy /
Dwight Furrow.
        p. cm.
    Includes bibliographical references and index.
    ISBN 0-415-91079-X (cloth). — ISBN 0-415-91080-3 (pbk.)
    1. Ethics, Modern—20th century. 2. Postmodernism. I. Title.
    BJ324.P67F87 1995
170—dc20   95-8031
                                                                    CIP

To Lynn

Contents

Preface

This book emerged from an abiding belief in the importance of ethics, and perplexity regarding its nature. For me, the field of ethics has always been a field of conflict in which deeply held beliefs and wild beatings of the chest feebly confront abject suffering; where often the best exemplars are inarticulate, and eloquence mere hypocrisy. My own perplexity has led me to feel a general dissatisfaction with the inflated claims of philosophical ethics. The most important thing to know is how fragile our moral judgments can be; what small comfort they provide; yet how essential to our humanity they are.

Although Chapter One is a review of antitheory arguments, subsequent chapters are each organized around the work of a contemporary philosopher whose thought brings to the surface the conflictual and sometimes tragic dimension of this complex and troubled domain. My ideas are enhanced by working through the texts of someone whose thinking is far more agile than my own. Thus, I employ a good deal of critical exegesis, using interpretations of others to generate my own conclusions. Readers already familiar with these writers under discussion, and impatient with exegesis might need only browse these sections, although I would guess that some of the interpretations will be surprising. The interpretations are, in any case, central to the argument of the book.

I owe a special debt of gratitude to Bernd Magnus, whose guidance, generosity, and wisdom have been a constant source of inspiration and insight. I would also like to thank John Fischer, Alexander Rosenberg, and Georgia Warnke, who have read and commented helpfully on this manuscript at various stages in its development. Finally, I have benefited

greatly from discussions with the participants in the 1991 NEH Summer
Seminar for College Teachers, "A Genealogy of Postmodernism," espe-
cially James Chansky, Robert Gall, Kevin O'Neill, Greg Schufreider, and
Joanne Waugh.

Introduction

The urge to theorize about the nature of things apparently is a defining feature of Western civilization. Certainly, we could not recognize our intellectual history without it. The history of ideas has not been univocal on the question of theory, however. Along the way there have been dissenting voices. Each era has its skeptics who, along with the occasional radical empiricist like Bacon, or the logical positivists, offer cautionary tales about the blindness of abstraction. Nevertheless, the success of the natural sciences attests to the power of theory, and the rest of culture generally pays homage, finding it hard to resist the aspiration to mimic this success by employing formal methods in philosophy, history, the literary arts, and the social sciences. In fact, it could be argued that even in practical reasoning, when normative issues are at stake, we tend to sustain this respect for science by internalizing a rough picture of the relationship between theory and practice. Theories (e.g., rational choice theory) produce an increasingly accurate representation of reality and, on the basis of this representation, generate prescriptions for practical action. Success of the action depends on the accuracy of the representation.[1]

Dissent is now being heard once again under various rubrics including "postmodernism," "poststructuralism," "deconstruction," or "pragmatism."[2] This dissent questions the very foundations of theory, challenging the intelligibility of any unifying theme or system and questioning the idea of accurate representation. Science and philosophy are submerged in textuality on this view, each a literary genre among others.[3]

Concurrent to this trend in contemporary thought is a less global critique of theory confined to the practice of theoretical ethics. This critique, largely influenced by the reemergence and rereading of Aristotle, questions the capacity of normative ethical theory to provide guidance on normative questions, challenging its relevance to the lived experience of moral agents. These critics of ethical theory also raise questions about theoretical unity and systematization—in this case, doubting its appropriateness to an object domain which may not exhibit the requisite systematicity.[4]

These two contemporary literatures have vastly different genealogies and methodologies, and appear to have little in common except an antipathy toward systematic, theoretical frameworks. Moreover, proponents of postmodernism and poststructuralism have been criticized for remaining silent on moral questions, and even for undermining the intelligibility of moral experience. Thus, articulating continuities between these two currents of thought seems improbable at best.

Despite the important differences between the literatures, common themes run through both and make an exchange of views between them fruitful. Moreover, much recent work that is loosely referred to as postmodern deals explicitly with moral and political questions. It will not be too misleading, therefore, to refer to an "antitheory" position, distilled from these disparate sources, that speaks specifically to the question of moral theory.[5]

My aim in this essay is to assess this attack on moral theory. I suppose there are two ways to go about such an assessment. One would be to rehearse the arguments given to date, and measure the objections of the antitheorists against the best theoretical work, in order to find gaps in the logic or ambiguities in the presentation that might lead us to reject the antitheory arguments. However, it is not obvious to me that tinkering with the arguments or characterizing the aims of theory in a way that will accommodate objections will advance the debate significantly. It is likely that the differences between theorists and antitheorists involve substantially different ways of thinking about morality and rationality that will not come to light merely by focusing on the negative side of the antitheory position. It is not so much the details of the arguments that are at stake as is the basic perceptions about what it means to respond to an obligation or act with a sense of justice. In other words, the antitheory position involves substantive commitments to a basic conception of morality that must be brought to the surface before any assessment can begin.

What we want at this date, if we take the antitheorists seriously, is an account of the implications for moral reflection. Assessment will be advanced by a comparison between two live options. Thus, rather than arguing *to* the antitheory position by adding epicycles to what others have written, I argue *from* this position by tracing its implications and assessing its promise. I will not, therefore, be devising counter-attacks to support the aims and aspirations of theory. Instead, I am concerned with spelling out a version of what it means to hold this antitheory position and its implications for moral reflection. In the end I think we gain some insight into the human condition from such an inquiry.

The antitheory position is motivated by the perception that when moral agents think about moral questions, they do so not in terms of abstract principles with an aim to systematize some large chunk of moral experience, but in terms of concrete relationships with other people within the context of their understanding of those relationships, histories, and the institutions in which they are embedded. Friendships, family relationships, religious and national heritage, economic status, and of course the slights, traumas, accomplishments, and joys of everyday life guide us in our complex judgments about morality. To the extent that we think about principles and rules, they are viewed as emerging from the aforementioned concrete relationships.

Theorists who aim to systematize these judgments can, of course, grant all this—for they are asking the further question of whether our judgments are rationally justifiable, irrespective of how we acquired them. But antitheorists will argue that the attempt to view these judgments systematically from an objective point of view in fact distorts the very phenomena it studies, and damages the ability of moral agents to make these ordinary judgments, whose appropriateness can only be viewed in their particular contexts. When we try to look behind our moral points of view to seek the principles that justify them, there is nothing that looks more reliable than the beliefs we seek to justify and the institutions and relationships from which they emerge. The antitheorists argue that there are no systems of principles more fundamental than those we happen to live by. Thus, if we understand moral prescriptions to be worth endorsing only if they conform to a theory, our moral judgments are undecidable. Consistent and intelligent theorists can argue either side of a case without result. Consider the abortion issue as a case in point—these theorists are no help at all to a woman worried about the moral status of the abortion she is considering. To varying degrees, antitheorists argue for the contingency of moral experience and for the absence of any rational principles more fundamental than the moral practices by which we happen to live, that will justify those practices.

I should mention at the outset that antitheorists are not of one voice on this question of contingency. Some antitheorists argue that although there are no systematic principles or underlying *logos* not subject to the vicissitudes of history to which we can appeal, the history of moral practice itself contains certain regularities, discoverable by philosophical reflection, that help us think more clearly about morality. The Anglo-American philosophers under discussion tend to adopt the latter view, while the continental thinkers take a less sanguine view of our capacity to utilize the history of institutions and practices as a guide.

Another feature of everyday experience that lends support to an antitheory position is the proliferation of ways of speaking about morality. The social institutions and the amalgam of cultures that make up contemporary society are hardly univocal on questions of morality. Religious, ethnic, and other minority groups not only disagree on moral and political questions, but disagree on what will count as a legitimate answer to these questions, even while defining themselves in terms of their differences. Lacking a set of common experiences, our moral and political discourse seems unable to articulate a common purpose. Instead, it focuses on special, narrowly defined interests, often in ways that do not allow for compromise. Thus, many of the antitheorists will argue that moral discourse is incommensurable—characterized by multiple, rival, incompatible paradigms of justification. Once again, antitheorists differ on the extent of incommensurability and our chances to overcome it. Much of this book is devoted to characterizing different versions of incommensurability and the degree to which it threatens agreement on moral questions.

My intention is not to provide a review of the antitheory literature, but rather to use this literature to try to understand the complexity of moral experience. Thus, I have been selective, choosing to discuss those writers whose work advances my argument. Chapter One is devoted to summarizing the principle themes and arguments that support the antitheory position, especially those providing a critique of analytic moral theory. Subsequent chapters attempt to assess what I consider to be the two primary alternatives to a traditional theoretical approach to ethics. Part One is devoted to a group of philosophers whom I will call the narrativists. I include among this group Martha Nussbaum, Alasdair MacIntyre, and Richard Rorty. They hold in common the view that a moral life takes the form of a narrative, and they emphasize the role of historical understanding or imaginative identification in recognizing and acting upon moral obligations. Part Two is devoted to postmodernism, represented here by Emmanuel Levinas and Jean-Francois Lyotard.[6] They argue that narrative is an inadequate vehicle for moral reflection, and endorse a rather novel account of moral obligation as a feeling of being bound by a presence that cannot be fully grasped through understanding or reason. I should note in passing that each of these writers, although skeptical about the hegemony of theory, differs in the role they think theory ought to play in philosophy and in practical reflection. Rorty wants us to lose the motivation for theorizing altogether or view it solely as a mode of self-creation. Lyotard wants us to acknowledge that theory cannot be action guiding, Levinas believes that all theories are a disguised form of egoism, while Nussbaum views theory as a helpful framework for commenting on literary texts. Their powerful characterizations of the limits of theory, and their keen sense of what might lie beyond it tie them together for my purposes.[7]

My own interest in these particular philosophers stems from a deeply puzzling phenomenon that emerges often in the course of human history, and which the antitheory literature helps us understand. Why is it that decent people who accept the guidance of morality in their lives perform or acquiesce to monstrous acts of cruelty? History is filled with acts of injustice and evil carried out in the name of a moral good. The crusades, the slave trade, the Nazi terror, to name just a few, were undertaken with at least the expressed aim to improve the human condition. None of these activities could have advanced except as an expression of public virtue embodied in social and legal institutions, and supported by the moral climate of their time and place.

What does this alleged complicity of goodness and evil tell us about morality? The standard answer likely would be that it tells us nothing about morality. It could be argued that these acts of cruelty exhibit the failure for humans to live up to moral ideals; the claims to moral justification a mere exercise in self-deception. But this response begs the question of how these ideals could be so massively misunderstood and misappropriated. I believe the interplay of goodness and evil suggests that morality has a tragic dimension, that even our most cherished moral ideals can generate an extraordinary moral blindness.

Each of the philosophers whose work I discuss plays a role in articulating the nature of moral responsiveness given this tragic conception of ethics. Furthermore, the tragic character of moral judgment best explains the difficulties in coming up with a consistent account of morality that coheres with lived experience, and therefore helps to explain the force of the antitheory arguments and exposes the presuppositions that support them. But it will also help to advance the argument I wish to make, that a critical skepticism toward one's own ideals is an essential part of a moral point of view, an insight that the postmodern alternative can articulate more forcefully than the narrativists.

This discussion of moral blindness raises the question of what sort of standard will serve to evaluate the works discussed here. To answer this question, I wish to engage a debate that overlaps this question of theory and has roots deep in the history of philosophy. Much moral reflection—both theoretical and practical—revolves around the question, In virtue of what do we have obligations? One way to draw a contrast between communitarians and traditional liberals, and such luminaries as Kant and Hegel, Hume and Aquinas, and Plato and Aristotle, is on this question of the source of obligation.

I will introduce this issue by raising a paradox that practical, moral reflection is concerned with working through. As I briefly note earlier, judgments about how one should live and interact with others are made in virtue of having internalized the norms of a particular community. These norms are meaningful to the extent that agents are cognizant of their place within a particular history and set of institutions that supply them with examples of moral conduct, and within particular relationships by virtue of which they incur obligations. On the other hand, our interaction with others is often a confrontation with "otherness," a confrontation with those who share neither our norms nor our history. Moral reflection, in this case, must take place outside the context that gives significance and value to those norms. Despite this loss of significance, success of the interaction may depend upon sustaining the possibility of cooperation, and the trust on which such cooperation depends. Thus, the paradox is that in confronting the "other," moral reflection either expresses this significance and value but risks misunderstanding and ineffectiveness, or is effective but suffers a loss of significance. This question of the confrontation with the "other" has been an ongoing concern within the continental tradition and is, therefore, the most promising issue with which to bring into conversation the analytic and continental approaches.

The Christian traditions and the Enlightenment solved this paradox by bestowing moral significance on everyone by virtue of being one of God's children or possessing the distinctly human capacity for free choice and autonomy. In matters of ethics every human being has the capacity to act morally, and all therefore are worthy of equal respect, a worth that other differences between people cannot diminish. Although the histories and institutions of particular communities give content and significance to ethical life, moral reflection and conduct is constrained by an absolute requirement to treat all moral agents with equal respect. In Western civilization, universal moral agency has become so deeply ingrained in the language of morality that the standard view of the meaning of moral terms is that

Anyone who says, meaning it, that a certain action (or person, or state of affairs, etc.) is morally right or wrong, good or bad, ought or ought not to be done . . . is thereby committed to taking the same view about any other relevantly similar action (etc.)[8]

Thus, moral reflection seems to pull in opposing directions: on the one hand toward the task of sustaining the local mores and practices that give moral life its content; on the other toward an aspiration to judge from a point of view representing all moral agents.

Modern moral theory, with the notable exception of some of Hegel's work, has concerned itself primarily with shoring up the argumentative scaffolding of this aspiration to judge from a point of view that represents all moral agents. Recently, however, this abandonment of the field of ethics to the universalists has come under a rather withering attack from those who think this way of arguing for universal moral agency sucks the very lifeblood from morality by ignoring institutions and practices that make morality meaningful.[9] The heart of this argument is that obligations appealing to an objective or impersonal point of view for their intelligibility lack the specificity that gives moral life its content. Instead, genuine moral obligations arise from obligations that participation in the institutions and practices of a society embodying a shared way of life imposes on an agent. Such participation in this common task itself is rewarding because the community becomes the expression of the agent's identity. For want of a better term, I will call this position "concrete ethics."[10]

It should be clear, at this point, why one would expect an overlap between antitheory arguments and concrete ethics. In arguing that theory overlooks important features of moral experience, we see that what is overlooked is precisely the features that proponents of "concrete ethics" wish to call to our attention. Doubts regarding the universalist conception of moral agency are not unrelated to the various currents of dissent that question theory *simpliciter*.

The difficulty with "concrete ethics" is that many of the practices and institutions that orient us toward our local folkways also express the requirement of universal and equal respect, so ingrained in our tradition. Thus, despite the attempt to reorient ethics toward something smaller and more local than the "community of humankind," the tension between these two moral points of view still exerts a considerable tug, even within the antitheory position. As will become evident later, despite antitheorists' arguments that the aspiration to occupy the universalist point of view erodes the significance of moral life, they nevertheless feel compelled to account for the intuition that universal moral agency is an important value. This muddles the distinction between theorists and antitheorists considerably.

The tension between concrete ethics and the aspiration to find a moral point of view from which all moral agents can be represented requires that we treat the distinction between theory and alternative forms of reflection as a continuum. In fact, what will emerge from this inquiry is that underlying the various positions on this continuum are varying perceptions of the nature and persistence of the problem of incommensurability. The resources available for overcoming obstacles to understanding and finding ways to live with alien points of view will lend plausibility to a conception of universal moral agency. I argue that it is on this issue of incommensurability that the Anglo-American antitheorists stumble, thus making the work of Lyotard and Levinas relevant.

In developing a characterization of what it means to hold an "antitheory" position, I argue for the persistence of the problem of incommensurability. Yet, I also assume that the aspiration to judge from a position in which all moral agents are represented is something for which moral reflection must make room. The capacity to account for this aspiration despite the persistence of incommensurability therefore serves as a standard by which to evaluate the antitheory claims. I feel justified in adopting a capacity to account for the universalist aspiration as a criterion because: (1) I do not know how to begin to argue for or against this aspiration without begging every question at stake; (2) all the philosophers whose positions I evaluate in this book implicitly endorse it; and (3) an idea so important to the moral discourse of Western civilization should not be given up without a sustained attempt to articulate it in defensible terms. Furthermore, it would seem that the best chance of mitigating the worries I mentioned earlier regarding moral blindness would rest with an account of a universal moral agency that avoids the abstractness and reductionist tendencies of theory.

However, to argue that what is at stake is a "position from which to judge all moral agents" is an unfortunate way of characterizing this aspiration. The antitheorists object to related notions like "objectivity" and "neutrality," which seem to naturally flow from this characterization. Thus, I will be appealing to the capacity to transcend the limitations of one's moral perspective as an appropriate, nonquestion-begging way of cashing out this aspiration.

In this brief discussion of universal moral agency I employ three different characterizations of it: (1) The capacity to judge from a moral point of view that represents the needs and interests of all moral agents; (2) the capacity to recognize and respect alien points of view; (3) the capacity to transcend the limitations of one's moral framework. These three characterizations are not equivalent. In fact, despite a resemblance between them, they each presuppose quite different assumptions about moral discourse. Part of the substance of my argument is that (1) and (2) presuppose conceptions of morality that are problematic and that (3) will provide the best characterization of universal moral agency. This argument will not be complete until the final chapter. Thus, the reader should bear in mind that the question of the characterization of universal moral agency is not being begged, but deferred until the conceptual apparatus is available for answering it.

As to the outline of my argument, I claim that antitheory arguments asserting that theories of universalist ethics overlook important features of moral experience are correct, but the commitment to "concrete ethics" that seems to follow from this assertion is unable to shed the problem of incommensurability. This undermines our conception of universal moral agency. However, by reconceptualizing the notion of obligation along lines suggested by Lyotard and Levinas, we can preserve both this aspiration as well as the insights of the antitheorists.

Broadly speaking, the argument has two parts corresponding to Parts One and Two of this text. In Part One I argue that the narrativists think of moral reflection partly as a search for a social identity, which MacIntyre, Nussbaum, and Rorty all think of as the search for a coherent historical narrative regarding one's life and culture. This search for a social identity as a source of obligation leads to a form of moral blindness, because the judgments we make in connection with this pursuit tend to be contrasting. They depend on the articulation of invidious distinctions between people as a condition of their intelligibility. This is often why when we act on our deepest, most well-intentioned moral commitments, our actions can have tragically harmful consequences. These contrast judgments are a form of incommensurability that stand in the way of the articulation of a conception of universal moral agency from within the narrativists' framework.

In Part Two I argue, using Lyotard and Levinas as a source of insight, that moral obligation involves a feeling of being bound to another person through a recognition of his or her capacity to suffer—a recognition that cannot be reduced to an instance of understanding, a system of principles or norms, or a coherent narrative. The inability to satisfactorily explain or justify suffering itself provokes a moral concern in those who are moved by obligation. This capacity to be shocked by others' suffering, and a resistance to settling for ersatz explanations of it, accounts for our capacity to transcend the limitations of a moral point of view, and provides us with a recharacterized sense of universal moral agency compatible with the main tenets of the antitheory position. The virtue of such a position is that it allows us to conceptualize an ethics and politics that depends only minimally on shared beliefs.

1

A Thematic Summary of Arguments

In this chapter, I accomplish three tasks. First, I provide a summary of the major themes developed by philosophers who subscribe to the claim that normative ethical theory cannot make a significant contribution to moral reflection or conduct. Second, I distinguish antitheory arguments from closely related arguments that support nonfoundationalist forms of justification compatible with a theoretical approach to ethics. Finally, I provide some motivation for the agenda in subsequent chapters. In connection with this latter task, I should mention that the overall aim of the dissertation is to gain some understanding of what moral reflection becomes once the force of the antitheory arguments has been recognized. I am less concerned about providing a general defense of the antitheory position against theoretical approaches, preferring to rely, instead, on work already accomplished in that area. The only exception to this is on the question of the status of nonfoundationalist forms of justification, against which antitheory arguments tend to be relatively silent. I try to supply some additional support for the antitheory position when such support is needed to mark the contrast with nonfoundationalism.[1]

The word "theory" has so many uses, and applies in so many different contexts, that it probably cannot be given a very precise definition capturing all of its instances. As a first approximation, we might say a theory is a hypothesis asserting that apparently diverse phenomena are dependent on an underlying unity, leaving the notions of "dependent" and "unity" unhelpfully unspecified. I doubt, however, that there is any univocal way of fleshing out these notions. It is therefore difficult to know what a general "antitheory" position is opposed to, because any useful discussion of

1

an "antitheory" position must specify the sense of "theory" being rejected. The particular kind of theory at issue here is normative ethical theory, and the use of the term "antitheory" herein should be understood to apply only to those theories falling under that rubric.

The dominant positions in normative ethical theory either claim explicitly or presuppose that moral phenomena exhibit a unity that can be adequately represented by hierarchical arrangements of moral principles.[2] Normative ethical theories typically offer the promise of applying principles supported by a theory to particular cases of moral decision-making, thereby helping to discover which of our moral beliefs or actions are justified and which are not. By "normative ethical theories," I mean at least the deontological tradition dominated by Kant, and including recent writers such as Rawls, Gewirth, and Donagan. I also refer to the utilitarian tradition beginning with Bentham and Mill, continuing through Brandt as well as rational choice theory. There are, of course, other normative theories, some of which are coming to dominate contemporary discussion, to which the above description of a normative ethical theory may not apply —virtue ethics, communitarian theories, and critical social theory come to mind. The question of whether antitheory arguments can be extended to apply to these other normative theories is part of what is being discussed in this dissertation. I will therefore leave aside this question pending the upcoming analysis.

The motivation to construct a normative ethical theory has its source in a certain picture of morality and related notions such as justice. To say that an action or belief is morally justified, or that a particular distribution of goods is just, is to say that a belief, action, or distribution conforms to what morality or justice really is. This presupposes that morality and justice can be characterized, at least to some degree, independently of what moral agents actually do. A justified action is one that mimics an ideal model or an essence. Thus, the primary job of the moral theorist is not to describe what moral agents do, rather it is to describe what agents should be replicating or conforming to in their actions. The prescription expressed by "should" derives part of its meaning from the implication that the ideal or essence of morality and justice do not always obtain. The description that the theorist provides is of a largely absent state of affairs that agents are enjoined to make present through their actions. Thus, the practice of morality requires theoretical understanding. In order to know what their conduct should conform to, moral agents must gain knowledge of this domain that is, to a degree, independent of their actions.

As I have just described, moral theory, despite its normative preoccupations, is very much a descriptive enterprise in that it seeks to describe those ideals to which we ought to conform. Even though philosophical ethics is usually not thought of as a science, its status as a theoretical inquiry would seem to prescribe some relationship to scientific methodology. Even Kant, who sharply distinguished the cognitive from the ethical, enjoined moral agents to act *as if* the maxim of one's action were a universal law of nature. Indeed, the equation of scientific methodology with reason *simpliciter* has infected much of contemporary culture and intellectual life, and philosophical ethics is no exception. Although it may not be accurate to claim that philosophical ethics has adopted a scientific methodology, it is not difficult to show a number of basic presuppositions made by most ethical theorists that are also basic to science, at least as traditionally conceived. Most important among these is the notion that the object domain can be understood to exhibit a relatively fixed, unified nature, independent of the inquirers seeking to discover that nature. This presupposition motivates the adoption of three methodological assumptions: (1) that diverse phenomena can be ultimately understood or explained by a few integrated, fundamental principles or laws; (2) the principles or laws must be universal; and (3) the credibility of inquiry depends on the duplication of results by any competent observer.

The history of normative ethical theory displays a preoccupation with universality, objectivity, and the autonomy of ethical phenomena from other aspects of life that makes moral philosophy's debt to science obvious despite the apparent disanalogies between physical and moral phenomena. It is testimony to the strength of this ideology that, given the extraordinary historical and cultural diversity of moral phenomena, and the failure of any theory thus far to attain genuine objectivity and universality in the face of it, hope that such a theory is attainable remains alive. In this climate, simply pointing to the diversity of these norms and the failure of past theories to display their systematicity is not a persuasive strategy for calling the quasi-scientific paradigm into question, for the easy response is that the diversity of ethical beliefs can best be explained by the incompleteness of prevailing moral points of view. If we were fully enlightened, the ultimate unity of moral beliefs would be clear. Thus, only an argument that shows why the scientific ideal is, in principle, unattainable in ethics would succeed at making the cachet of science appear less attractive as a model for moral reflection. Given the dominance of a scientific paradigm, it seems natural to begin to explore the antitheorist position by considering such an argument.

Antiobjectivism

In *Ethics and the Limits of Philosophy,* Bernard Williams argues that the difference between science and ethics centers around "the best hopes we could coherently entertain for eliminating disagreement in the two areas."[3] If and when there is convergence of belief in science, it will be because of "how things are." This is because there is reason to think that the scientifically formed belief that the world has certain properties is best explained by the fact that the world, indeed, has those properties. Such an explanation would be part of what Williams calls the "absolute conception of the world," and includes not only our settled scientific beliefs about the world, but also evolutionary theory and neurological science, which explain how we came to acquire those beliefs about the world.

This "absolute conception" provides us with a justification for seeing the world in terms of our settled scientific beliefs. We can give causal accounts of why the world appears to us as it does, even in cases such as color predicates, in which we might expect quite different creatures to attribute different properties to the world. By showing why a certain kind of perceptual mechanism yields a particular perception, we can determine when the lack of a specific perception means something has gone wrong with the mechanism, thereby distinguishing a defective mechanism from a different mechanism. Moreover, the absolute conception would be able to account for the evolution of various mechanisms and understand their features in terms of underlying physical properties, etc. Most importantly, we would have no reason to conclude that investigators different from us would have different scientific beliefs. If they did, we could explain this divergence: We could give an account of our own ability to comprehend science. In short, we know our representation of the world is correct to the extent that we can explain our capacity for representation. Scientific theories justify as well as explain because they help establish the objectivity of the beliefs in question. It should be noted that Williams is not claiming that such a convergence within science has been accomplished or even that it is in sight. His point is that such a convergence is readily conceivable given what science has accomplished to date.

Moral theory, according to Williams, can never aspire to this sort of explanation. Any attempt to sustain the analogy between science and ethics must provide an account of moral belief acquisition that explains the cultural diversity we find with respect to moral practices in a way that explains the acquisition of correct moral beliefs. Regardless of the merits of social scientific explanations, they will only answer the question of how these particular agents in fact acquired the beliefs they hold. They will not answer the further question, Is this a good way of living compared to others? An answer to this question would require an ethical theory lacking the explanatory power of a scientific theory.

> It might rationalize some cultural differences, showing why one local concept rather than others was ethically appropriate in particular circumstances. . . . But while it might explain why it was reasonable for people to have these various ethical beliefs, it would not be the sort of theory that could explain why they did or did not have them. It could not do something that explanations of perception can do, which is to generate an adequate theory of error and to account generally for the tendency of people to have what, according to its principles, are wrong beliefs.[4]

The conclusion at which Williams arrives from these considerations is that we cannot give an explanation of correct, *moral* belief acquisition such that deviations from a norm could be explained as an error. Therefore, the conditions that establish objectivity in science are simply not present in the moral case.

The Priority of Lived Experience

If Williams is correct regarding the absence of a plausible theory of reliable belief-acquisition in ethics, he casts a good deal of doubt on the intuition that ethics is a matter of giving an account of a fixed, unified object domain, for we no longer have a reliable means of distinguishing "how things are" from "how they appear." Moreover, the absence of a neutral standard of comparison against which competing beliefs can be measured means we can never get outside the set of moral dispositions we've acquired through living in a particular culture in order to gain a genuinely independent perspective.

> The belief that you can look critically at all your dispositions from the outside, from the point of view of the universe, assumes that you could understand your own and other people's dispositions from that point of view without tacitly taking for granted a picture of the world more locally familiar than any that would be available from there; but neither the psychology nor the history of ethical reflection gives much reason to believe that the theoretical reasonings of

the cool hour can do without a sense of the moral shape of the world, of the kind given in the everyday dispositions.[5]

Moreover, the attempt to find such neutral ground on moral questions might ultimately be destructive, according to Williams, in that it threatens to become an alien, dominating ideology destroying our capacity to exercise moral dispositions that help us sustain social reality. Thus, Williams argues that we should resist the demands placed on ethical reflection by the ideal of scientific objectivity.

In rejecting objectivity as a meaningful goal for moral inquiry, Williams is committed to the view that there are no moral facts independent of the beliefs of particular groups of moral agents. Moral reflection must begin from inside some particular moral point of view—from within the norms, values, and ideals each agent has acquired from living within a certain culture or tradition. Indeed, it is hard to imagine a process of socialization and language acquisition that did not impose on agents a moral vocabulary constituted by substantial agreement on the meanings and referents of moral terms and shared exemplars of problem solving and cooperation. Moral reflection begins with a commitment to a particular set of values, norms, and ideals on which the process of evaluation and assessment must rest.

However, this initial privileging of a particular perspective introduces circularity into the process of evaluation and assessment, and creates tension with what would seem to be the point and purpose of moral reflection. There are many contexts in which moral reflection would seem to be helpful. We seek to allay doubts about a belief we hold, adjudicate conflict between competing prescriptions, evaluate obligations to be sustained or suspended, judge the actions of others, defend our actions to others, etc. What we seek in each case is a reason for thinking or doing one thing rather than another. The point of calling this search for reasons "reflection" is that the reasons sought are not self-evident. The application of received opinions, embedded cultural norms, action-guiding principles, and ordinary extensions of moral terms are often open to question. They cannot be immediately applied, but must be thought through and reassessed in light of the circumstances that give rise to the pressure to choose. However, because the antiobjectivist position claims that there is no external point of view from which to proceed, the only criteria available for this reassessment, at least initially, will be drawn from the very beliefs and principles that are in question. It follows that what is put into question in the act of reflection cannot be global. Reflection has inherent limits because there is no way to put one's whole perspective in question all at once.[6] Against both the moral skeptic and the critic whose moral perspective is radically different from the one in question, there is no noncircular defense, no ultimate, argumentative recourse to justifying one's moral beliefs. As Williams points out, this goes against the grain of much of the tradition of normative ethical theory, which has taken the problem of defeating the moral skeptic seriously.

To Williams, and others such as Richard Rorty, this inherent circularity in moral reflection suggests a strong antitheory position. Rorty will argue that once we accept that we must work from within the perspective of some particular group of moral agents and do so without a noncircular justification, we are confronted with two options: Either we attach a special privilege to our own community, or we pretend an impossible tolerance for every other group."[7] Although some might take seriously the conclusion that in the absence of objective criteria all beliefs are roughly on a par, this would require that we sacrifice "habits of thought" on which our cultural identity depends—the Enlightenment legacy of tolerance, free inquiry, and democracy. Rorty advocates that we grasp the ethnocentric horn of the dilemma, privileging our own group and thereby recognizing that there are "lots of views we simply cannot take seriously."[8] By "our own group" Rorty means "those who share enough of one's beliefs to make fruitful conversation possible."[9] Thus, in Rorty's view, the priority of lived experience, which follows from antiobjectivism, leads directly to "mild ethnocentrism" because the only other alternative—sophomoric relativism—is self-defeating.

However, this "mild ethnocentrism" will make philosophical theory largely irrelevant, according to Rorty, especially with respect to matters of public concern expressed in the political arena. For us—that is, for Rorty's readers who are primarily Western intellectuals—"mild ethnocentrism" entails some commitment to democratic ideals. However, the possibility of political community within a democracy requires a public discourse within which some agreement on issues of policy and procedure can be attained. In this political context, philosophical disputes about the existence and characteristics of human nature, the meaning of life, and the nature of personhood and moral obligation are useless because they are apparently undecidable. The history of philosophy is largely a history of interminable, unresolved disagreement. Once we adopt the ethnocentric view that democratic ideals are of paramount importance, the incessant disputations of philosophical theory are unreliable participants in the forging of a political consensus.[10]

It is important to point out, however, that accepting the claim that there is no objective standpoint does not necessarily commit one to the antitheory position. Although I think Williams successfully shows why the attempt to gain a genuinely objective point of view that is independent of all competing ethical perspectives is bound to fail, his attack on theory, like Rorty's, seems primarily directed toward foundationalist approaches to moral justification. Nonfoundationalist theories that attempt to begin from within a particular ethical perspective, working outward to explore common ground with other perspectives, require neither the antecedent identification of a privileged class of statements that issue from an objective point of view nor conclusive positions on canonical problems in philosophy. Despite the absence of a genuinely independent perspective, the theorist can still seek to codify the moral perspective of the particular agents in question, including their conception of personhood and moral motivation, demonstrate the logical and evidentiary connections exemplified in this perspective, and test these intuitions described by sociological and historical investigations against available normative theories and alternative moral conceptions seeking regularities that transcend parochial concerns. Although antecedent criteria for adjudicating conflicts between perspectives may not be available, the process of searching for regularities may identify areas of agreement that will serve as criteria. Thus, despite the attack on objectivity, there is still substantial room for moral theory. However, the upshot of the antiobjectivist argument is that such a theory must operate under the following constraint: At least some beliefs of the actual moral agents whose beliefs are at issue must be assumed to have some initial credibility if the theory is to get off the ground. The degree to which theoretical principles cohere with the lived experience of moral agents will be an important element in the justification of such a theory.

This description of a nonfoundationalist theory loosely describes Rawls's conception of wide-reflective equilibrium. The point of invoking wide-reflective equilibrium here is that it represents a mode of theoretical justification that is not dependent on the epistemic priority of theory, and is quite compatible with nonobjectivism and the privileging of lived experience. Because this sort of justification has gained currency in recent years, a successful critique of normative theory must apply to it as well. Consequently, a genuine antitheory position must rest on more than antiobjectivism and the priority of lived experience. In fact, antitheorists will argue that moral phenomena resist the sort of codification that wide-reflective equilibrium requires.

The Uncodifiability Thesis and Reflective Equilibrium

Reflective equilibrium is a strategy of justification that appears to avoid antitheorists' objections. Justification is the result of a process that requires the mutual comparison and revision of both theoretical principles and considered judgments. Because it assigns initial credibility to the considered moral judgments of the agents in question and requires the revision of theoretical principles in light of those judgemnts, it utilizes the lived experience of moral agents without the constraint of an independent or neutral point of view.

However, some philosophers have argued that moral judgments cannot be codified into moral principles without losing their action-guiding capacity. I will call this the "uncodifiability thesis," following John McDowell.[11] In this section I want to explore the extent to which the uncodifiability thesis threatens the strategy of justification in reflective equilibrium.

Reflective equilibrium, as first articulated by John Rawls in *A Theory of Justice,* has two versions—wide and narrow—that differ with respect to the theoretical commitments involved. I will consider both.[12]

In narrow-reflective equilibrium, an individual's considered moral judgments—made under conditions that tend to minimize error—are compared with various competing sets of moral principles. We go back and forth between considered judgments and moral principles, modifying each in light of the other until we arrive at an equilibrium point described as the best fit between judgments and principles.[13] Judgments and principles are justified to the extent that they can be brought into this state of equilibrium. Considered judgments are assigned some initial credibility because, upon reflection, they seem to play a central role in defining one's personal or social identity.[14] Any principles that systematize them would acquire credibility as well. Thus, there is some pressure to revise principles to accommodate as many judgments as possible. Similarly, a particular considered judgment will gain credibility if, under the scope of a principle, it can be shown to be consistent with other considered judgments also fitting under that principle. Thus, a consistent set of principles that systematizes a number of considered judgments will exert revisionary pressure on recalcitrant or novel considered judgments, while judgments to which we are strongly committed constrain and exert revisionary pressure on the principles. The principles not only serve the function of demonstrating a systematicity in the judgments that went previously unobserved but, through the process of revision, shape judgments to cohere with these patterns. Principles and considered judgments are justified if they survive this process of amendment.

The uncodifiability thesis calls into question the capacity of principles to revise judgments. It asserts that coherent patterns in a moral agent's behavior are not instantiations of a rule or principle but are dependent on the perceptions of similarity and difference that involve the agent's entire conception of how to live.[15] According to McDowell, in a practical syllogism, an appeal to a rule or principle (the major premise) plus a description of the situation (the minor premise) will not explain why an agent performs one action rather than another.[16]

> It is by virtue of his seeing this particular fact rather than that one as the salient fact about the situation that he is moved to act by this concern rather than that one. . . . A conception of how to live shows itself, when more than one concern might issue in action, in one's seeing or being able to be brought to see, one fact rather than another as salient.[17]

A similar point can be made with respect to legal norms and the collective judgments embodied in social practices. Annette Baier argues that a principle like "Do not kill" does not represent our conduct since we frequently accept its violation, especially with regard to animals. However, qualifying the principle to "Do not kill humans" will not suffice either. War is an obvious counter-example, among others. We must then go to something like "Do not kill the innocent," whereby we are forced to list the ways in which someone can forfeit his or her right not to be killed. Yet even this long list of exceptions to the principle "Do not kill innocent humans" will not summarize our attitudes toward killing since we allow some degree of killing caused by unsafe products, polluted air, and the like. So we must be applying a rule such as "Don't kill unless you can't help it, except at unreasonable cost."

> The "innocent" who are protected by this rule turn out to be a dwindling group, those whom we choose to save, just as "Don't eat people" can be accepted by cannibals, who protest that they eat only their enemies, who are not real people, not *fellow persons*.[18]

Baier's discussion suggests that moral principles run out rather quickly, thus initiating a process of deliberation in which the principles play little role.

The judgments invoking an entire "conception of how to live," and the judgment of salience that issues from them, cannot be fully articulated.

> Any attempt to capture it in words will recapitulate the character of the teaching whereby it might be instilled: generalizations will be approximate at best, and examples will need to be taken with the sort of "and so on" which appeals to the cooperation of a hearer who has cottoned on.[19]

McDowell and Baier are suggesting that in addition to principles and situation descriptions, complex deliberative processes are at work in applying a principle to a situation. However, this does not constitute an objection to reflective equilibrium. Proponents of reflective equilibrium need not deny the importance of deliberation, insisting rather that principles play an important role in that deliberation. Within the process of revising considered judgments, the defender of reflective equilibrium could argue that moral principles perform two important functions. First, principles are a kind of shorthand for representing large groupings of clear cases—judgments that fit under a principle unproblematically. The point of invoking a principle or competition between principles is to bring clear cases to bear on the particular case at issue. In demonstrating the range of cases that must be revised in order to bring a particular judgment under a particular principle, the costs and benefits of various proposed revisions can be assessed. Second, the principle imposes a demand for integrity on the process of revising considered judgments, which, in the absence of a principle, would amount to little more than trade-offs between judgments. Presumably, moral integrity requires that some moral judgments not be compromised in the face of competing judgments.[20] Thus, the principle is a kind of heuristic device—a helpful oversimplification—that represents clear cases for the purpose of testing considered judgments. It is a summary of the perceptions of similarity and difference that guide action, but a summary, nonetheless, that has a role to play in the critical assessment of considered judgments.

However, despite the compatibility of McDowell's conception of deliberation and reflective equilibrium, there is a difference of emphasis. McDowell thinks of deliberation as a "bottom-up" affair, with perceptions of particular situations dominating the deliberative process. In reflective equilibrium, deliberation is both "bottom-up" and "top-down"—a matter of reflecting on individual cases, fixing the concepts that can be generalized into principles, and then extending those principles to new cases until further reflection on individual cases requires further modification of the principles. Moreover, it is not obvious that the principles' capacity to force revisions of considered judgments has been sufficiently articulated. If moral principles are merely heuristic devices without any independent justificatory weight, what is the warrant for forcing revisions of our considered judgments?

I want to extend the uncodifiability thesis by arguing that principles do not have the capacity to revise considered judgments, and within the process of deliberation there is only a highly restricted role for principles to play.

Considered moral judgments in reflective equilibrium are judgments about particular cases or generalizations from particular cases.[21] Moral principles are constructed from a series of considered moral judgments, as well as a process of generalization through which we come to see our actions as having special moral value by virtue of some repeatedly instantiated property they possess. Such properties are candidates for generalization if they are morally relevant, by which I mean that their presence makes a difference in the evaluation of the action in question. For instance, having respect for the choices of others is often relevant to evaluating an action. This would be generalized into the principle, "Respect the rational autonomy of other human beings."

In reflective equilibrium, a principle supported by a generalization is thought to be useful for evaluating particular cases. It is a necessary condition of the principle being relevant to a particular case that the proposed action in that case possess the property referred to in the principle. For instance, if a proposed action would be a display of kindness, the necessary condition for the principle "Always perform acts of kindness" would be satisfied. Thus, the action-guidedness of principles is dependent as a necessary condition on the presence, in a particular case, of a property referred to by the principle. What I want to argue is that only in rare cases can a sufficient condition be satisfied.

The problem in satisfying the sufficient condition lies in the nature of a generalization. Generalizations, because they identify properties characteristic of a wide range of situations inevitably leave out much of the detail of the circumstances under which these properties appear. Part of what is left out is the morally relevant, *competing* properties present in the particular cases from which the generalizations are constructed. The fact that respecting the rational autonomy of moral agents is significant in so many contexts gives it the status of a moral principle. However, the relative weight given it *vis-à-vis* other morally relevant considerations within the particular cases on which this generalization is based is not part of the generalization. These other considerations are precisely what is subtracted in the process of generalization.

Because the generalization does not make reference to competing properties, the action guide represented in the principle is highly restricted.

(1) A principle is action-guiding in a situation just in case the property expressed in the principle is present, and there are no morally relevant competing properties.

Given the complexity of life, this condition on the action-guidedness of moral principles is seldom satisfied because most particular cases involve competing, morally relevant properties. (1) is hardly helpful in justifying revisions of recalcitrant considered judgments.

However, things are somewhat more complicated than this, because principles are often stated with their exceptions and qualifications, and it could be argued that this more complex principle, with its priority rules for determining which properties are more relevant than others, would generate a more substantive action guide.

Exceptions are dependent on generalizations as well, although these generalizations will be two-term relations as they refer to both the property touched on in the principle and the property creating the exception. The generalization will be constructed out of considered judgments based on particular cases in which the exception-creating property was judged more significant than the property referred to in the principle. Yet just as in the case of generalizations that support principles, the generalization supporting an exception will not make reference to competing morally relevant properties. For instance, we can list properties that typically create exceptions to the principle of respect for rational autonomy—usually some limitation on or impairment of rational faculties like age, inadequate information, emotional duress, or the effects of drugs. But these are not consistently applied except in extreme cases. More importantly, inconsistencies can usually best be explained by the presence of morally relevant competing properties unrelated to those that support the principle or its exception.[22]

For example, human interaction in many contexts—education, friendship, the workplace, etc.—involves a delicate balance between respect for autonomy and coercion. A regulation in the workplace may be an exception to the principle of respect for rational autonomy. However, the relevant property supporting the exception may have nothing to do with

limitations on or impairment of rational functioning and everything to
do with the requirements of the task to be accomplished, the need to
maintain uniform standards of fairness, or the need to solve cooperation
and coordination problems. An action's properties that are related to
what is important and possible within a particular situation compete for
the choices of others with the property of respect. Yet they are also unrelated to the properties of dysfunction that typically create exceptions to
respect for autonomy. The point here is that properties related to what is
possible and important to accomplish cannot be generalized in a manner
supportive of a moral principle or an exception, because they are too
closely tied to the contingencies of circumstance. Generalizations, including those that create exceptions, by their very nature leave out reference
to these properties. These considerations entail the following set of
action-guiding conditions:

> (2) An exception to a moral principle is action-guiding in a situation
>   just in case (a) the property referred to in the exception is pre-
>   sent; (b) the generalization supporting the exception contains
>   properties the moral significance of which is invariably greater
>   than the property referred to by the principle; and (c) there are
>   no morally relevant competing properties present.

(1) and (2) are extraordinarily strong. They suggest that moral principles
are not action-guiding in any case requiring deliberation. This entailment
is because generalizations supporting principles and exceptions neither
represent all the morally relevant properties of a proposed action nor
provide us with nomological regularities that would support the priority
of a particular property in *all* cases. The fact that a property is decisive in
the absence of morally relevant competing properties does not give me a
reason to think it will decide in the presence of competing properties. The
principle provides us with no device for attaching weight to a particular
property, independently of evaluating the significance of that property in
the present situation *and in situations like it.* This last point is absolutely
crucial. I am not claiming that the properties referred to by principles do
not have the significance we normally attach to them, nor am I claiming
that moral evaluation is restricted to situations. I am claiming that moral
evaluation is not mediated by principles, but proceeds by exploring the
similarities and differences between situations and considered judgments,
noting the shades of contrast and nuances that emerge from competing
descriptions. As McDowell claims, what "keeps us on the rails" is the

shared sense of what is similar, and the capacity to sustain that sense across situations.

To maintain this thesis, I must assume a certain burden. Given that appeals to principles are pervasive in moral discourse, I need to explain why they are so pervasive in light of their disutility. I said earlier that principles play a certain limited role in deliberation, bringing clear cases to bear on particular situations and maintaining a sense of moral integrity. Nothing in this argument for moral particularism disputes the existence of clear cases or their importance in moral conduct. However, these clear cases emerge from concrete situations, and it is the availability of these situations that figures in the deliberative process. An appeal to a principle is a handy way of invoking these clear cases, since clear cases are less likely than others to present morally relevant competing properties. Still, an appeal to a principle carries no justificatory weight independently of those clear cases.

Moral integrity and the role principles play in preserving it is a complicated phenomenon that I will discuss in later chapters. It will suffice here to point out that the invocation of a moral principle expresses the strength of conviction an agent feels with respect to clear cases. This would account for the pervasiveness of appeals to principles. However, on my analysis, moral principles do not prevent erosion of a moral point of view in the face of mere tradeoffs among competing values. Staying "on the rails" is not a matter of adherence to a principle but of sustaining a complex description.

This argument for a kind of moral particularism obviously has an impact on the plausibility of narrow reflective equilibrium from which this discussion began. The very process of generalization by which principles are constructed out of considered judgments undermines their capacity to revise the considered judgments. Moral principles, restricted in application to cases lacking morally relevant competing properties, can hardly exert a significant degree of revisionary pressure on recalcitrant considered moral judgments that are recalcitrant just because they contain such properties.

It is, however, generally acknowledged that narrow reflective equilibrium is inadequate as a justification and must be supplemented by wide reflective equilibrium.[23] It might be the case that the virtues of moral principles become apparent only against a wider background of institutions and cultural practices that support our moral attitudes and frame what McDowell calls "a conception of how to live." If these principles can be made to cohere with an account of this background, then perhaps additional justificatory weight is transferred to the principles. Moral particularism will fail as a defense of the uncodifiability thesis if wide reflective equilibrium is able to demonstrate a wider role for moral principles. Norman Daniels' formulation of wide reflective equilibrium is the most useful one for my purposes.

> The method of wide reflective equilibrium is an attempt to produce coherence in an ordered triple of sets of beliefs held by a particular person, namely (a) a set of considered moral judgments; (b) a set of moral principles; and (c) a set of relevant background theories.[24]

Instead of being content with the best fit of principles and judgments:

> . . . we advance philosophical arguments intended to bring out the relative strengths and weaknesses of the alternative sets of principles (or competing moral conceptions). These arguments can be construed as inferences from some set of relevant background theories. . . .[25]

The principles that produce the best fit with the considered moral judgments in narrow reflective equilibrium are tested against inferences from relevant background theories. The background theories identify particular properties as morally relevant, thus supporting principles that agree with the theory. For instance, in Rawls's theory of justice, theories of the person, a well-ordered society, and the role of morality within society pick out properties that define the choice situation in the original position from which the two principles of justice are derived. In this view, principles supported by background theories exert revisionary pressure on the considered moral judgments, and to the extent that judgments, principles, and theories are mutually supportive, i.e., brought into equilibrium, the principles and judgments are justified.

Wide reflective equilibrium assumes a heavy burden in order to demonstrate the acceptability of the particular theories on which the justification of a principle depends. Rejection of one of the supporting theories would considerably weaken support for the principle. As Daniels formulates, part of the acceptability of the theory is its contribution to the coherence of the system as a whole.

> Most generally, what justifies us is the coherence of those theories with the other beliefs we think justified in wide equilibrium (including some account of how we have acquired them.)[26]

Thus, wide reflective equilibrium can sustain its nonfoundationalist credentials.

The theories contributing to the support of the principles are themselves generalizations of considered judgments. Yet it is not obvious why the regularities discovered by these theories would carry additional justificatory weight if they were simply reformulations of the original generalizations. Daniels addresses this problem by introducing an additional constraint on the theories. They must satisfy an "independence constraint" such that given the original set of judgments (a):

> The background theories should have a scope reaching beyond the range of the judgments in (a). Suppose some set of considered moral judgments, (a*), plays a role in constraining the background theories in (c). Then we are asking that some interesting, nontrivial portion of (a*) should be disjoint from the set (a) that constrains the principles in (b).[27]

The independence constraint requires that background theories, in order to play a role in systematizing a given set of considered judgments, must also be constrained by an independent set of considered judgments.

Satisfaction of the independence constraint will mitigate, at least to a degree, the problems of narrow reflective equilibrium that I raised above. Satisfaction of such a constraint gives us reason to think that the morally relevant properties identified by the theory are significant across a wider range of experience. This lends some support to the claim that the properties identified by the principles are a relatively fixed reference point with a *prima facie* claim over subordinate properties. The wider the scope of the generalizations that satisfy the independence constraint, the more reason we have to think that situations can be most usefully assessed by consideration of clear cases, giving weight to the similarities across situations rather than the differences between them. As Daniels points out, satisfaction of the independence constraint gives us reason to think that the generalizations are not accidental.[28] The regularities are stronger and more akin to nomological generalizations. This supports the claim that principles play a dominant role in deliberation. Moreover, the wide justificatory net cast by wide reflective equilibrium, although dominated by a theoretical perspective, need not be viewed as alien to the lived experience of moral agents. The sense that diverse areas of one's life form a coherent, intelligible whole might in itself be a reason to adopt those principles mutually supported by background theories as action-guiding principles. By requiring generalizations to achieve a wider scope through satisfaction of the independence constraint, moral principles exert considerable revisionary pressure on moral judgments.

From this account of wide reflective equilibrium, it appears that at least one dominant theoretical approach has succeeded in assimilating the antitheorists' concerns with respect to objectivism and lived experience, without sacrificing the virtues of theory. However, the antitheorist is not without recourse. The virtues of wide reflective equilibrium are dependent on the assumption that there are such regularities of wide scope discoverable by the background theories, an assumption that the antitheorist denies.

Rorty has given us reason to think that these background theories are undecidable. Much of Rorty's corpus is an attempt to persuade us, by pointing to 2,500 years of interminable debate, that philosophy cannot provide us with answers to philosophical questions. As I noted earlier, wide reflective equilibrium, as Rawls and Daniels have articulated it, is entirely dependent on the offering of an account of a particular theory's superiority on such issues as the nature of persons, what counts as a well-ordered society, and the role of morality in society—traditional philosophical questions. In fact, Daniels argues that one of the virtues of wide reflective equilibrium is the relative decidability of these philosophical issues when compared to ethical theories.[29] This strikes me as a preposterous claim, given the history of philosophical reflection on these issues. However, the antitheory position requires some account of why we should not expect consensus on these issues in the future if they are to be effective against wide reflective equilibrium. To this end, I will argue that doubts about the tenability of a theoretical approach can be explained by doubts about the degree and durability of the regularities that social reality exhibits.

Contingency and Morality

If there is a single objection to theory that unifies the antitheorists, it is the claim that the motivational states of moral agents are impenetrable to theoretical discourse. This claim has been implicit in much of the foregoing material, but I have not said much about antitheorists's view of motivational states. Although this objection has traditionally been lodged against Kantian and utilitarian moral theories, especially by those who endorse an Aristotelian view of moral motivation, I want to show here that there is available a more comprehensive antitheory position that objects to any systematic rendering of moral motivation. As will become evident, this involves a commitment to a controversial understanding of the nature of morality.

Antitheorists tend to view social reality as unpredictable, absent of regularities of wide scope, and subject to forces beyond the control of agents. The infirm and desultory character of public discourse, the diversity of life circumstances and moral perspectives across cultures and through history, the continual challenge of new predicaments undreamt of by the practitioners of traditional norms, not to mention the sheer complexity of human life, are obstacles to the systematic rendering of morality that theory attempts to accomplish. I intend all of these obstacles to be captured by the term "contingency." I will argue that the contingency of social reality will explain why judgment cannot be primarily a matter of constructing and extending moral principles. Thus, the contingency thesis will prove to be one feature of the antitheory position that clearly separates it from theoretical approaches, including those of a nonfoundationalist variety.

In the face of the aforementioned impediments to the discovery of an underlying system in our moral judgments, moral theories typically employ idealizations to determine what moral agents are enjoined to do under ideal circumstances. This is because, in addition to minimizing the degree to which the norms described by the theory might be the result of bias, prejudice, or parochial interest, idealizations isolate just those general properties of situations the theorist wants to discuss, while discounting the messy details that bring ambiguity and complexity to the lived experience of ordinary agents. Although this idealizing strategy can be constrained, as it is in Rawls's theory, to reflect only the ideals of a particular group (thus avoiding William's argument against objectivism), it is not obvious that the minimal gains in objectivity achieved by the strategy are worth the losses it sustains with respect to standards of relevance. Such a strategy often fails to explain the force of recommendations under the nonideal circumstances faced by actual moral agents. As Annette Baier points out, although we can attempt to devise perfect responses to nonideal circumstances—norms of Samaritanism or punishment, for instance—when we are confronted with imperfections in these latter responses, we hardly know how to respond. Ideal responses to bad Samaritans and poor administrators are not salient in our moral code, despite the frequency with which we are confronted with the less-than-perfect.[30]

This suggests a more general reason why not only idealizations but indeed the background theories that support them are not very useful in the codification of moral practices into discursive principles. Morality must play its functional role in regulating our conduct by responding to a world of imperfection and corruption. To quote Baier once again,

> Morality controls our responses in this situation of vulnerability and danger, staving off the outright barbarity of the unregulated life of all against all. . . . Moral feelings control by positively reinforcing our responses to the good of cooperation, trust, mutual aid, friendship, love, as well as regulating responses to the risk of evil.[31]

Good and evil are inseparably linked because the possibility of evil is the rationale for having a morality in the first place. Morality "responds to a situation in which hope and fear are properly inspired by one and the same situation."[32]

That the opportunity to do good exists only if the risk of evil is incurred suggests that morality itself is pervaded by contingency, for our sense of vulnerability is conditioned by the circumstances under which it arises. We feel threatened by particular harms just because they are novel, unpredictable, because our grasp of them is tenuous, and our control over circumstances unsure. Vulnerability is almost always thoroughly dependent on contextual factors, and so must be moral judgment. Moreover, I doubt that any general theory of human imperfection is possible, since the human imagination seems endlessly fecund in finding new forms of going off the rails. There would appear to be myriad ways in which corruption might seep into our lives, for even our best intentions can be twisted by a world resistant to our aims.

This suggests that the attempt to describe morality as a function of permanent, widely shared features of the human condition, even when tested against local considered judgments, overlooks the role that morality plays in the economy of life. I say "suggests" because, if the particular harms and dangers we face share common features that demand a common response, then recognition of this element of contingency should not dissuade us from pursuing grand theoretical strategies. However, if our fears and vulnerabilities arrive individuated and plural, and as irreducible to a single dimension as the goods we seek, then moral reflection must pursue a different strategy, for in that case morality is unlikely to display the kinds of regularities that a theory demands. Thus, the issue will turn on the regularities displayed by human responses to vulnerability and threat.

The appeal to contingency, if it is to support the antitheory position, must show that the capacity for a moral life, when viewed against this background of vulnerability, cannot be articulated, explained, or justified by appeal to relatively fixed, widely shared, structural features of human nature discovered through theoretical reflection. Richard Rorty comes closest to articulating such a view.

Rorty's Contingency Thesis

As Nietzsche pointed out, the human being is the meaning-giving animal that must endlessly suffer the fruits of its labor. The source of human vulnerability is not merely the ever-present possibility of death, but the recognition that the things we think are significant will die with us. Our sense of what is important seems to have only a tenuous existence, and its loss as threatening as death. "The world can blindly and inarticulately crush us; mute despair, intense mental pain, can cause us to blot ourselves out."[33] One way of finding meaning in life despite the black humor of a disenchanted universe is to become attached to some larger context, something permanent and transcendent, with a significance that cannot be destroyed by mere mortality. For Rorty, philosophers exemplify *in extremis* this desire for transcendence. Philosophy is an attempt to "speak nature's own vocabulary," thereby gaining a measure of control over inarticulate forces. More concretely, philosophy encourages us to revise our judgments on the basis of what reality and human beings are "really" like—on the basis of how things are. Much of Rorty's corpus has been devoted to explaining why this attempt at philosophical transcendence is mere hubris. Philosophy cannot serve as our connection to a larger purpose or secure a fixed reference point from which the essence of what it means to be human can be represented.

According to Rorty, at the heart of the theoretical enterprise is a picture of the relationship between language, self, and reality that is dominated by metaphors of representation. Language is a medium that represents reality to a subject. This way of looking at the relationship between word and world assumes that some ways of speaking represent reality more accurately than others, and the justification for speaking one way rather than another includes the presence of a causal connection between word and world, on the basis of which criteria of adequacy can be established.

This assumption, however, cannot be given any substantial support. We cannot form an idea of the world that is not a representation or description of that world; thus, we have no independent means to determine the accuracy of the description except by means of another description, the accuracy of which itself cannot be independently verified. Inquiry, therefore, must be a matter of comparing one description with another, not a comparison with "reality's own language."[34] Moreover, when comparing competing descriptions of reality, although it is appropriate to think of the world as containing the causes of "our being justified in holding a belief" when we have clear and uncontroversial standards for adjudicating disagreement, such criteria are lacking when the disagreement is between two quite different ways of looking at the world, when the competing descriptions are too far apart to share common assumptions.[35] Because the criteria of adequacy associated with the old way of speaking will be questioned with the proposed revision, we are left with no criteria in terms of which to judge the comparison. Thus, on Rorty's view, when revising our beliefs involves substantial changes in vocabulary—global shifts in meaning—we should not describe this as a process of justification. We cannot explain our holding the beliefs we do as a process of getting closer to what reality is in itself. Our linguistic practices are contingent—a series of historical accidents—because without the hypothesis of a "made true" relationship between world and word, there is nothing deeper than history that will explain our holding the beliefs we hold. To use Rorty's example, since we can't plausibly justify speaking the vocabulary of democracy rather than the vocabulary of aristocracy by appealing to a causal relationship between word and world, we can only appeal to purely historical causes as explanations for why we speak the language of democracy.

Rorty's thesis regarding the contingency of language ought to make us question background theories' authority to force revisions of considered judgments in reflective equilibrium. However, as I noted previously, the theories included within wide reflective equilibrium need only satisfy coherence constraints imposed by the demand that the theories be open to revision from considered judgments at all levels of the equilibrium. They need not satisfy the demand that justified beliefs be "made true" by what the belief represents. Hence, the contingency of language will not in itself mark a serious objection to wide reflective equilibrium. Nevertheless, Rorty provides an interesting thesis about conceptual change that points to the limits of theory as responsible for revising beliefs. If Rorty is correct, widespread conceptual change cannot be explained by theoretical reflection because substantial doubt about one's beliefs brings substantial doubt about the criteria one uses for demonstrating the superiority of one belief system over another. I will have occasion to discuss this problem in the section on incommensurability, which follows. Before turning to that issue, I want to look at Rorty's discussion of the contingency of the self. It is here, I think, that Rorty succeeds in drawing the sharpest contrast between antitheory and nonfoundationalism.

The representationalist epistemology that Rorty is attacking has another side to it as well. Language not only represents reality, it also expresses the beliefs and desires of a human self, and thus serves as the vehicle for representing what is distinctly human. Since Plato, the question of what sort of language best expresses our humanity has been hotly contested. Poets and philosophers are the main adversaries in this debate, which Rorty uses as a means of explicating alternative modes of confronting mortality—alternatives that nonphilosophers and nonpoets embody to a degree.

Philosophers typically seek to discover universal properties that constitute the meaning of being human, thereby establishing a connection with an entity larger than oneself.

> One could die with satisfaction, having accomplished the only task laid upon humanity, *to know the truth,* to be in touch with what is "out there".... Extinction would not matter, for one would have become identical with the truth, and truth, on this traditional view, is imperishable.[36]

In Rorty's thumbnail sketch of the philosophical tradition, this project typically has taken the form of splitting the self into two parts: reason, which all humans potentially share, and a less important, idiosyncratic part of the self that harbors contingent desires and emotions and is useless for purposes of seeking the constitutive properties of human experience. This bifurcation of the self is another instance of philosophical attempts to corral the unpredictable, uncontrollable, and inarticulate forces that foster our sense of vulnerability.

Poets, on the other hand, seek consolation by trying to figure out what is distinctive about oneself, to find the words that will demonstrate why one is not a copy of someone else. We should "seek consolation at the moment of death, not in having transcended the animal condition but in being that peculiar sort of dying animal who, by describing himself in his own terms, had created himself."[37] The poet's awareness of her past is not a matter of discovery but of self-creation, of creating a new vocabulary with which to describe herself, since the use of an inherited vocabulary will fail to demonstrate the uniqueness that the poet seeks. After 2,500 years of metaphysical debates, the philosophical questions look unanswerable to Rorty, and the attachment to something trans-human increasingly tenuous. This loss of what Nietzsche called "metaphysical comfort" suggests that only the alternative offered by the poet is viable.

The contrast between philosopher and poet on questions of the ultimate meaning of life is reinscribed at another level connecting directly with moral philosophy. On the conflict between public responsibility and private ends, between a common moral conscience and individual self-expression, the respective tasks of poets and philosophers seem to diverge. Moral theory has usually attempted to resolve this conflict by demonstrating that, even while pursuing private ends, we are committed to a common moral conscience by threat of irrationality. Once again, this can only be accomplished by reducing the contingency of human experience. Kant accomplishes this by positing a part of the self that is independent of space and time, and thus not dependent upon contingent private ends. Utilitarians achieve similar results by claiming to speak from the point of view of an ideally clairvoyant, disinterested observer.

Rorty appeals to followers of Freud, who make the resolution of this conflict between public and private psychologically accessible by showing that "compassion is not identification with a human core, but is channeled in specific ways toward specific people." In this view, the self becomes a "tissue of contingencies" rather than a "well-ordered system of faculties."[38] Rorty's point here is that what is most human in us and what accounts for the person each of us has become is a history of human attachments. What is important about this history is that each relationship has its own character, provokes a unique emotional tone, engenders its own set of specific obligations and permissions, and provides a unique perspective on what is important and what is not. There may, of course, be features common to most human relationships, features that can be analytically distinguished and given a general description, that divide the soul into parts or faculties. Yet these will not explain why we have become the individuals we are. The formative power of these attachments—the capacity of these relationships to shape a personality or character—is in their singularity and uniqueness.

Rorty claims significant explanatory power for this account of moral motivation.

> He [Freud] helps explain how someone can be both a tender mother and a merciless concentration-camp guard, or be a just and temperate magistrate and also a chilly, rejecting father . . . why we deplore cruelty in some cases and relish it in others. He shows us why our ability to love is restricted to some very particular shapes and sizes and colors of people, things, or ideas.[39]

In contrast to the Kantian notion of rationality, which involves subsuming particular cases under general principles, Rorty's Freud would have us focus on the particular, identifying idiosyncratic contingencies from the past, and redescribe ourselves in light of this knowledge, thereby breaking free from the past.

The Freudian vocabulary enables us to sketch a richer and more fine-grained narrative of our moral experience than the traditional categories in moral philosophy. By exhibiting the complexity of our unconscious strategies,

> [Freud] makes it possible for us to see science and poetry, genius and psychosis—and, most importantly, morality and prudence—not as products of distinct faculties but as alternative modes of adaptation.[40]

In so doing, Freud demonstrates that the exclusive rights to the task of redescription are not held by the poets. Freud's contribution to civilization is to make this task of redescription accessible to us all. The unconscious life of everyman is a source of creativity that transforms everyday encounters into symbolic expressions. Thus, the poet is merely a special case:

> Somebody who does with marks and noises what other people do with their spouses and children, their fellow workers, the tools of their trade . . . the music they listen to, the sports they play or watch, or the trees they pass on their way to work. . . . Any such constellation can set up an unconditional commandment to whose service a life may be devoted—a commandment no less unconditional because it may be intelligible to, at most, only one person.[41]

The self, therefore, is no less contingent than language—that is to say, the formation of character, personality, and a sense of autonomy associated with self-reflection and agency are more usefully explained by tracing a particular history than by positing a substantial, underlying essential nature accessible to philosophical theory.

The obvious objection to this moral psychology is that it makes a mystery out of our attachment to the larger community. If compassion is channeled in specific ways through specific people, how do we account for the "social glue" that binds larger groups of people through impersonal political institutions? It follows from the contingency of the self that a concern for justice, or lack thereof, is somehow a function of past human attachments. This leads Rorty to assert, rather glibly, that "Allegiance to social institutions is like the choice of friends."[42] Moreover, it follows from the contingency of language and the aforementioned objections to objectivist justifications that philosophical criteria will not help us understand the social bond either. The social bond, "human solidarity," is not explained by appeal to an "essence" or a faculty, nor is it explained by some in-dwelling logos operating throughout history. Rorty's answer to the question of the social bond is that the beliefs we hold about who counts as a moral agent, and the appropriate conduct toward a human agent, are the result of those institutions we happen to have adopted throughout the history of Western civilization. Although this history is shaped by Christianity and the philosophical tradition, both of which assert a deeper level of explanation (one that appeals to divine inspiration, an "essential human nature," a metaphysical self or some other foundational principle), Rorty argues that we can dispense with these explanations. We must understand ourselves as products of history rather than something beyond time, products of a civilization that just happens to value individual freedom and abhor cruelty. No further explanation is possible or required.[43] Moral conscience does not rest on philosophical foundations. Community, too, is the result of time and chance.

Rorty's appropriation of Freud deepens and extends the contingency thesis, because it strengthens the inference from the contingency of the circumstances human beings confront to the contingency of the responses to those circumstances.[44] In Rorty's treatment, vulnerability and desire not only condition morality, but do so without forming regular patterns of response that might be explicable through theoretical discourse. The harms and dangers we confront are neither universal nor even widely shared, and our coping strategies are as idiosyncratic as the fears and vulnerabilities on which these strategies rest.

This suggests that among the capacities the possibility of a moral response to conditions of deficit requires is a particular kind of historical sense, as well as a fecund imagination. As the significance of life, for Rorty, is to be understood in terms of attachments to particular episodes from one's past, framed against a background of vulnerability, and because any of these attachments can be the source of "an unconditional commandment," moral reflection requires a historical sensitivity directed toward these particular formative episodes. However, because the contingency thesis precludes an explanation that would reduce this history to a system of laws or principles, the only power we have over this past is the power of redescription. When confronted with the unpredictable and uncontrollable, and in recognition of the brute inarticulateness of what

Rorty calls the "blind impress" that unwittingly shapes each of us, we can only attempt to recreate ourselves by redescribing the authority figures who have influenced us. Liberation from the dead weight of the past requires the resources of the poet who can, through the use of metaphor, induce in us novel forms of self-understanding.

It is important to emphasize that the contingency of the self does not guarantee a *moral* response to contingent circumstances, since presumably there is no intrinsic relationship between idiosyncratic impulses and moral conduct. Rorty's appeal to Freud does not define what counts as morality, but only points to the context in which moral reflection must gain a purchase. Rorty's presentation of a moral perspective is richer than is indicated here, and I will return to Rorty in Chapter Five to remedy this deficiency. However, this account of the contingency of language, self, and community is sufficient to sharpen the distinction between anti-theory and wide reflective equilibrium.

Recall that the function of background theories in wide reflective equilibrium is to help determine which facts about individuals and societies are morally relevant, thereby supporting the generalizations represented by the moral principles that are to be included in the equilibrium. Baier effectively argued that, to the extent these theories are idealizations, there is reason to doubt the degree to which they support action-guiding principles because moral agents typically do not respond to ideal circumstances. Rorty's rather idiosyncratic understanding of moral motivation widens the scope of this objection to include even theories of the self and community that are not dependent on idealizations but rely instead on empirical generalizations. If it is the case, as Rorty claims, that the self is a "tissue of contingencies" in which almost anything can be the source of an "unconditional commandment" supplying the locus of meaning for one's life, then it is difficult to imagine how any theory of the self, or conception of community grounded in such a theory, could convincingly identify just those morally relevant properties required by particular moral principles. It would be difficult, with this conception of the self in particular, for Rawls to argue that a theory of persons identifies properties possessed by choosers, in the original position, as the morally relevant properties with respect to principles of justice. Any theory of persons will appear excessively reductionist in light of Rorty's description of the self.

In accordance with his claim that argument, as traditionally conceived, is less persuasive than redescription, Rorty fails to give substantive philosophical arguments for his conception of the self. To serve his purposes, he simply gives us an alternative way of looking at the self. The power of redescription notwithstanding, this is likely to be unconvincing to some-one who is not antecedently committed to the picture he paints. Part of the agenda of subsequent chapters will be to explore the kinds of continu-ity a human self requires for moral conduct to be intelligible. Despite the absence of conclusive arguments, which would in any case be incompati-ble with Rorty's views on the contingency of language, his redescription of the self succeeds in sharpening the contrast between nonfoundationalism and antitheory. Underlying much of the writing that can be broadly con-strued as antitheoretical is the worry that theory tends to disconnect rea-sons from motivational states. We saw this theme in Williams's and Rorty's expressed worries about theoretical imperialism, in McDowell's claim that the practical syllogism could not explain moral conduct, and in Baier's discussion of the limits of moral principles. Rorty's contingency thesis, then, can be viewed as an attempt to explain the disconnection between theory and motivational states. In Rorty's view, whatever motivation we find to act morally will arise only from our concrete relations with others.

The recognition that contingency pervades morality begins with the recognition that the possibility of good is linked to the possibility of evil. This suggests that the primary role of moral agency is to regulate our responses to conditions of vulnerability and threat, and that moral judg-ment is constrained by imperfect information, parochial interest, limita-tions on material and emotional resources, and our deficient capacities to predict and control the forces of nature and human nature. The cumu-lative effect of these claims produces a picture of morality as a collection of strategies for coping. Rorty, however, claims that the harms and dangers we confront are neither universal nor even widely shared, and our coping strategies are as idiosyncratic as the fears and vulnerabilities on which these strategies rest. In summary, the distinction between non-foundationalism and antitheory can be most clearly marked by the claim that theoretical principles are not responsive to the conditions to which morality is a response. I return to Rorty in Chapter Five and discuss his view in more detail.

Incommensurability

The final element in the antitheory position is the incommensurability thesis. The incommensurability thesis's importance to the antitheory position is connected to the extent and nature of moral disagreement, and the prospects for resolving that disagreement. In its most general formu-lation, incommensurability refers to a disruption in communication across theories, vocabularies, or perspectives that renders rational assessment difficult or impossible. Because it is part of the conditions of adequacy for any theory that it explains, and it justifies the full range of moral judgments agents typically make, the claim that competing moral perspectives cannot be rationally assessed would cast doubt on the basic aims of the theoretical enterprise. Consequently, if true, the incommensurability thesis would represent a serious objection to theory. However, there has been much debate on exactly how to characterize "incommensurability." Before we turn to the question of whether the thesis can be defended, we have to be clear about what the thesis comes to. Furthermore, it is part of this book's aim to defend a particular version of the incommensurability thesis. Thus, I will not attempt a comprehensive defense here but will focus on beginning to clarify my understanding of the term.

Since the term "incommensurability" gained currency in connection with the work of Kuhn and Feyerabend in the philosophy of science, "incommensurability" has been the source of much confusion. Although it clearly involves a disruption in the ability to communicate across alternative conceptual frameworks, the controversy lies in the appropriate characterization of the disruption. Although I cannot here rehearse the details of its various formulations, I will attempt to give a quick summary in order to clarify its relevance to the antitheory position in ethics.

In the first instance, "incommensurability" means that the meaning or reference of key terms in one theory or vocabulary cannot be equated with those in another. Thus, no judgment of superiority between competing theories or vocabularies is possible, since we would not know the meaning of at least some of the terms being assessed. This has suggested to some philosophers that the problem of incommensurability is one of translation, and that inquirers are locked into linguistic frameworks, unable to communicate with those trapped in alternative frameworks.[45] Donald Davidson has shown, however, that extreme cases of either sort of incommensurability cannot exist, since we cannot recognize something both as a language and as untranslatable, nor can we recognize a conceptual framework with absolutely no relation to our own as a conceptual framework.[46] Thus, the only coherent form of incommensurability of this sort involves partial intranslatability.

Partial intranslatability suggests there is some overlap in the descriptions allowing coreference to go through, and the question of assessment will revolve around how much semantic overlap is required for comparisons to be made. However, the question of coreference can be avoided entirely. If we agree with Davidson that learning a language is a matter of correlating the sounds speakers make with observable features of the world, there is no reason to think any of these correlations will be, in principle, inaccessible to a translator. Thus, the problem of incommensurability, if it exists at all, is not one of translation.[47]

In fact, Alasdair MacIntyre argues that it is our prodigious capacity to translate the canonical texts of diverse traditions that helps to explain incommensurability.[48] In discussing a hypothetical speaker of a premodern language who frees herself from the limitations of her traditional culture by learning to speak the language of modernity, MacIntyre writes:

> But the culture that is able to make such a language available is so only because it is a culture offering, for the relevant kinds of controversial subject matter, all too many heterogeneous and incompatible schemes of rational justification. . . . Hence our imaginary person, whose acquisition of one of the natural languages of modernity . . . was to rescue him or her from the relativism imposed by his or her previous condition, cannot find here any more than there, albeit for very different reasons, any genuinely neutral and independent standard of rational justification.[49]

Here, the incommensurability thesis refers to the presence of numerous conflicting procedures of justification that prevent a commitment to any of them. This passage from MacIntyre suggests that the obstacle to rational assessment characteristic of the incommensurability thesis is the absence of a set of criteria independent of the competing viewpoints being assessed. This is another standard definition of incommensurability, shared by some commentators who understand the thesis asserting there are no permanent, neutral, universal standards of rationality.[50] This definition of incommensurability is problematic because, at least in the face of moral questions, it tends to collapse into the antiobjectivism of Williams, a discussion of which I began this chapter. In that discussion, I claimed that antiobjectivism did not present a hurdle to nonfoundationalism since the latter did not require such a set of neutral standards. Thus, if this is all to which the incommensurability thesis comes, it would not be distinct from the many Hegelian, hermeneutic, and nonfoundationalist critiques of objectivism that have gained currency. It would not, therefore, have the radical consequences of the possibility of communication it is purported to have, nor would it advance the antitheory position.

In fact, the previous quote from MacIntyre is somewhat misleading. In referring to neutral, independent standards of justification, MacIntyre apparently makes reference to the aspirations of modernist theory and its failure to supply modern agents with genuinely neutral criteria. When MacIntyre turns to the question of how incommensurability can be alleviated, he argues that judgments of rational superiority do not require neutrality, but instead require the resources of a tradition; specifically, a set of canonical problems intrinsic to that tradition, in terms of which its progress, or failure to progress can be assessed. Accompanying this is the recognition that failure may necessitate the appropriation of resources from outside that tradition. This suggests that incommensurability can be defined in terms of the breakdown in norms associated with rational assessment within a tradition, a phenomenon brought on by the emergence of modernism's ideal of neutrality and its hostile attitude toward tradition, according to MacIntyre.

In this view, incommensurability is an empirical phenomenon, itself a product of a particular history. It differs from nonobjectivism in that the obstacle to justification is not the absence of independent or neutral criteria. The difficulty is in the absence of criteria internal to the tradition that warrant judgments of progress or decline. However, MacIntyre's conception of incommensurability is dependent on the claim that the presence of multiple, rival, incompatible paradigms of justification precludes a commitment to any one of them, and on the claim that traditions are unified by the presence of explicit, canonical paradigms of assessment. Both of these claims are controversial, and the incommensurability thesis would be strengthened if it could be made to rest on less controversial ground.[51]

Bjorn Ramberg's account of incommensurability preserves the claim that incommensurability is an empirical phenomenon based on the erosion of norms, while avoiding the claim that the source of incommensurability lies in the absence of explicit criteria. Moreover, Ramberg's characterization of incommensurability preserves its original attachment in Kuhn's writings to questions of meaning, which tend to get lost in MacIntyre's concern with paradigms of justification. Ramberg argues that:

> the conventions of a language are diachronic generalizations of linguistic practice. . . . We rely on conventions to understand and make ourselves understood. Incommensurability, as a communication breakdown, can be understood as a breakdown of linguistic conventions, caused by changes in use that are too abrupt to be absorbed smoothly, or changes that a particular set of conventions are too rigid to accommodate. Semantically, then, incommensurability is

a disruption in the ongoing interpretation-through-application of our linguistic conventions.[52]

It's important to see that the source of communication breakdown in this account of incommensurability is not linguistic meaning itself, but the production of meaning. Regardless of how effortless is our deployment of linguistic conventions in ordinary contexts, these conventions are sometimes unhelpful in clarifying the meaning of speakers. At that point of breakdown, further communication will depend on the capacity for interpretation that is distinct from the deployment of conventions on Ramberg's Davidsonian account of language, and must proceed without recourse to those conventions. Incommensurability refers to this semantic obstruction caused by the failure of prevailing linguistic norms to successfully produce the meaning required for communication. However, intranslatability is not a consequence of this breakdown because, in Ramberg's Davidsonian view of language, our linguistic capacity to correlate utterances with observable features of the world remains intact.[53] Incommensurability is, therefore, not a total breakdown in the capacity to communicate, only a breakdown in those conventions that make communication effortless.

Thus, incommensurability is not a relation between conceptual schemes or structures but "a symptom of structural change" that is manifested by failed attempts at communication, and can occur within a tradition or paradigm as well as between them.

> In my analysis this incommensurability is not a particular relation among the different moral vocabularies, it is a characteristic of the discourse that results when we proceed *as if* we are using the same vocabulary, and so interpret others by applying linguistic conventions to which they are not party.[54]

Ramberg's explication reshapes, to a degree, the debate surrounding the incommensurability thesis. It has less to do with justification *simpliciter* and more to do with the communicative practice that justification requires. The source of incommensurability is not the absence of criteria, although this might be a consequence. Its source lies at the intersection of the pressures for linguistic reform and the resistance of linguistic norms to those pressures.

The final version of incommensurability I want to consider is that of the French philosopher Jean-Francois Lyotard. I will call this radical incommensurability. Thus far, the forms of incommensurability we have looked at have had their source either in the absence of criteria for justification or at the point at which linguistic conventions fail to produce meaning. Lyotard, instead, focuses on the performative aspects of language and discovers incommensurability at the heart of all linguistic practice.

Incommensurability, for Lyotard, is a function of the ambiguity of language and of the fact it serves a multitude of purposes. In Lyotard's conception of language, speakers utter phrases that can be classified under various phrase regimes—descriptives, prescriptives, questions, exclamations, etc. Phrase regimes are then linked in ways that are teleologically determined by an idea imposing unity on these regimes. This teleological determinate is called a genre.

> For example, dialogue [a genre] links an ostension (showing) or a definition (describing) onto a question; at stake [the purpose] in it is two parties coming to an agreement about the sense of a referent.[55]

Interlocutors, however, can place phrases under various genres. In response to some utterance that falls under a particular regime and genre, interlocutors are free to respond in any number of ways that may or may not be in accord with the speaker's intentions. There is no need to respond in a particular way. Thus, by responding with a phrase within one genre, a number of other possible genres are suppressed, giving rise to what Lyotard calls a *differend*.

> A case of *differend* between two parties takes place when the "regulation" of the conflict that opposes them is done in the idiom of one of the parties while the wrong suffered by the other is not signified in that idiom.[56]

For instance, laws and norms respecting property rights might describe as theft the removal of an icon from a Native American burial site located on private property. However, the Native American may not recognize such property rights with respect to objects of worship. In a court of law, the Native American cannot prove legal ownership, and the sense in which the icon "belongs" to him cannot be expressed in the idiom of the court. Hence, a *differend* exists between the two parties, the result of a conflict over genre. Similarly, in Lyotard's preferred example, the silence of survivors of the Holocaust cannot find expression in the cognitive phrase regime that seeks to understand the Holocaust as a historical event among others. Since the silence provides no evidence for the existence of the Holocaust, the sense in which the Holocaust transcends all explanation is suppressed.

In all complex forms of communication and deliberation, genres succeed and suppress each other as they contend for supremacy. The threat of a *differend* is always present, although it is most acute when the ethical, political, and cognitive genres are in play.

Lyotard's work will play a significant role in the argument of this book. These sketchy remarks on *differends* will serve here only as background to a somewhat different conception developed later in this book, beginning with Chapter Three. For Lyotard, incommensurability is not simply a breakdown in the effectiveness of linguistic norms. It is, instead, an essential feature of them, and this will reinforce a point in which I made a brief allusion to Ramberg. Incommensurability need not refer to conflicts between distant cultures or entire vocabularies—in Lyotard's view, it characterizes conflicts in the bedroom and workplace as well. When carried to its extreme, incommensurability calls into question the sense in which a culture rests on shared beliefs.

The incommensurability thesis raises questions about the content and aspirations of moral theories. Even if we accept the premise that moral reflection must begin from within a point of view, it does not follow that moral discourse is only applicable within that point of view, or that expressions of moral concern referring beyond one's own point of view are nonsense. Thus, a moral theory, even one that begins from within a moral perspective, must be able to demonstrate its relationship to other perspectives, explaining disagreements and discrepancies as well as identifying points of agreement. Moreover, a moral theory that could not clarify the moral status of those who shared different moral perspectives would be seriously deficient, especially in a culture such as our own, which is deeply influenced by universalist moral and religious beliefs.

Returning to the status of nonfoundationalist approaches to moral theory, incommensurability would certainly be an obstacle to wide reflective equilibrium's capacity to satisfy these aspirations of a moral theory. As Williams writes in response to contractualism's commitment to wide reflective equilibrium:

We can less and less appropriately rely on those intuitions that belong distinctively to the local *we*, since the theory is now to be a theory for an *us* that includes agents existing far away from our local folkways.[57]

The general criteria of coherence and wide scope would be restricted to a narrow range of considered judgments, depending, of course, on the severity of the incommensurability.

It is important to see what follows if the incommensurability thesis of MacIntyre or Ramberg is defensible. In that case, if we wish to sustain the aspirations of theory and the criteria of wide scope and systematicity, we will be forced to relax the initial credibility of our considered moral judgments to accommodate greater diversity. We will, then, have to rely more heavily on background theories to support those considered moral judgments and to reestablish an equilibrium. However, the incommensurability thesis asserts that prevailing criteria and norms—the very background articulated by the background theories—will not produce the requisite intelligibility for the proposed justification. Thus, if the incommensurability thesis is defensible, wide-reflective equilibrium is impotent, except within a very narrow range.

The situation with theory is exacerbated if Lyotard's more radical incommensurability thesis is the case. Then there is no reason to think there are shared, considered moral judgments from which moral principles can be generalized.[58]

This concludes the summary of antitheory arguments. Throughout the course of this chapter, I was concerned about marking the difference between nonfoundationalist attacks on foundationalist moral theories and antitheory arguments against normative ethical theory in general. As I noted at the beginning of the chapter, my intent was not a sustained defense of the antitheorists, except where some additional support was needed to mark the contrast with nonfoundationalism, nor did I intend to point out flaws in the position. Instead, my intent was to lay the groundwork for a further exploration of the shape of moral reflection once we accept the basic thrust of the antitheory arguments. However, it should come as no surprise to the reader that I am in agreement with the position as rendered thus far.

As I remarked earlier, I do not intend to forgo assessment of the antitheory approach but will pursue that assessment by raising what I take to be the single largest obstacle to accepting the position—it cannot account for the central notion that all moral agents are worthy of equal respect and concern. It should be clear by now that antitheorists presuppose a conception of morality that I called "concrete ethics" in the introduction. The absence of an objective point of view, the importance of particularity, and the openness of the human condition to contingency and incommensurability leave little for morality to represent except those obligations incurred through participation in a history of institutions and specific relationships. But if these are the origins of our moral obligations, it is not immediately obvious how we are to understand obligations to the radically "other"—those who do not share a tradition or who owe allegiance to a different community. My worry is that antitheorists have no adequate response to this objection. Is it part of the antitheory position that we should stop pursuing this aspiration, or is theory only a failed means to a worthy end for which alternative means are available? The writers who raise objections to theory almost universally acknowledge the power of this intuition, and devote considerable space to articulating the alternative ways of accounting for and sustaining this intuition. However, the arguments do not proceed by attempting to ground this intuition in an unassailable moral principle (unassailable because it is deductively generated from an objective point of view). Rather, they try to show how it is continually possible to transcend one's point of view by gaining a critical perspective allowing one to both perceive the limitations of it and formulate novel approaches that sustain moral progress.

In the following chapters, I will take up this question of transcending one's moral point of view in light of these doubts about moral theory. In turning to this issue, however, a number of related questions arise that I will take up in conjunction with the issue of transcending limitations. One of the more interesting claims that emerges from this literature is the suggestion that narratives are a richer resource for moral reflection than theory. I will assess that claim as well, beginning with the work of Alasdair MacIntyre.

Part One

Narrative and Ethics

2

MacIntyre: The Claim of History

The moral point of view to which antitheory arguments seem to lead is this: Moral agents act on the basis of the concrete detail of lived experience that gives moral reflection its content and purpose. I have suggested that this conception of moral agency might be unable to account for the attribution of universal moral agency that has become central to our moral point of view. Alasdair MacIntyre's work is concerned with getting through this tension, and this chapter will also in part be devoted to assessing his success. However, the chapter will serve another purpose. MacIntyre makes some very suggestive remarks regarding how the notion of narrative structure casts light on the nature of human agency. Because it is my aim to begin to articulate an alternative view of moral reflection, I will consider in some detail MacIntyre's remarks on narrative. These two aims will not be incompatible, because I wish to pose the question of whether the concept of narrative helps resolve this tension between concrete ethics and universal moral agency.

MacIntyre provides us with one way of articulating what it means to attend to the concrete details of moral life. He argues that answers to moral questions can be intelligibly addressed only from within a particular historical tradition, and that an understanding of this history plays an essential role in moral reflection. Thus, MacIntyre seems to endorse at least some elements of the antitheory position articulated in Chapter One. However, the difficulty with any moral perspective taking history and tradition as the source of moral commitment is that it seems too parochial to capture the intuitions of our Enlightenment heritage that encourage the attribution of universal moral agency, and is, consequently, open to charges of relativism and narrowness of vision. It seems reasonable to demand of a moral perspective that it express our sense of humanity and confer full moral status on those who have different histories and traditions; that it express the virtues of tolerance and openness; and that it possess resources for self-criticism and correction, especially in light of the destructive cultural traditions staining human history. Because these demands require that we achieve some critical distance from our history and tradition, the historicist's task is to articulate a capacity for transcending the limitations of one's history—a capacity that can also remaining embedded within that tradition.

I want to explore MacIntyre's conception of the role of history in moral reflection, especially focusing on this tension between embeddedness in a tradition and the aspiration to transcend that tradition. MacIntyre fails to resolve this tension satisfactorily, and his proposed resolution in fact undermines what he wishes to assert; namely, that history exerts a claim on moral reflection. My argument will emphasize the stringency of the constraints history places on moral agents, in MacIntyre's view. Thus, I will begin by summarizing his account of the ways in which our lives, both individually and collectively, require historical awareness for their intelligibility.

The question of the importance of historical understanding for moral reflection arises in the context of MacIntyre's perception of a moral crisis affecting the modern age. In often apocalyptic tones, MacIntyre argues that modernism has undermined the rich and varied religious and intellectual traditions that once nurtured our capacity for moral reflection and judgment. He tells a finely textured story of how the rejection of the idea of a natural *telos* characterizing both ancient and medieval thought, and the subsequent emergence of modern liberalism's emphasis on individualism and freedom of choice, has left us with only fragments of a moral vocabulary that cannot be effectively used to resolve disagreement on moral issues. Specifically, according to MacIntyre, Enlightenment science, by replacing the teleological, Aristotelian world view, severed the connection between fact and value resting on that world view. The result, embodied in both the philosophy and social institutions of modernism, is an "emotivist self" issuing moral judgments without the aid of a relatively fixed social identity providing standards of judgment for resolving practical questions. The principles and norms expressed in our moral vocabulary are inadequate for the tasks of moral reflection because we lack agreed-upon paradigms of justification to resolve conflicts between them. In the absence of such agreement, the content of morality is simply a matter of choice for individual agents, who may accept or reject any aspect of it on purely subjective grounds. Although we often use the moral vocabulary inherited from our various traditions and originally employed to enable humanity to achieve its *telos,* this vocabulary is, in the absence of such a conception of human nature, useful only for covering up the arbitrary assertion of will that lies at the bottom of our moral choices. Consequently, contemporary moral reflection must either affirm the arbitrary assertion of subjective will or return to the essentially Aristotelian idea of a natural *telos.*

As a result of this global indictment of modern liberalism, MacIntyre assumes the burden of providing a genuine alternative that corrects the principle defect of liberalism—the arbitrariness of moral choice. Yet MacIntyre does not have available to him a credible version of the *natural* teleology that provided a functional role for the moral virtues in Aristotle's scheme of things, given the rejection of Aristotle's metaphysical biology by modern science. Instead, MacIntyre finds this functional role for the virtues within the history of our social practices and traditions. Consequently, the most important component of this alternative to liberalism is MacIntyre's claim that only a moral perspective that takes historical understanding seriously will correct liberalism's central defect—the arbitrariness of moral choice.

History and Social Identity

In this section, I will begin to explicate the connections in MacIntyre's work between historical awareness and a form of moral reflection that promises nonarbitrary moral choice. Despite MacIntyre's desire to distance himself from Aristotle's metaphysical biology, he nevertheless finds Aristotle's functional account of human flourishing useful in establishing the connection between fact and value. He argues that, to the extent the moral concepts we employ are functional concepts embodying a goal or purpose, we can move from factual premises to evaluative conclusions. A good (x) is one that performs its function well. Because the performance of certain functions essential to social life will require virtues, MacIntyre can argue that the goods that are acquired through, or are constitutive of these functions can be achieved only if one cultivates virtues.

This connection between a functional account of human flourishing and virtues is spelled out in three stages that identify features of social reality and the goods associated with them, attainment of which will require virtues. The first stage concerns the relation between social practices and virtues—qualities of character that enable agents to acquire the goods internal to those practices. For instance, the practice of friendship requires the virtue of honesty, the practice of teaching requires a sense of justice (a sense of what is due to whom), and the protection of individuals and communities requires the virtue of courage, etc.[1] However, specification of the qualities required to achieve goods will fail to mitigate the arbitrariness of moral choice, because it gives us no reason to prefer one practice over another. The second stage attempts to respond to this lacuna by establishing a connection between virtue and what MacIntyre calls "the narrative unity of a single human life." At this point MacIntyre must assert the importance of history as a central component in the conceptual background of virtues, because at stake is the way in which virtues contribute to the unity of an individual's entire life. What is interesting and unique about MacIntyre's account of the unity of an individual life is his claim that our sense of personal and social identity through time has the form of a historical narrative.

According to MacIntyre, a central component of our understanding of social relations is historical awareness. We are able to make sense of the actions of ourselves and others, and can hold ourselves and others responsible for our actions, only if historical awareness is presupposed. Our ordinary explanations of individual actions are enhanced by our capacity to situate them in a history that exposes the long-term intentions of an agent, and the intelligibility of these intentions depend further on our understanding of the history of the context in which an action takes place. Furthermore, we make sense of how others respond to us, in part, by making reference to facts about the past—most notably, that each of us begins life by occupying identifiable social roles defined by family, country, religion, and ethnicity.

In addition to these intelligibility conditions, there are identity conditions that can be satisfied only by historical awareness, according to MacIntyre. That the episodic course of my life is subject to description by others imposes strict identity conditions on me by demanding that I be the single subject of various actions at disparate times and places—past actions for which I can be held accountable despite physical or psychological transformations. To account for personal identity and responsibility is therefore to tell a story unified by the persistence of a character that is the subject of these actions over time.

Most importantly, for MacIntyre, the attachment to social roles, especially those acquired at birth, represent a set of commitments from which moral reflection begins and to which it must remain committed.

[W]e all approach our own circumstances as bearers of a particular social identity. . . . I inherit from the past of my family, my city, my tribe, my nation, a variety of debts, inheritances, rightful expectations and obligations. These constitute the given of my life, my moral starting point. This is in part what gives my life its own moral particularity.[2]

Obligation, for MacIntyre, is thus defined, at least in part, in terms of the demands of social roles that make reference to the past. His principal complaint against modern individualism is the ease with which we put into question our attachments to the past, as evidenced by the refusal of some modern Americans to assume responsibility for the effects of slavery.

As occupants of these social roles, we come to understand what is important, and learn to what ends our actions are directed. Unlike the arbitrary, criterionless choices wrought by liberalism, judgments about the sorts of practices that have significance, and the norms of conduct appropriate to those practices, are conditioned by the above-mentioned intelligibility and accountability constraints sustaining a unified social identity. Choices are nonarbitrary because, once we understand the goals and purposes inherited along with these social roles, we can evaluate qualities of character on the basis of those that tend to help us realize these aims. Desirable character traits will be those that help sustain our place within the network of practices and relationships that make up a particular form of social life. Thus, MacIntyre insists that "what is good for me has to be good for one who inhabits these roles."[3] Social roles are part of the independent facts of social life that define what counts as a virtue, prescribe a specific function for the virtues, and guide us in practical reason.

Thus, in MacIntyre's view, if social life and my own role in society is to make sense to me, if I am to acknowledge the judgments and attitudes of others with whom I share a social life, and if I am to accept responsibility for past actions, the legacy of the past cannot be viewed as the consequence of a series of choices that can be discarded or sustained at will. In fact, that legacy is as much a part of me as my physical characteristics. The point and purpose of a good deal of our social activity, and the qualities of character that support this activity, make sense and can be sustained only if we acknowledge obligations to the past and the relative fixity of the aims these obligations impose. Of course, one might not accept the antecedents of these conditionals, but in that case we are back on the ground of liberalism with its arbitrary, subjective choices.

MacIntyre's view that we are deeply embedded in our histories, and dependent on the obligations imposed by history for the qualities of character required to sustain social life, is dependent on our ability to specify goals stable enough to organize the episodes of a life into a coherent unity. However, the claim of history articulated thus far cannot fully account for the capacity for moral judgment. Moral judgment requires us to project future states of affairs and to give an account of what ought to be, not merely what is or has been. Moreover, our lives are unfinished and unpredictable and the ends we seek not yet fully known; thus, it cannot be that we must simply adopt those ends assigned to us by the social roles inherited from the past. Despite our responsibility to the past, the demands of intelligibility and unity also require that our goals be responsive to the vicissitudes of chance. If our lives have the structure of a narrative, that structure must be sensitive to both the claim of history and the unpredictability of life. To understand how narrative unity contributes to moral judgment, we have to probe more deeply into MacIntyre's notion of a narrative.

Narrative History

MacIntyre never clearly explains what he means by narrative history. He obviously means neither a mere chronology of events nor a retrospective recounting of causal influence, because he insists that "human transactions in general" have "beginnings, middles, and endings just as literary works do."[4] Plus, he suggests that the significance of events is, in part, dependent on how they are situated in this temporal structure, a significance that cannot be reduced to causal influence and one that has more structure than a chronology.[5] Apparently, MacIntyre refers to the unity described here as a *narrative* unity, because the significance of the episodes of one's life are determined by how they contribute to, or undermine, progress toward an implicit goal. Just as the episodes of a novel gain significance in light of the plot development directed toward the end of the story, the significance and description of an action or event—whether past or contemplated—will depend on its temporal position within a story.[6] For instance, plans can be judged to be carried out, hopes dashed, and misfortune redeemed only from a point of view that anticipates the end of a story, since these descriptions require a sense of finality in order to be intelligible. Events that appear to be utterly insignificant take on importance if they can later be described as the beginning of a chain of dramatic events. Events stand out or recede into the background because of their location in this web of stories. Thus, the sort of history MacIntyre thinks is essential to personal and social identity is teleological in form. The significance of the past is dependent on how it contributes to subsequent events. Moreover, narrative history in MacIntyre's scheme of things cannot be purely retrospective, for human transactions, to the extent that they involve choices, point to an anticipated future.

> There is no present which is not informed by some image of some future and an image of the future which always presents itself in the form of a *telos*—or of a variety of ends or goals—towards which we are either moving or failing to move in the present.[7]

Therefore, the best interpretation of MacIntyre's view of narrative is that the kind of historical awareness framing our conception of social reality has the organization of a narrative-in-progress, the minimal features of which include a structure of beginning, middle, and *anticipated* end.

Many philosophers might argue that narrative form only becomes apparent retrospectively, and consequently cannot be a part of the lived experience of agents who make judgments in light of an anticipated future.[8] In this view, narrative history requires the notion of a completed story, retrospectively conferring intelligibility on actions because their relationship to the end is well understood. Because we know what happened, we can more reliably infer how or why it happened. Obviously, MacIntyre cannot rely solely on retrospective narrative histories, since most of our stories are ongoing, yet-to-be-completed ones.

However, this would not seem to be a telling objection against MacIntyre's conception of the use of narrative. Over their course, stories display tendencies or trends that emerge from the events themselves and transcend the plans and interests of the individuals involved. W. B. Gallie argued that this emerging theme allows the reader to "reassemble and reassess different possible relevances, links, dependencies, [and] still unexplained juxtapositions" through contingent and surprising events, understanding that these events lead to this promised but unrevealed conclusion.[9] Hence, the story's "followability" is as much responsible for the unity of the story as the end.

In this analysis of narrative unity, a life, through the interaction of characters and events, might exhibit patterns of interest and conduct that share a family resemblance. Therefore, we might attribute a dominant theme to that life—a persistent dedication and contribution to a profession, or a courageous fight against injustice, for instance. This theme, along with our background understanding of human action within a particular social context, might allow us to identify a range of possible endings to these patterns—even going so far as to identify the narrative genres in terms of which these patterns can be best understood. As MacIntyre states:

> We allocate conversations to genres just as we do literary narratives. . . . But if this is true of conversations, it is true also *mutatis mutandis,* of battles, chess games, courtships, philosophy seminars, families at the dinner table, businessmen negotiating contracts—that is, of human transactions in general.[10]

Furthermore, we might then be able to make judgments about some endings that would be more plausible than others given what we know about that theme, the characters involved, and the range of genres available. Such a judgment would constitute an argument in favor of acting one way rather than another, since certain choices would make a more coherent story than others.

By analogy with the judgments of a reader, a moral agent would seek to identify a range of intelligible endings that coherently link past, present, and future as a process of development toward his or her long-term intentions. The agent's decisions regarding storyending will be a function of the constraints on followability—plausibility judgments that situate the emerging theme within a web of overlapping narratives comprising an individual's life. Events out of which this narrative is constructed are described in light of the most plausible anticipated endings, but with the understanding that contingencies might force significant changes in how we describe these events.

The functional role of the virtues, then, is understood against this background of narrative unity, for such a narrative represents failure and reversal as well as triumph and success. Also the qualities of character that allow agents to persist in their endeavors can be assessed in light of this narrative. The anticipated ending to the various stories of which one as a part functions as a *telos* in terms of which success and failure can be defined, and which gives significance to contingent events that confront characters with obstacles against which the virtues get defined. This teleological and temporal structure, along with the qualities of character that sustain it, constitutes part of what MacIntyre calls the "narrative unity of a single human life."[11]

One might object, at this point, that the notion of narrative unity has no moral content. It has not provided us with a genuine telos, for what we wish to know is not simply that our various goals determine standards of success and failure; rather, we want to know which goals are appropriate to have. In the absence of such an account, MacIntyre's analysis under-determines the virtues. However, it is important to emphasize that a significant component of narrative unity is MacIntyre's insistence that obligations to the past are imposed by the requirements of intelligibility and accountability. He unequivocally asserts that if we are to make sense out of our lives, we must acknowledge that our aims and purposes are, in some sense or other, inherited from the social roles we occupy as a conse-quence of our history. That our individual narratives are embedded in the narratives of others, in part accounts for the unity of moral character. Thus, it is not narrative structure alone supplying the background for virtues, but the narrative structure that emerges from a life actively striv-ing to sustain obligations inherited from social roles. Narrative endings are terminal points in the extension and development of the obligations inherited from those social roles that give moral content to the standards of narrative coherence—standards that would otherwise seem to be purely aesthetic criteria.

Thus, in MacIntyre's view, to be embedded in a history is to discover the range of possibilities that inherited social roles make available, as well as the specific actions and qualities of character that are appropriate in the context of these social roles. The specific role narrative plays is to bring out the developmental structure of our relatedness to past, present, and future. Narrative structure describes how possibilities understood as anticipated story endings and informed by obligations incurred in the past, control a process of development that both transforms our concep-tion of the end and gives specificity to the descriptions of the virtues required to achieve it.

This wedding of substantive moral content and narrative structure, however, will not yield the determinate conception of the good that MacIntyre seeks. This is because his account of narrative history harbors within it conflicting considerations that threaten the unity of this account. On one hand, MacIntyre argues that only an acknowledgement of our obligations to historically constituted social roles supplies a determinate conception of the good that will resolve the moral conflicts within liberal-ism. Although religious, ethnic, national, familial, and occupational asso-ciations are central features of a modern life, it is the ease with which we dispense with the constraints of our social roles to which MacIntyre objects. We no longer take our social roles to be defining characteristics essential for personal identity, nor do we see them as absolute constraints on our choices. We consider the obligations associated with historically constituted social roles to be optional, part of a wide range of considerations in practical reason rather than a central factor. Thus, part of the point of invoking the claim of history is to argue that social roles inevitably impose constraints on our choices, and to treat these with disdain, irony, or indifference is to invite a loss of personal identity, a sense of meaninglessness, and a sense of alienation from one's community.

Nevertheless, this conception of a social environment in which individuals occupy fixed social roles surely is not responsive enough to the contingencies and unpredictability of life. Given this unpredictability, we cannot expect to be confronted only with difficulties that have been anticipated and for which clear solutions have already been decided by the norms that govern our social roles. Thus, on the other hand, by invoking the narrative structure of life, MacIntyre seeks to explain how these social roles can be transformed by our projections of a possible future—by an image of the good life. However, if that image of the good life must itself be drawn from these historically constituted social roles, if the only criteria available for judging which ends are appropriate are these very social roles at issue, it is not obvious that MacIntyre leaves room for the critical judgment required to open traditional social roles to new possibilities. Apparently the inherited obligations, along with the aforementioned identity and intelligibility conditions that constitute the claim of history, place severe constraints on the kinds of goods at which we can legitimately aim.

To make the same point somewhat differently, in MacIntyre's view, genuine morality must be embodied in a narrative of loyalty and faithfulness—for only then will we avoid the criterionless choices of a discredited liberalism, and only through such faithfulness can we develop the moral dispositions that help sustain the unity of our lives. However, this preference for a certain kind of story has nothing to do with narrative structure. Stories that have betrayal and disintegration as their end are as intelligible as stories of loyalty and faithfulness. One could live a life that has as its aim the undoing of all one's ties to the past without violating the intelligibility of the narrative, and a life lived in disregard for basic moral norms could conceivably be as unified as any other life. Moreover, there is nothing in this notion of narrative unity that would prevent each individual from having a substantially different conception of what narrative unity requires. In fact, there is reason to think that coherent, followable stories will allow for a number of plausible but quite incompatible endings, with no criteria but subjective preference to guide decisions. Narrative unity and the unity of moral character, as MacIntyre understands it, seem quite distinct; in fact, they seem at odds, the analogy establishing only that goals confer intelligibility on actions and qualities of character but supplying no content to the notion of an end or goal. Thus, narrative structure doesn't offer any independent reason for endorsing the claim of history. The argument must rest entirely on the importance of inherited social roles for the intelligibility and accountability of social life.

In summary, MacIntyre's position incorporates two independent considerations that are in conflict. On one hand, the content of our moral life is to emerge out of our attachments to the past. On the other hand, the narrative structure of life suggests a more extensive range of possibilities unbeholden to the constraints of morality or the stability of moral character, that rely on the spontaneous, generative resources of the imagination. There is tension within this marriage of narrative and morality, for if the claim of history is a necessary condition for moral judgment, and the only source of specificity for the virtues, MacIntyre cannot allow that claim to be suspended in the face of a contingent future without admitting the arbitrary, criterionless choices of liberalism he is bound to set aside. The introduction of narrative unity cannot explain how we transcend the limitations of inherited social roles without severely discounting their value.

Tradition and Human Flourishing

Thus far, I have referred to only two of the three stages in MacIntyre's account of the background conditions for the virtues. In the third stage, his account of tradition, he attempts to take up some of the previously raised objections. MacIntyre will grant that there are some obligations, some inheritances from the past, that may not be worth preserving, but he will argue that traditions typically have the built-in capacity to rationally distinguish what is valuable from what is not. In fact MacIntyre defines a tradition as a "historically extended, socially embodied argument, and an argument precisely in part about the goods constituting that tradition."[12]

MacIntyre begins this account with a curious yet instructive maneuver. He claims that it is the systematic asking of two questions, "What is the good for me?" and "What is the good for man?" that provide the moral life with its unity and final end.[13] In light of the fact that MacIntyre has just argued that the recognition of the point of the virtues is dependent on the recognition of our indebtedness to a particular history and tradition, one would have thought that the relevant question might be, "What is the good for those of us who share in this history?" Hence, one wonders what licenses this move to a question about the universal "good for man," and why a tradition, limited as it is by time and circumstance, is the sort of social entity that can address such a question.

Although it is not clear what licenses this move, it is clear what motivates it. MacIntyre writes:

> Notice also that the fact that the self has to find its moral identity in and through its membership in communities such as those of the family, the neighborhood, the city and the tribe does not entail that the self has to accept the moral *limitations* of the particularity of those forms of community. Without those moral particularities to begin from there would never be anywhere to begin; but it is in moving forward from such particularity that the search for the good, for the universal, consists.[14]

We arrive, therefore, at the problem I raised at the beginning of this essay. How is embeddedness in a historical tradition made compatible with the capacity to transcend the limitations of that history, to advance toward universal moral agency [An aspiration, I noted earlier, it seems reasonable for a moral point of view to have]? MacIntyre's rather stunning answer to this question is that traditions have built-in resources for overcoming themselves, that it is in the nature of traditions to seek the good for man. The commonly held notion that traditions are resistant to change is simply a prejudice promulgated by an unholy alliance of conservative political theorists and Enlightenment rationalists, according to MacIntyre.

MacIntyre wants to claim on one hand that a morality is grounded in the particular historical and cultural conditions that produce it, and on the other hand that the incommensurability and relativism such a view entails are potentially resolvable by virtue of the resources a tradition possesses to engage in rational inquiry into the "good for man." His strategy is to provide an account of how the rational superiority of a tradition over competing systems of beliefs can be demonstrated from within that particular tradition in a way that makes us believe such rational superiority is an advance toward a conception of the "good for man"—a conception of the good, it turns out, that will exhibit salient features of an Aristotelian and Thomistic ethic.

In *Whose Justice? Which Rationality?*, MacIntyre offers an extensive account of the resources for moral reflection supplied by a tradition that further strengthens the claim of history. He argues that the shared linguistic resources of a tradition serve to fix the meaning of moral terms by recounting the contrasts against which a particular assertion was thought to be significant. This is a task requiring detailed historical exposition. Without this rich historical context, moral doctrines are cut off from the reasons for which they were advanced in the first place. Moreover, the attachments and loyalties that constitute the particularity of a tradition are fully embodied in the language of that tradition, such that "languages-in-use" are essentially untranslatable and entail a range of commitments only adherents to that tradition can share.[15] What follows from this fixity of meaning and unambiguous reference is a stable collection of fundamental agreements that allow agents to be certain of their judgments.

It is clear from MacIntyre's remarks on Aristotle that certainty with respect to one's judgments is the most significant element in tradition-informed moral reasoning. MacIntyre argues that,

> we recognize the necessity and the immediacy of rational action by someone inhabiting a structured role in a context in which the goods of some systematic form of practice are unambiguously ordered. . . . It is thus only within those systematic forms of activity within which goods are unambiguously ordered and within which individuals occupy and move between well-defined roles that the standards of rational action directed toward the good and the best can be embodied.[16]

This unambiguous ordering of social roles is enhanced by another virtuous feature of traditions—stable and authoritative political institutions. MacIntyre will argue that moral reasoning can only arrive at a determinate conception of human flourishing that allows individuals to reason effectively regarding the relative importance of the various goods they seek, if such reasoning is carried out within a political community already expressing that conception of human flourishing. Apparently, for MacIntyre, a nonarbitrary moral justification of a good requires a prior commitment to political institutions embodying that good.

> From within and only from within a given *polis*, already provided with an ordering of goods, goods to be achieved by excellence within specific and systematic forms of activity, integrated into an overall rank-order by the political activity of those particular citizens, does it make sense to ask: "In the light of the evaluations and the resources of dialectical reasoning which we now possess can we construct a better account of the supreme good than any hitherto suggested?"[17]

The third resource that a tradition supplies, and the one on which I want to focus, is the capacity for internal criticism that will, according to MacIntyre, vindicate his claim that the quest for the "good for man" can only be pursued from within a tradition. Traditions sufficiently advanced enough to have a history of argument over some of their central beliefs embody a process of criticism, reformulation, and revision by which the superiority of revised beliefs can be demonstrated, and for which a claim to truth can be justified. Thus, MacIntyre's account of tradition promises an answer to the question of how we distinguish arbitrary choices from rational decisions, and consequently transcend the limitations of a particular tradition so we can advance toward a universal moral conception.

The primary vehicle for such revelations of truth is what MacIntyre calls an epistemological crisis—periodic episodes in which a tradition, according to its own standards of evaluation, can no longer resolve the problems with which it is confronted because continued adherence to those beliefs issues in more incoherence. Resolution of this crisis can only take place when some available alternative set of beliefs satisfies the following conditions:

1. The "new and conceptually enriched scheme . . . must furnish a solution to the problems that had previously proved intractable in a systematic and coherent way."

2. The new scheme must explain why the previous beliefs rendered the tradition "sterile" or "incoherent," or both.

3. Future beliefs must preserve some fundamental continuity with the beliefs that have defined the tradition up to now.[18]

The alternative scheme that resolves the crisis can be the product of innovation, it can be resurrected from the history of the tradition in crisis, or it can be appropriated from an alien tradition. The latter case is the most interesting because it is a tradition's capacity to correct itself, by appealing to an alternative tradition, that supports MacIntyre's claim to have overcome relativism—and, if it is cogent, that will establish the transcendence he seeks. Thus, I will concern myself exclusively with the case in which a tradition corrects itself by appealing to an alternative tradition. In this case, MacIntyre stipulates that the third condition requiring continuity with previous beliefs need not be satisfied. Thus, rational justification of this change of belief devolves from the first two criteria. Satisfaction of these conditions demonstrates the rational superiority of the successor beliefs, while preserving the claim that a tradition's standards of assessment are internal. When these conditions are satisfied the rationality of tradition requires an acknowledgment by those who have hitherto inhabited and given their allegiance to the tradition in crisis that the alien tradition is superior in rationality and in respect of its claims to truth to their own.[19]

It is important to recognize that, in this account, rational change in belief is in part a process of historical explanation, especially with respect to the second criterion. As a prior condition of this change in belief, the new scheme must provide a better historical account, when compared with other available explanations, of why "given the structures of inquiry within that tradition the crisis had to happen as it did and does not itself suffer from the same defects of incoherence and resourcelessness. . . ."[20]

The plausibility of this condition is enhanced by a restriction that MacIntyre places on this historical explanation. The adherents of the tradition in crisis must find this explanation "cogent and illuminating" *by the very same standards* by which they judged their own beliefs to be incoherent—that is, according to the prevailing standards of explanation *prior* to acceptance of the superiority of the alternative tradition. This restriction allows MacIntyre to claim that the satisfaction of these conditions resolves the problem of incommensurability, since the rational superiority of a competing viewpoint can be judged from within the tradition in question.

There is reason to think, however, that those who adhere to a tradition need not affirm the rational superiority of an alternative tradition despite their satisfaction of these conditions. Charles Taylor has argued that some traditional cultures make no distinction between understanding the world and being attuned to it, i.e., understanding their place in that world and acknowledging it as a desirable way of life.[21] Such a world view might well have persistent difficulty explaining certain natural phenomena, and might come to recognize the superior explanatory power of modern science. MacIntyre's criteria would demand that to resolve the crisis, and, if it is to avoid irrationality, this tradition adopt beliefs held by an alien culture, such as those of a modern technological society.

However, as David B. Wong has argued, it may nevertheless be rational to hold on to the traditional belief system if the form of life dependent on attunement to nature is valued highly enough, if the costs of giving up this view of nature are too high.[22] MacIntyre's criteria for rational change in belief presuppose agreement on the relative value of explanation as the primary justification of a belief, as if this were a tradition-neutral standard by which to measure competing belief systems. Yet it is part of

MacIntyre's thesis that there are no tradition-neutral standards, and he fails to show why the sort of explanatory adequacy associated with epistemic notions of truth *must* outweigh the value of attunement.

Similarly, we may well grant on liberalism's own grounds the incoherence of liberal thought, and with MacIntyre assert that the interminable disagreement on moral questions that characterizes modern society is a crisis that constitutes the failure of modernism. Yet we may decline to endorse the rational superiority of alternative traditions, including the Thomistic and Aristotelian traditions that MacIntyre endorses. We might decline on the grounds that the relative freedom accorded the individual within liberalism is worth preserving, despite having to put up with the incoherence and disunity that seem to accompany it. It is not obvious at any rate that such a judgment is irrational. The virtues of pluralism and of individual freedom are as readily apparent as their vices, and the quest for unity and agreement has vices of its own, as history makes readily apparent.

MacIntyre wishes to show that the modernist conception of a tradition-neutral rationality is bankrupt. However, his discomfort with the relativism that his historicist position seems to entail leads him, once again, to assert the stringent claim of history with one hand while attempting to deny that claim with the other. Just as his discussion of narrative unity fails to show how obligations to the past are compatible with our response to an unpredictable future, in this case he fails to show how adherence to the internal standards of a tradition are sufficient to explain rational change in belief. In both cases, avoiding the limits of historicism seems to require adoption of the modernist/liberal scheme he wishes to set aside. MacIntyre seems to think a tradition that values some feature of its way of life more highly than its capacity to guarantee the unity of understanding has lost its capacity for rational reflection; this exposes the underlying assumption that drives MacIntyre's thought. The regulative ideal governing moral reflection for MacIntyre is that the "good for man" must ultimately form a single, coherent unity, and the conception of rational inquiry as the process of discovering this unified object domain is no less important. Neither of these assumptions receive a defense in MacIntyre's work, and they beg precisely the questions at issue between MacIntyre and the liberals.

These considerations show that MacIntyre's criteria are too weak to support his claim that, within traditions, there is a distinctive form of inherent rationality that successfully avoids relativism, since explanatory adequacy and the unity of understanding are not the only standards a tradition might value. However, this argument rests on the controversial claim that there are goods that can be rationally valued more highly than those of unity and explanatory adequacy. Since this claim is likely to evoke conflicting intuitions on what counts as "rational," it is preferable that the argument rest on less controversial premises.

I think a more secure argument can be made against MacIntyre's position by showing that his second criterion, which I will refer to as the "best explanation" criterion, is in conflict with the very claim of history on which his conception of obligation depends. I will argue that the historical explanation of why the epistemological crisis had to happen as it did, and why the new scheme does not itself suffer from the same difficulties, is incompatible with the significance of tradition for social identity and moral conduct MacIntyre otherwise wants to endorse. As a consequence, what MacIntyre calls rational superiority cannot be demonstrated from within a tradition, since the conditions that must be satisfied for such a demonstration deny the normative force of that tradition. The upshot is that MacIntyre fails to resolve the conflict between embeddedness within a tradition and the capacity to transcend the limits of that tradition and his claim to have overcome relativism cannot be vindicated.

It might be helpful at this point to reiterate what I mean by the claim of history, for my argument depends crucially on the stringency of this claim, as MacIntyre conceives it. As I have been using the phrase, the "claim of history" refers to MacIntyre's account of the historical conditions that contribute to an individual's sense of personal and social identity, and the obligations, allegiances, and commitments incurred because this social identity presupposes a set of social relations providing the content of one's moral life. Thus, it includes what I referred to as identity and intelligibility conditions, the particularity of "languages-in-use," the unambiguous ordering of social roles and the political authority that supports them, and the sense of certainty that agents acquire by reasoning within the context of a tradition. I refer to attachment to one's tradition as a "claim," because the factors constituting a tradition are neither optional features of a genuine moral life nor chosen by agents from a range of alternatives. Rather, they are part of the "given" of moral life, unarticulated background conditions (prejudices or prejudgments, to use Gadamer's terminology), stored up and transmitted across time, that determine prior to the raising of questions what counts as a question, and prior to the assessment of value what counts as a good. In MacIntyre's view of a tradition, acknowledging the authority of what history has handed down to us can only help sustain our moral reasoning. The foundations of moral reasoning lie so deeply embedded within language, institutions, and practices that to call them into question is to call into question who one is. To discount such authority is to dispense with the only criteria we have available to adjudicate competing moral claims. This is precisely where MacIntyre locates the poverty of liberalism, for in dispensing with the necessity of the public quest for the best account of human flourishing, there are no longer any criteria by which to judge the plethora of pretenders to that throne; therefore, the good is relegated to the status of private preference. The result is interminable moral debate and the social pathology of *anomie* that pervades modern society.

Narrative and Historical Explanation

Despite the claim of history, MacIntyre argues that we need not be subject to the moral limitations of a particular tradition because traditions in good order have their own capacity for internal critique. As I noted earlier, I will claim that this capacity is insufficiently critical. My argument for this conclusion depends on the claim, endorsed by MacIntyre, that historical explanations are narratives. I will make use of the characteristics of narrative histories to bring out a tension in MacIntyre's work between his account of the role tradition plays in moral reflection and the resources for overcoming the limits of a tradition.

As a general thesis, the claim that historical explanations are narratives simply asserts that the meaning or significance of historical events are conditioned by their role in a story, so that structural features of narrative—especially location within the temporal sequence of beginning, middle, or end—explain the significance historical events possess.[23] To use the standard example, the 1914 assassination of Archduke Ferdinand in Sarajevo is significant because it marked the beginning of the story that we would later call WWI. One of the virtues of characterizing historical explanation in terms of narrative categories is that it helps explain the processes of selection that historians employ in the writing of history. The selection of events to be included in the story, and decisions about the description under which a particular event is relevant, are determined by the relative impact of these events and descriptions of the story the historian elects to tell, as well as its thematic content.[24]

What follows from this consideration of narrative structure, and the process of selecting events for inclusion within the story, is that both the occurrence of unexpected events and the recognition of previously unobserved processes in history will result in different stories being told. Events formerly thought insignificant become salient in the light of subsequent developments, and those formerly thought significant recede into the background. For example, Aristarchus's prescient description of a heliocentric universe became part of the story of astronomy only after the Copernican revolution made his contribution seem important. Ancient astronomers working within the Ptolemaic system became largely irrelevant. Retrospective realignments of the past are commonplace within history.

The appeal to an alternative tradition in the resolution of an epistemological crisis constitutes such a shift in plot development, although the end that confers significance on the past will be an anticipated future. Traditions are extended arguments about the "good for man," and conflict between traditions is conflict about the ultimate aims of human endeavor, in MacIntyre's view. In anticipating adoption of an alternative system of belief, adherents of a tradition are being asked to consider a different set of ends—a range of novel possibilities constituting the ultimate aims of human endeavor that will guide their conduct. According to MacIntyre's criteria, these are live possibilities to the extent that they render the history of the tradition in crisis more coherent. Yet, this change in belief about what is possible and important also provides the adherents of a tradition with a different set of categories with which to describe their pasts. This feature of such a dramatic conceptual shift is troublesome for the sense of obligation to the past that MacIntyre claimed was central to moral agency. It is not obvious why the resolution of an epistemological crisis—which requires the retrospective realignment of the past in light of this transformed conception of the "good for man" as a condition for its resolution—would not distort the very history that was argued to be central to identity and intelligibility. This is because the telling of this new story would yield vastly different reference points for the selection of events and event descriptions. The social roles inherited from the past [which were understood by MacIntyre to be the source of obligation], the historical context that helps to fix the meaning of moral terms, the social and political institutions that express the shared beliefs of the community, and the persistence of moral character over time exemplified by the virtues are all subject to redescription and reevaluation with respect to their significance. In fact, it would seem that even those criteria by which the tradition judges its own beliefs inadequate would be subject to reevaluation as well. Consequently, there is no longer a way to characterize the story as a search for "the good," because the normative significance of the history in question is tied to commitments to social roles that have been displaced and subverted.

Examples of the sort of thing I have in mind abound. For instance, the rapid advances in transportation technology in the 20th century, and the consequent interest in a mobile lifestyle as an important element in our conception of the good, have had a significant impact on the importance of an extended family rooted in a particular geographical location. It could plausibly be argued that this transformed conception of the good, when confronted with this technology, has caused a significant rupture in the salience of kinship bonds and communal attachments among traditional cultures. This modifies everything from the skills and capacities required for productive labor to the esteem accorded the elders in the community, whose profound yet parochial wisdom seems no longer adequate to the demands of such mobility. Moreover, the justification for this substantial change in our conception of the good life might well have been generated by an awareness of the limitations of the communal ties within those traditions, when confronted with economic competition and military threat.

To the degree that events of the past are viewed as significant in light of newly formulated ends adopted from an alien tradition, they will likely exhibit different salient properties than they did within the conceptual framework being replaced. Because the obligations and sense of indebtedness were dependent on this latter narrative, resolution of the epistemological crisis calls these obligations into question—a result that MacIntyre should not welcome, given his insistence on the importance of these obligations. The narrative of obligation that forms the basis of moral character is a narrative of what a person cares about. There simply is no reason to think that a narrative recounting the story of a reconceptualized "good for man" would be the same narrative, despite the fact that standards for judging the cogency of explanations are held fixed.

If this argument is correct, MacIntyre's claim to have solved the problem of relativism, by demonstrating the rational superiority of an alternative conceptual framework from within the perspective of one's own tradition, has been purchased at a cost. He has succeeded in explaining how a tradition can overcome its limitations—only by licensing a redescription of that tradition threatening to discount much of what is important about traditions. As I argued previously, the capacity for moral reflection is dependent on an acknowledgement of the allegiances, loyalties, and obligations imposed by one's past; the stability and authority of political institutions; the rigorous ordering of social roles; and the certainties of meaning and reference passed down by means of "languages-in-use." Yet the meaning and significance of all these features of a tradition are dependent on a particular conception of the "good for man," in MacIntyre's account. Once we have recognized the poverty of that conception, and adopted the beliefs of an alien tradition—and thus a different conception of the good we have also adopted a new way of attaching meaning and significance to the social roles, institutions, practices, relationships, and even the language on which moral reflection depends. All of our former attachments are now available for redescription. MacIntyre cannot, therefore, claim to have explained how embeddedness in history is compatible with the capacity to transcend the limits of that history, for once we transcend the limitations as prescribed by MacIntyre, we are no longer embedded in the tradition that supplied the necessary background for moral judgment. I fail to see how agents successfully negotiating this crisis differ from modern victims of *anomie.*

The Plausibility Objection

The difficulty with MacIntyre's characterization of tradition thus far is that he has given it such a central role in moral reflection, it is hard to see how one might dispense with it regardless of its limitations. He therefore must either modify his account of the importance of tradition and the claim of history, or restrain the capacity of traditions to overcome their limitations. In fact, traditions are less capable of overcoming their limitations than MacIntyre thinks because conceptual difficulties render any account of history that satisfies the "best explanation" criterion less plausible than its natural rivals. Thus, MacIntyre's second criterion for demonstrating the rational superiority of rival traditions cannot be satisfied. At issue in this objection is the structure of the explanation MacIntyre proposes. The "best explanation" criterion requires for its satisfaction a historical explanation that explains, better than the available rival explanations, both why the epistemological crisis had to occur as it did and why the successor beliefs are not similarly incoherent or limited. This suggests that the judgment satisfying the "best explanation" criterion will compare the explanation that uses the resources of the alternative tradition with competing explanations, and the claim that the former is more "cogent and illuminating" will have to be supported with reasons for telling the story one way rather than another. This would apparently include both a description of failed attempts by social and political institutions to resolve disagreement in light of the events that constitute the history of this tradition, and an account of how the conceptual resources of the new framework can, more effectively than competitors, locate the source of that disagreement—and suggest plausible alternatives that would not have displayed similar inadequacies. Unfortunately, the structure of the explanation MacIntyre envisions is flawed, and gives us no reason to think it would exhibit more plausibility than its natural rivals.

Once again, my argument will rely on the features of narrative history that have to do with the selection and description of events constituting the narrative. As I noted before, it is commonplace that, for the historian, events usually have significance in light of succeeding events. Because a historian is typically writing narratives, the beginnings and endings of which are both in the past relative to the historian's point of view, the historian will know how things turned out. He therefore will have available resources for describing and selecting important events that historical agents do not possess. Therein lies the explanatory power of a historical narrative. Whether or not an event has significance, and the way we describe that significance, depends on how things turn out—and to the degree historians are writing about the past, they are in the epistemic position to judge that significance.

For MacIntyre, however, the kind of historical explanation he requires differs from standard historical explanations in that the significance of the events figuring in the explanation is not solely determined by their relevance to subsequent past events constituting completed stories. An entrenched epistemological crisis might qualify as a completed story that would confer meaning on events leading up to it. This would allow an intelligible story to be related about why, given the conceptual resources available, the epistemological crisis had to happen as it did. Yet the "best explanation" criterion will only be satisfied if it can be plausibly argued that the alternative conceptual framework does not "suffer from the same defects of incoherence and resourcelessness" as did the conceptual framework being replaced. In other words, the explanation must show that if the principles of the new scheme had been acted upon, an epistemological crisis either would not have occurred or would have been resolved by the new conceptual framework.

This does not have the structure of a historical explanation, and it is difficult to see how one would be defensible. Such an explanation would confer significance upon events not by virtue of some later event to which the earlier events contribute but by virtue of a set of beliefs drawn from an alternative tradition—beliefs that posit an alternative but uninstantiated past. Satisfaction of the "best explanation" criterion requires a defensible counterfactual to the effect that if alternative beliefs had been available, the course of events would have been different. This explanation looks at the past entirely from the point of view of the road not taken. However, it is not obvious that there is an epistemic position from which to defend such a claim. A historian cannot know what the past is capable of until she sees what emerges from that past. And because what, in fact, emerged from that past was an epistemological crisis, judgments about the significance of preceding events must stem from that fact. Historians can identify the causative factors that contributed to the epistemological crisis, and argue that had one or more of those causative factors not been present, the crisis would not have occurred. Yet one cannot with confidence say very much about what course an alternative history might have taken had a different conceptual framework been in place, or whether that alternative history would have resulted in more or less incoherence or lack of resourcefulness. At best, she can make some tentative speculations about what might have been, but these would hardly be more plausible than the competing explanations proceeding from actual events. Historians simply have more resources available when working with completed stories than "not-yet-completed" ones. I conclude from this that MacIntyre's second criterion for rational change in belief cannot be satisfied, and therefore such global changes in conceptual frameworks, should they occur, are not rational, at least in the sense of "rational" adopted by MacIntyre.

A Second First Language

In this section I will briefly take up a possible response available to MacIntyre. I have argued that in the process of satisfying the criteria for demonstrating the rational superiority of an alien tradition, MacIntyre seems to require members of the tradition in crisis to give up the loyalties and commitments that provided the substance of their moral point of view, thus undermining the very criteria in terms of which moral judgment is possible. MacIntyre might grant me this, but argue that one of the conditions of this rational change in belief is that the agents in question adopt the language of the alien tradition as a "second first language." By "second first language," MacIntyre means:

> Knowing the culture so far as is possible, as a native inhabitant knows it, and speaking, hearing, writing, and reading the language as a native inhabitant speaks, hears, writes, and reads it.[25]

This sort of competence involves an understanding of cultural history, of the nuances and allusions employed by native speakers, of "knowing how to go on and to go further in the use of the expressions of a language," and a knowledge of the authoritative texts that supply paradigmatic examples of the language-in-use of an alien tradition.[26]

MacIntyre insists that between the language of one's own tradition and the alien tradition, there are not only substantive differences that preclude translation but genuine incompatibilities.

> The multiplicity of traditions does not afford a multiplicity of perspectives among which we can move, but a multiplicity of antagonistic commitments between which only conflict, rational or nonrational, is possible.[27]

Thus, the confrontation between the two languages-in-use, both of which are thoroughly understood by an inquirer, will be a genuine test of rival world views in which one exposes the unsupported assumptions and untested beliefs of the other. MacIntyre argues that only when the members of a tradition in crisis understand the language of the alien tradition as a second first language can the criteria for rational change in belief be satisfied. The sort of cultural immersion required in order to learn a second first language supplies the agents with the fixity of meaning and reference, paradigms of justification, and ways of going on that I have argued they will lose in satisfying the "best explanation" criterion.

If MacIntyre is correct that adoption of a second first language provides a critical perspective from which to assess the relative value of competing traditions, and if the agent acquiring the second first language is sufficiently socialized into the alien tradition, then the force of my first objection to the "best explanation criterion" is mitigated. However, I think we need to be suspicious of the degree to which the acquisition of a second first language would constitute a genuine test of competing moral views. As MacIntyre characterizes it, this second first language is not a genuine language-in-use. It is described as a work of the imagination that does not enable an inquirer to understand social reality, as those in the alien tradition do.

> To possess the concepts of an alien culture in this secondary mode, informed by conceptual imagination, differs in important ways from possessing the concepts which are genuinely one's own. For insofar as one disagrees upon whether or not a particular concept has application . . . because one's own conceptual scheme precludes its having application, one will only be able to deploy it in the way in

which an actor speaking his part may say things which he or she does not in his or her own person believe.[28]

These acts of imagination are hardly the sort of thing that could count as a rigorous test of one's own tradition, especially given the degree of communal self-congratulation that MacIntyre has built into his notion of a tradition. For MacIntyre, the lived experience of one's own tradition is the condition upon which the possibility of moral reflection rests. Regardless of how sympathetic an observer one is, and regardless of the facility one has in recognizing how a particular concept or argument is employed by members of an alien tradition, an observer of that alien tradition is unlikely to share the evaluative interest of the members. On MacIntyre's own grounds, there is an important difference between knowing the associations and resonances a word has and having those associations and resonances as one's own, as part of the nonoptional set of commitments and obligations to which members of a tradition have been delivered over by their collective history. Despite the fact that the observer will understand certain associations as reasons, she will not know what it is like to *endorse* these associations as reasons, since they do not contribute to the background of beliefs and normative pre-conceptions that condition her understanding of what is salient and significant.

To use MacIntyre's example, the Irish Protestant may know that what she calls "Londonderry" is called "Doire Columcille" by the Irish Catholic. She may also understand the historical usages of "Doire Columcille," understand the lineages of kinship referred to by the name, and recognize and appreciate how the presence of that location in the literature and history of Ireland confers political legitimacy on the institutions that preserve the name in the eyes of Catholics. However, there is no reason to think that this understanding in itself will carry with it the same reason-giving force that it has for the Catholic, whose own past cannot be understood without those associations in question. Part of the reason-giving force of these associations can only come about as a result of membership in that tradition.

MacIntyre continually asserts that any healthy tradition must be open to the fact that some other tradition may be superior in rationality. He argues that the superiority of one tradition over another can be demonstrated only through a dialectical confrontation between the two rival, incompatible traditions, a confrontation that presupposes the acquisition by both parties of the rival's language as a second first language. Through this confrontation, the limitations of one or the other tradition is exposed since they presuppose incompatible schemes of justification and because MacIntyre insists on the constraint that there be only one best answer to the questions provoked by this confrontation.

However, given the cumulative effects of tradition—the claim of history—it is difficult to see how that identity is to be surrendered in order to absorb the standards and norms of an alien tradition, without at the same time sacrificing the very ability to put alternative moral conceptions in dialectical relation. This ability is conditioned by the very substantive beliefs that are being sacrificed. It is important to repeat that MacIntyre's assumption is not that there is an underlying level of agreement between two traditions, sustaining the compatibility at a deeper level. Instead, traditions are resolutely incompatible with other traditions. Thus, to genuinely absorb what another tradition has to offer would require that one give up the substantive beliefs generating the conflict in the first place.

There is, then, a real danger that attempts to understand an alien tradition, even with the good intentions advanced by MacIntyre, are little more than a process of imaginatively drawing the beliefs of the alien tradition into the orbit of one's own by rendering the unfamiliar into a more familiar conceptual framework. Emphatically, this is not MacIntyre's intent—in fact, quite the opposite. MacIntyre explicitly argues against the Davidsonian view that to understand another culture one must presuppose that they are to a significant degree like us.[29] I don't see how such a presupposition can be avoided, despite the availability of a second first language.[30]

The Ambiguous Legacy of History

The conclusion to draw from the foregoing is this: If moral reflection is as strongly rooted in history and tradition as MacIntyre claims, he offers no reason to hope for a historicist perspective that will alleviate worries about parochialism or incommensurability. My argument suggests that to recognize the claim of history is to resist the recognition of the rational superiority of alternative traditions. Thus, the appeal to narrative as rendered by MacIntyre will not show how the particularity of moral judgment is compatible with universalist aspirations.

However, although concrete ethics may be the only plausible moral perspective given the presuppositions of historicism, this conclusion does not support the claim of history as MacIntyre understands it either. If we are to understand moral obligations as constraints imposed on us by virtue of our attachments to a particular history, we cannot dispense with judgments concerning the future. After all, "ought" statements refer to a state of affairs not yet realized, and a history that is to serve as a premise for an "ought" statement must be written from the vantage point of the present anticipating a possible future. Therefore, to the degree that history is made to serve a moral or political agenda, it will have the narrative form of a "not-yet-completed" story, the details of which will be a consequence of the story endings anticipated in the future. Because these projections of future states of affairs confront the contingency of that future even as they supply standards for describing and assessing the past, the legacy of history and its claim on us will be ambiguous at best. There are, both within a tradition and between traditions, as many rival histories as there are potential story endings, and the contingency of experience suggests a multiplicity of endings. Thus, from within the perspective of narrative history, *pace* MacIntyre, our relationship to tradition should be neither an endorsement nor a rejection but rather a recognition of the tenuous hold memory exerts on our judgments.

This ambiguity in the meaning of history should lead us to be suspicious of the claim that the primary source of moral obligation is a tradition. A judgment of what counts as possible and important will risk rendering invisible the people and events that do not fit the patterns prescribed by the chosen *telos,* thereby silencing what may have a legitimate claim on our attention if the future takes an unanticipated shape. A kind of moral blindness seems to be built into the structure of narrative histories because the sort of moral obligations they generate are tied to partial, contingent perspectives.

However, this accusation of moral blindness will stick only if these alternative histories are incommensurable, if there is no inclusive story in which the various alternative stories are represented. In Chapter One I argued that incommensurability is not a conceptual difficulty but an empirical phenomenon. Consequently, my argument does not (and need not) demonstrate that these rival histories are *necessarily* incommensurable. It does not show that resolutions of epistemological crises *in principle* cannot preserve the common reference points that will sustain a continuous conflict-resolving discourse between rival histories. However, it does strongly suggest that there is no reason to think conventional norms that make agreement possible will be preserved. Because the resolution of an epistemological crisis does not leave everything else fixed, but instead produces significant shifts in patterns of salience, there is no reason to think that the separate quests carried out by distinct traditions, or within each tradition at different times, have a common objective and a shared sense of what is possible and important. If this is the case for norms that help resolve conflict, it is true *a fortiori* for norms that warrant judgments of moral progress with which MacIntyre is especially concerned, for neither is there a canonical set of problems and solutions that allow us to characterize these resolutions as progress toward a single conception of the good. Incommensurability and contingency remain obstacles to philosophical attempts to impose unity on moral phenomena, even when philosophy is supplemented by narrative discourse.

3

The Ethics of Tragedy

In Chapter One I argue that the heart of the antitheory position in ethics is this: The moral life is characterized by contingency and incommensurability, and these factors severely restrict moral theory's capacity to provide criteria on which to rationally assess one's own, as well as alternative, beliefs. In Chapter Two I begin to assess the claim that reflection on these recalcitrant features of moral life must proceed by means of a fundamentally different form of discourse, one that has the features of a narrative. I argue that one attempt to overcome these difficulties of contingency and incommensurability, by supplementing theory with the resources of the temporal structure of a historical narrative, fails. In this chapter, I assess the extent to which the resources of literary narrative help us cope with these difficulties.

It has long been argued by literary figures—Trilling and T. S. Eliot come immediately to mind—that literary fiction has a special role to play in the formation of moral character. Recently, this claim has been advanced within philosophy by Martha Nussbaum and Richard Rorty. In both cases, the significance of literature is supported by a conception of morality that can best be described as tragic. This connection between morality and tragedy is explicitly acknowledged by Nussbaum, who has devoted considerable attention to the representation of morality within tragic literature. In Rorty's case the connection is less salient, although I shall argue it is no less important in understanding the moral point of view that emerges from his texts. In chapters Three and Four, I will consider Nussbaum's work; Rorty will occupy Chapter Five.

Luck and Ethics

Moral philosophy is typically concerned with only those actions an agent is responsible for performing, for it is only those actions for which an agent can be held deserving of praise or blame.[1] However, Nussbaum argues that such an orientation seriously distorts morality, and that philosophical accounts of morality must be cognizant of the degree to which our activities of praising and blaming take luck into account. She argues that moral philosophy must take very seriously this question of luck: "How much *should* we live with, in order to live the life that is best and most valuable for a human being?"[2] She persuasively argues that, because of the role of luck as it is expressed, especially in tragic literature, moral character and moral goodness are fragile and always in danger of coming apart. Yet she will also argue that certain qualities of character, exhibited best by literary characters and justified by a significantly revised conception of moral theory, enable agents to sustain moral character and moral goodness in the face of this fragility. I will counter that although Nussbaum is right about the fragility of moral goodness, she fails to give a convincing account of moral character that can be sustained despite tragic conflict. My argument will show that identifying the components of "the life that is best and most valuable for a human being" presupposes a form of incommensurability that precludes an account of universal moral agency. This will lead me to draw different conclusions concerning the role that tragic literature can play in moral reflection.

Tragedy and Moral Conflict

The importance of tragedy in moral reflection rests on two prominent features of human experience, according to Nussbaum. The first is the sheer contingency of experience. It is a stubborn fact of life that the order of things is organized with contempt for our intentions and deserts. The good person can do everything he or she is morally obligated to do and things might still turn out badly. One consequence of this is that the good person can be harmed. There appears to be no tendency for happiness and morality to coincide, a result that has troubled many a moral theorist, including Plato and Kant. A second consequence of this "openness to fortune" is that agents cannot control their exposure to moral conflict. The vicissitudes of life, often through no fault of our own, regularly place conflicting moral demands on us. In acting to do the right thing, we may be forced to do harm as egregious as the "right thing" was obligatory.

The second feature of human experience that suggests a tragic dimension to our moral lives is what Nussbaum calls the noncommensurability of the goods we value.[3] This thesis of noncommensurability asserts that there is a rich diversity of goods on which we place value, and no standard for comparing these goods in choice situations. This is because the sorts of things that would count as a standard of comparison are incompatible with having the goods in question. For instance, we might compare rival goods according to some common feature they both share, such as price or utility, of which the more highly valued good will have more or less. Nussbaum argues that in situations in which we must choose between alternative courses of action, often there is no quality common to each that would allow such a comparison. Many of the things we hold in esteem are qualitatively distinct from other goods, and it is precisely in this qualitative distinctness that their value lies. Friendship, love, liberty, the pursuit of knowledge, creativity, aesthetic experience, and enjoyments of various sorts are characteristically valued for their own sake, not for what they share with other goods.

The degree to which competing goods bring about some desirable state of affairs also might count as a standard of comparison. Once again, Nussbaum argues that this is an inappropriate standard for those goods valued for their own sake. If I act in accordance with justice only because I will be rewarded for it, I am thereby not acting out of a sense of justice. To act out of a sense of justice requires that I understand the intrinsic value of justice, that I understand how it differs from acting out of a desire for reward.[4] Because there are some goods that are desired precisely for what they do not share with other goods, and because they are not valued as instruments for bringing about some further end, there is no standard in terms of which they can be compared. They are noncommensurable.[5]

The qualitative distinctness of goods, and the salient role of luck in determining the situations moral agents typically confront, suggests that philosophical reflection on morality must take seriously the kind of moral conflict we find most readily in tragic literature. In such conflict, an agent is confronted with two alternative courses of action, each of which the agent is morally obligated to pursue. The conflict arises because the unfortunate agent confronts circumstances that prevent the satisfaction of both claims. Because the good embodied in each alternative is desired for its own sake, there is no alternative path that would achieve an outcome of equal value. Thus, no matter what the agent chooses to do, she cannot satisfy both obligations, and a wrong will have been committed. In such cases, Nussbaum claims, a wrong act is committed with full knowledge and without physical compulsion by a person whose character would otherwise dispose her to reject the act.

In situations of tragic conflict an agent cannot avoid doing harm, and because goods are noncommensurable there is no way of assessing which harm is greater. Is there any course of action that is preferable? Nussbaum claims that there is, for what is important in situations of tragic conflict is that the agent emerge with her character and moral integrity intact. For Nussbaum, this means that the agent should *not* try to solve the dilemma by revising her commitments to the people and ideals in conflict, for to do so would be to discount something of extraordinary and irreplaceable value.

> If we were such that we could in a crisis dissociate ourselves from one commitment because it clashed with another, we would be less good. Goodness itself, then, insists that there should be no further or more revisionary solving.[6]

Instead of thinking of tragic conflict as a puzzle to be solved, Nussbaum argues that the demands of morality can be satisfied by genuinely expressing the appropriate emotional response to one's inevitable moral failure. In doing so, moral agents maintain the force of the value not acted upon, because it is by expressing emotion that we recognize and express the value things have. As this recognition sustains our ongoing commitments to the people and ideals we value, the dispositions and virtues that help sustain those commitments are strengthened. Thus, moral failure is not limited to the tendency of our actions to do wrong or to cause harm, but instead includes moral integrity's erosion by the failure to sustain ongoing commitments to what is most valuable in life — despite the vicissitudes of circumstance.

This conception of moral failure and moral integrity, Nussbaum will claim, is also a theme within tragic literature. This makes it an important vehicle for moral reflection. She will argue that when tragic heroes meet their demises, their failure is often in part a moral failure — for in their attempts to solve their dilemma, they revise their commitments, thereby suffering a loss of integrity. She illustrates this thesis using Aeschylus's *Agamemnon* as an example.

In this play, Agamemnon is enjoined by Zeus to avenge a breach of hospitality by attacking Troy. His ships, however, are stayed by the hand of Artemis, who calms the seas and protects Troy from the assault. This delay deeply concerns Agamemnon because it places his men at some risk. It turns out that only the sacrifice of Agamemnon's daughter, Iphigenia, by Agamemnon's own hand will move Artemis to allow the ships to sail. Thus, Agamemnon is torn between piety to the Gods and his love for his daughter. He cannot act without destroying something he values deeply.

As Nussbaum reads this play, Agamemnon's dilemma is not of his own making. Agamemnon is, on Nussbaum's reading, a man of exemplary character.[7] The dilemma results from the confluence of contingent circumstances over which Agamemnon has no control. Agamemnon chooses to sacrifice his daughter, thereby committing a wrong he would not otherwise have committed. But for Nussbaum, this is not Agamemnon's moral failure.

> We can see that one choice, the choice to sacrifice Iphigenia, seems clearly preferable, both because of consequences and because of the impiety involved in the other choice. Indeed, it is hard to imagine that Agamemnon could rationally have chosen any other way.[8]

Rather, his failure was in failing to show the appropriate remorse for his act. Once Agamemnon makes his agonizing decision, he seems to endorse his course of action without remorse.

> Pain both ways and what is worse?
> Desert the fleets, fail the alliance?
> No, but stop the winds with a virgin's blood,
> feed their lust, their fury? — feed their fury! —
> Law is law! (212–17)

He then proceeds with cold efficiency to cooperate with his fate, preparing his fleet for battle without expressing the grief expected in such circumstances. Agamemnon has chosen what he judges to be the lesser of two wrongs. However, his decision has a finality, as though the correct resolution of the dilemma had been discovered and the competing value of the path not chosen thoroughly discounted once the decision was made. Agamemnon's need to oversimplify his moral situation, to suppress the confusing and conflicting emotions that would complicate his choices and induce doubt about his chosen course of action, the lack of remorse, regret, or grief—all these are what Nussbaum finds objectionable about Agamemnon's conduct.

It is precisely this commitment to a problem-solving adventure that Nussbaum finds objectionable about moral theory, for moral theory, too, assumes there must be a right answer to moral questions. However, assessing alternative courses of action on the basis of independent criteria such as degree of utility would violate the qualitative distinctness of the conflicting goods by reducing differences in quality to differences in quantity. Attempts to solve moral dilemmas by employing hierarchical arrangements of antecedently formulated moral principles will be excessively reductionist as well. These attempts to show that one obligation is more fundamental than another, and should therefore take priority in all cases of moral conflict that are relevantly similar to the one in question, will fail to be responsive to novel situations with which we are likely to be confronted. The diversity and heterogeneity of goods makes confrontation with unexpected and novel comparisons likely, and the qualitative distinctness of goods suggests that many choices will be unique to particular situations. Such attempts to reduce the heterogeneity of goods will "do away with the nature of these goods as they are, and hence with their special contribution to the richness and fullness of the good life," according to Nussbaum.[9]

Tragic literature emphasizes our openness to fortune, in contrast with a theoretical approach to moral conflict, which will advocate a course of action that regulates an agent's exposure to moral conflict by discounting something the agent values. It treats a particular kind of moral conflict as a salient and irrepressible component of life rather than a puzzle to be solved. In showing conflict to be irrepressible and pervasive, tragic literature reveals the fate of characters who lose sight of this feature of the human condition, and thus compound their inevitable moral failure as they attempt to solve their dilemma by revising their ongoing commitments. Tragic literature reveals the need for a more complex form of cognition, in which judgment and emotion conspire to sustain as much as possible of what is valuable in life.

Moral Perception and Tragic Conflict

Nussbaum's treatment of Agamemnon seems to suggest that the aim of moral judgment is the preservation of ongoing commitments. However, she does not understand these commitments to be inflexible moral conventions or inviolate fixed points that function as prior constraints on conduct. In fact, Nussbaum argues that tragic literature often supplies a model of complex moral perception in which the recognition of novel, unique, and nonrepeatable features of situations shape ongoing commitments in ways that sustain these commitments, despite tragic conflict.

Only when our ongoing commitments and standing obligations are suitably modified, by a perceptive and emotionally responsive understanding of how those commitments can meet the demands of a particular situation, do they constrain us in the appropriate way. It is by means of such responsiveness that moral integrity is preserved.

This virtue of perceptiveness is best illustrated in the work of Henry James, especially in the actions of Maggie, one of the principle characters in *The Golden Bowl*. Maggie's bond with her father, Adam, is so consuming that it prevents her from fully participating in her marriage to Amerigo. He has reacted to this barrier erected by father and daughter by renewing a rather passionate affair with Charlotte, a former lover, and more recently a friend of Maggie's as well. As the story develops, Charlotte and Adam also marry, although their marriage appears to be a marriage of convenience. Thus, each character is obligated through marriage while simultaneously sustaining a passionate relationship with someone from the past. Although each of the characters has a genuine concern for the others in this tightly knit circle of friends and lovers, both marriages are harmed by the father-daughter relationship and Maggie's naiveté regarding its destructive effects.

It is Maggie's realization that her husband is having an affair with her friend Charlotte that provides the impetus for the final denouement. Through subtle manipulations Maggie resolves to untangle this web, but must tread lightly in order to avoid harming someone she cares about. Both Maggie and her father come to realize they must part ways; she is tormented by the thought of separation from her father, who has nurtured her throughout her life. His daughter's rejection would not be taken lightly—it might condemn him to a lonely and unhappy life—but she cannot love her husband, nor restore his wounded dignity, except by rejecting her father. Maggie has to distance herself from her father without rejecting him, while reinvigorating the affection of her husband. Resolution comes with the decision that Adam will go to America with Charlotte. Adam will have to sacrifice for the sake of Maggie's marriage. Yet, for this to be a genuine resolution, it has to be offered in such a way as to avoid the emotional scars that will result if it is handled badly.

The conflict that confronts Maggie has the structure of a tragic conflict. No matter what she does she will fail to honor an obligation she has incurred, and someone about whom she cares deeply will be harmed. According to Nussbaum, Maggie's judgment and increasing moral maturity in resolving these conflicts is a paradigm of moral reasoning. It illustrates the importance of gestures, of subtle feeling and expression, and of attention to the minute details of how one communicates to sustain the significance of human relationships. Only if Maggie gets these right can she induce each character to act in a way that preserves everyone's dignity and minimizes the harm to each of them. Moral failure is the result of inattention.

Quoting from James's own comments on his work, Nussbaum claims that the main project in a moral life is to make ourselves people "on whom nothing is lost."[10] Without the ability to interpret concrete particulars, Maggie and Adam could not figure out which rules and commitments are operative. Thus, the ability to see makes it possible to act from the appropriate motivation.

> What makes their embrace a wonderful achievement of love and mutual altruism is not the bare fact that it is an embrace; it is the precise tonality and quality of that embrace: that it is hard and long, expressive of deep passion on his side, yielding acceptance of that love on hers; yet dignified and austere, refusing the easy yielding to tears that might have cheapened it.[11]

The perception of particulars shapes moral ideals, virtues, habits of thought, and judgment in order to induce these qualities of character to conform to the contours of the situation. Ongoing commitments, norms, and dispositions make moral perception possible because they form the foundation of moral character. However, the perception of particularity enables the agent to sustain the ongoing commitments by shaping those commitments to fit the particular situations containing elements of surprise and novelty. The right-making characteristics of an action, in Nussbaum's view, are irreducibly particular because the general moral understandings put into play in deliberation are uniquely modified to conform to the exigencies of the situation.

The moral perceptiveness exhibited by Maggie is Nussbaum's answer to the question of how moral agents transcend the limitations of their moral points of view. Neither Maggie nor Adam can rely on the routines of interaction that have characterized their relationship in the past. They are in uncharted waters and must find a responsive way of dealing with the novel situation. Moral blindness, the inability to perceive pain, need, wounded dignity, or humiliation is the cardinal vice of Jamesian heroes and of Nussbaum's treatment of tragic heroes. The perceptive individual is capable of seeing beyond the particular relationships and norms that form the substance of a moral perspective, while sustaining what is valuable in them as well. Thus, Nussbaum demonstrates how moral integrity is compatible with this aspiration to transcend our limitations.

In summary, for Nussbaum tragic literature represents the structure of moral conflict by presenting characters confronted with the inevitability of their doing harm. It also locates a primary source of moral failure in the inability to sustain ongoing commitments, and provides us with a model of deliberation and judgment in which general commitments and ideals are made to conform to the contours of particular situations by means of moral perception.

Moral Value and Moral Blindness

Like Nussbaum, I endorse the importance of tragic literature in moral reflection. However, I take issue with the particular way in which Nussbaum articulates this importance, especially her conception of moral failure, for I think tragedy harbors an insight much less flattering to her conception of moral integrity than her readings suggest. Tragic literature expresses an implicit critique of the very commitments that constitute moral integrity for Nussbaum, and provides us with a perspective from which to view the limitations of any moral point of view.

The limitations of Nussbaum's thesis can be best addressed by returning to her readings of *Agamemnon* and *The Golden Bowl*. Nussbaum argues that both Agamemnon and Maggie make defensible decisions, but Agamemnon fails to preserve his moral integrity while Maggie succeeds. Nussbaum locates moral failure in the tendency of agents to seek a "science of measurement" that attempts to determine an unequivocally correct answer to moral dilemmas—an approach to moral decision-making that, in its quest for control over contingent circumstances, disrupts moral character and fails to preserve the intrinsic value of the goods in conflict. Thus, Agamemnon reduces the variety and intensity of the things he cares about, ignoring the loss of Iphigenia in his pursuit of victory, while Maggie, through her perceptiveness, is able to preserve the value of the competing claims on her. Nussbaum's judgment that Maggie is a moral exemplar and Agamemnon is not apparently is grounded in the contrast between a deliberative style that discounts something of value in order to reduce conflict—what we might call the ideology of calculation—and a deliberative style that sustains value by exhibiting perceptiveness and emotional responsiveness.

However, despite Maggie's perceptive deliberative style, she fails to live up to the moral ideal that Nussbaum articulates—to be someone on whom nothing is lost. Many losses are incurred, especially by Charlotte, as the result of Maggie's manipulations. The wounds caused by Maggie's relationship with her father can only be healed if Charlotte and Adam depart for America. Charlotte must end her passionate relationship with Amerigo and can no longer sustain her friendship with Maggie. Charlotte loses her lover and her friend in return for a more or less aimless journey with a less than ideal companion many years her senior. Despite their friendship, Maggie never succeeds in clearly perceiving Charlotte's situation and the obvious harm that will befall her given Maggie's "solution." In fact, one could argue that, at bottom, Maggie's motivation is revenge against Charlotte's dalliances with her husband.[12]

Maggie wishes more than anything to mend the fissures in these relationships, symbolized by the shattered pieces of a bowl lying near a mantle as the novel approaches its conclusion. Commenting on Nussbaum's treatment of this book, Mary Ann Caws writes:

> As the demand of "restoration and constancy of the past" . . . so we might read Maggie's hopeless and heartfelt naive demand about her own past—as wife wanting to be unbetrayed, as daughter wanting to be unbetraying, as constancy observed and lauded and believed in— as itself, in the limits posed by James, the violation occasioning both tragedy and terrible blindness to tragedy.[13]

Maggie's reconstruction of her fragmented moral world is made possible by a perceptiveness that rests on blindness and a concern motivated by revenge.

Nussbaum treats Maggie's blindness as an instance of her increasing moral maturity and recognition of her own finitude. According to Nussbaum, the novel shows that a great love in one direction may produce a "tragically necessary blindness."

> The demands of the new ideal of seeing are not always compatible with an adequate fulfillment of each of our commitments, for some loves are exclusive and demand a blindness in other quarters. . .we may, in fact, have to become, as lovers, grossly insensitive and careless with respect to other, incompatible claims.[14]

This response muddies the waters. Up to this point, the implication was that Agamemnon had failed where Maggie had succeeded. Agamemnon's attempt to simplify his dilemma led to moral blindness, while Maggie's

deliberations were exemplary because they exhibited the virtue of perceptiveness. But if Maggie, too, exhibits moral blindness, why is she nevertheless a moral exemplar and Agamemnon a failure, in Nussbaum's view?
Does not Maggie fail in her moral task just as Agamemnon did? Although
Iphigenia's life may impose a greater moral claim on Agamemnon than
Charlotte's feelings and prospects impose on Maggie, thus making his
silencing a more egregious omission, this could not account for their
different statuses. Nussbaum does not condemn Agamemnon for taking
Iphigenia's life, but only for failing to express the appropriate sense of
loss—in part, what Maggie fails to do as well. Maggie, like Agamemnon,
fails to preserve the value of the competing claim.

It is, of course, part of Nussbaum's thesis that the good person can do
harm, that contingent forces prevent the realization of every good that we
seek, and in fact makes the performance of a wrong unavoidable. That
Maggie failed to realize completely her ideal of perceptiveness is not
in itself an objection to Maggie's character or to Nussbaum's view. Yet
Nussbaum owes us an account of the circumstances under which the good
person remains "good" despite moral failure. It cannot simply be the presence of a perceptive, deliberative style, since that too is compatible with
the discounting of something of value.

I want to argue that the moral blindness exhibited by both Maggie and
Agamemnon is not the result of their deliberative style at all. Rather, it is
related to the structure of moral ideals themselves. This is implicitly
recognized by Nussbaum when she argues that Maggie's love for Amerigo
is the sort of ideal that demands exclusivity and insensitivity to incompatible, competing claims. A similar blindness resides in the ideals that frame
Agamemnon's dilemma. Agamemnon's capacity to silence the claims of
Iphigenia is a product of the very ideal on which he chooses to act—the
ideal of piety. Piety encourages the silencing of competing claims because
its form of commitment tends to resist qualification. The point is not that
piety considered in the abstract conflicts conceptually with a genuine concern for others. Still a sustained commitment to piety does seem to
require absolute faith in the power and omniscience of divine commands,
leaving little room for doubt about the rightness of the course of action
commanded. Divine command generates its power to influence, in part,
from its capacity to simplify moral choice, to silence competing considerations when they conflict with the virtue of piety. It encourages a kind of
single-mindedness that overwhelms other sources of value. To demand of
piety that it recognize that the object of devotion should at times be
discounted to avoid harmful consequences is to give up piety as a virtue.

Such a demand would fail to recognize piety's special, unconditional force. Thus, Agamemnon's tendency to avoid remorse and discount genuine feelings is not the result of an independent commitment to a "science of measurement," as Nussbaum would have it, but is instead built into the virtue of piety itself.[15]

Regarding my alternative reading of *Agamemnon*, this tragedy does not illustrate, for the contemporary reader, the importance of the virtues or the worth of our commitments to time-honored values. Instead, it suggests a more intransigent imperfection in these values rendering them more tenuous than even the fragile values Nussbaum articulates. This explanation of Agamemnon's conduct suggests that it is often our virtues, our good moral character, the things we hold in highest esteem, that create the conditions for moral failure. It is precisely those commitments we think are the least questionable that sometimes threaten to impoverish our lives. Tragedy harbors the insight that moral ideals or qualities of excellent character can be the source of moral failure, and it leads us to recognize the importance of a critical perspective from which to assess our deepest commitments.[16]

This understanding of tragic figures will have implications for our conception of moral integrity and character. If sustained commitment to a moral value is the source of insensitivity and moral blindness, then the highest aim of our deliberations and emotional responsiveness should not be to preserve a commitment to that value. Moral integrity cannot be defined primarily in terms of the preservation of ongoing commitments if those commitments can themselves be the source of moral failure. Rather than support a conception of moral integrity, tragic literature may represent a boundary across which such a concept cannot gain a foothold.

Judgments of Contrast

I argue that tragic literature represents the dark side of our moral ideals. It suggests that ideals themselves may be the source of a certain kind of moral blindness, and that moral integrity may be impossible to sustain. However, if a general claim about this sort of moral failure is to be warranted, I need a more systematic account of it. In this section I will try to show why moral ideals typically issue in a form of moral blindness.

Part of the lived experience of most humans are attachments that lie so close to defining who we are as individuals and as members of a community that they dominate and give structure to the course of our lives. These include the obvious—bonds to family and friends, to one's nation, religion, profession, life projects, artistic pursuits, political causes, money and power, etc. We might also include on this list of what is most significant attachments to more personal, idiosyncratic experience—aesthetic experiences, pleasures of all sorts, aspirations and goals, as well as resentments, slights, psychological trauma, and other misfortunes that can consume our attention and energy.

Some of these consuming interests may be "deep loves" like Maggie's unconditional love for Amerigo or Agamemnon's devotion to Zeus. Moral values are also an important part of these attachments, although we need not restrict a list of things that have this kind of significance to those with a moral dimension. Some may be candidates for inclusion within a conception of a good human life. Others are "goods" only in the sense that they are objects of desire. We pursue them with energy and commitment (sometimes obsessively), although looked at impartially, upon reflection, we might not endorse them. The point here is that the range of things humans find worthy of unconditional attachment are many and diverse, and not restricted to goods defined as such by impartial, evaluative criteria. By "unconditional" I mean that in becoming an object of devotion or an organizing theme around which one's life revolves, these attachments cannot easily be disengaged from that life without massive conceptual and emotional transformation. They provide a *prima facie* motive for acting, and occupy a center around which the activities and episodes of one's life revolves.

It is part of the tragic vision that unconditional attachment to any one of these objects of devotion can compromise our capacity to become attached to the others. We cannot choose to pursue everything, as Maggie discovers when she allows her concern for Charlotte to recede behind moral curtains. However, this insight is not peculiar to tragic literature; rather, it characterizes the sort of narratives out of which the story of a life is constituted. The requirement that we subordinate the importance of some goods while advancing the importance of others is generally a salient feature of human experience, the high drama of tragedy being perhaps its most sublime expression.

This common feature of experience is easily explained by its narrative structure. As I indicated briefly in Chapter Two, life's narratives are constructed out of beginnings and endings, a context of significance into which we must place contingent experience. In choosing to act in a certain way, we move toward dimly perceived story endings, constructed out of our unconditional attachments, that help to determine what is possible and important. Part of what makes some attachments unconditional is the practical impossibility of shedding or reversing the choices we make. As we approach the end of any of the stories that make up our lives, what had seemed possible earlier is no longer available. The course of life produces its own subordinations—encounters seem more or less important, alliances more or less useful, bonds of association more or less captivating depending on their location in the temporal structure of the narrative. The judgment that some attachment is less important than another is demanded by the way goals are continually being transformed by our actions.

The subordinations produced by Agamemnon and Maggie, their failure to preserve the value of the competing claim, are not redeemable. This is because after their fateful decisions they become characters in their respective narratives, which take their points of demarcation *from* these decisions. The narrative fragments that included Iphigenia and Charlotte have reached their completion. They no longer mark a *telos* for Maggie and Agamemnon but the beginning of other narrative fragments, guided by other ends, which forbid the discarded characters from playing a major role no matter what appropriate emotions have been expressed.

Nussbaum's pluralism with respect to value, her concern that we sustain the rich diversity of human goods and avoid reducing the things we value to a single dimension, when combined with this conception of the narrative structure of a life tends to work against the notion of moral integrity she endorses. Any of the multiplicity of goods can function as a *telos,* organizing a life into a certain pattern that makes the value of other goods impossible to sustain. The limits of this diversity are prescribed by the narrative structure of life. Because the things we value have the capacity to subordinate—to focus attention on one thing rather than another—and to do so with a level of intensity that is sustained over time, they give meaning and intelligibility to life. There is, therefore, tension between the integrity of moral character, when understood as the capacity to sustain a diversity of ongoing commitments, and the narrative structure of life that inevitably makes certain commitments difficult to sustain.[17] The revisionary solving that fractures character is accomplished, not only by a misguided conception of practical reason, but by life itself.

Thus, given the claim that assignments of value are structured like narratives, it seems implausible that expression of the appropriate emotion is sufficient to sustain the integrity of moral character. It seems to me that nothing can salvage the significance of values not acted upon, given the way the episodes of a life tend to fall into patterns of possibility and dead ends. Emotion may sustain memory, and that may be morally significant, but it will not sustain the significance of possibilities foregone.

This tension between diversity and significance highlights the underlying structure of the virtue of perceptiveness. In Nussbaum's view, our capacity to perceive the uniqueness and special qualities that things have is essential to leading a good human life. In recognizing how particularity and novelty are central features of the things we value, and how these values can respond to the shape of the world, our commitments are reinforced. My account of narrative structure is that part of the uniqueness and special value of a good is its capacity to subordinate the less significant. To view one's beloved as unique; to sense, in a moment of intense pleasure, that there is nothing else on earth with that particular quality; to recognize in an art object the mark of incomparable originality; or to appreciate the singular contributions that one's community has made to humankind, is to mark off those experiences from the rest of life. This contrast makes these experiences special and worthy of high regard. The contrast is essential to recognizing quality, because the notion of "quality" picks out degrees of excellence that presuppose a contrast between higher and lower.

The tendency to subordinate, to distinguish that which has value from that which does not, seems built into the virtue of perceptiveness. To the degree that perceptiveness focuses on the recognition of quality and value, it relegates the mundane and insignificant to the background. Thus, a central component of the virtue of perceptiveness, the capacity to recognize qualitative distinctions, seems incompatible with the aspiration to be "someone on whom nothing is lost." Perceptiveness is not independent of value judgments, but an important component of them. The recognition of value itself presupposes a hierarchy in which something is diminished or reduced.[18]

I argue for the hierarchical structure of value judgments without drawing a distinction between moral and nonmoral value. I suspect that moral and nonmoral values are not so much distinct from each other as they are part of a continuum, with clear cases at each end and a substantial middle ground fraught with considerable ambiguity. There is a related distinction, however, indicating a fruitful way to draw the distinction between moral and nonmoral. There are some judgments that, in addition to giving structure and meaning to life, are judgments their bearers think others ought to share as well. Those who don't share them are subject to a degree of censure, and are often the objects of contempt. Moral judgments clearly are among these, although they need not be restricted to what we commonly think of as moral judgments. Religious beliefs, political ideologies, and choices regarding values and lifestyles often fit within this category. Other beliefs or judgments that may be equally central to a person's life do not carry with them this additional burden of a prescription directed at others. Judgments about the value of one's occupation or consuming interests are usually in the latter category, although human psychology is such that counterexamples can surely be advanced.

This distinction between judgments carrying the prescription that others ought to share them and judgments that are not deepens the sense of unconditionality noted previously. It is characteristic of the former that one must endorse them regardless of what other goods one values. This suggests that part of the belief system making these judgments possible is that some actions or judgments are inherently of higher value than others.[19]

When we consider judgments that have moral content or that carry with them this additional prescriptive force, the tension between an omniscient perceptiveness and the recognition of special quality, as well as the aforementioned tension between diversity and significance, becomes open conflict. Moral judgments, I will argue, are dependent upon judgments of qualitative contrast that prevent the realization of the Jamesian ideal to be someone "on whom nothing is lost."[20]

The judgment that everyone ought to value a certain moral standard, independently of whatever else they value, need not be based on some universally shared property such as rational autonomy or an interest in pursuing happiness. The judgments that interest me here are based on the belief that a certain standard, activity, or kind of life is higher in quality, more admirable, etc. than others that may deserve only our contempt or indifference. Only someone who pursues that activity or acts on that standard is worthy of respect and admiration. The force of the "ought" is that others ought to frame moral issues in this way as well—the standard or activity is inherently admirable. Charles Taylor provides some interesting examples of this sort of moral outlook.

1. Personal integrity—The state in which one's life expresses what one truly thinks is important, admirable, and desirable.
2. Agape—Having the power to heal divisions among men and to go beyond the limits of their love for one another.
3. Liberation—Achieving dignity through being self-directed; avoiding domination by others.
4. Utilitarian rationality—Clarity regarding one's goals and a capacity to objectify oneself and one's world.

These represent ways of framing moral issues that dispose agents to certain kinds of conduct compatible with their respective outlooks. What is important is that the contrast between higher and lower exhibited by these examples is essential to the judgment. In order to have these goods, one must decline to trade them off against other considerations. Not only must one be willing to sacrifice other considerations to sustain these goods, one must recognize that there is a contrast involved as well. Recognizing the higher value, acting out of a sense of its higher value, is an essential part of having it. As Taylor puts it, "The aspiration to achieve one of these goods is also an aspiration to be motivated in a certain way, or to have certain motivations win out in oneself."[21] The recognition of "standing out" in opposition to something corrupt is part of the motivation for acting. This suggests, for instance, that having integrity involves having a special sensitivity to integrity and a revulsion to its compromise. The implication is that without both the sensitivity *and* the revulsion one could not be a person of integrity.

The important point for my purposes is that the intelligibility of and commitment to the higher value is dependent upon one's resistance to sharing some dimension of experience for which one feels contempt or indifference. It is in the nature of contrast judgments that they subordinate dimensions of experience lacking the special quality to which a particular agent's perceptions are attracted. As Taylor notes, someone who wishes nothing more fervently than to have her life express only that which is admirable must guard against the temptations of conformity. Similarly, one whose actions exhibit *agape* not only will fail to see clearly the hopelessness of a situation or the virtues of solitude, but *must* fail to do so to remain committed to *agape*. Someone who sees reality as ultimately conforming to the clarity of insight and human reason must remain untouched by the mystery of experience, and fail to acknowledge the impenetrability of irrationality or the vulnerability of the human condition. Thus, someone who acquires the goods associated with these judgments of qualitative contrast will be prevented from acquiring other goods—for if the incompatibility were denied, one would have the wrong motivations for acting on the judgment.

A contrast judgment, then, is a judgment that rests on the belief that a significant good has intrinsic value, and that part of the value of said good, and/or the motivations for acting on that good, depend on the devaluing of other goods. This suggests that there are at least three different kinds of contrasts a judgment might exhibit. (1) A good is conceptually incompatible with other goods because of the qualitative judgment involved; that is to say, because the notion of "quality" picks out a degree of excellence, it presupposes a contrast between higher and lower. (2) A good is incompatible with other goods because, if the contrast were denied, one would have the wrong motivations for acting on that good. Finally, (3) a good is incompatible with other goods because it is valued as the result of the narrative structure of experience, which precludes the valuing of other goods.

These sorts of judgments, and the second-order motivations that accompany them, play a central role in explaining adherence to moral rules and our dispositions to act in accordance with them. Contrast judgments go to the heart of what it means to value something. Taking this view, agents' beliefs are hierarchically structured to reflect both the importance they attach to certain values, and their indifference or contempt for activities that contrast with these values. Although a single agent may have a tendency to employ a number of these judgments of contrast in her practical reasoning, they often lead to incompatible courses of action and the possibility of tragic conflict.

Thus, this notion of a contrast judgment provides a general framework for explaining the subordinations involved in the judgments of many tragic characters. As I noted previously, Agamemnon's piety not only made it possible to discount Iphigenia but actually required that it be done. Creon's commitment to civic virtue and progress are not only incompatible with the personal and tradition-bound but rest on their rejection, just as Antigone's devotion to dead family members must rest on her chill, dismissive attitude toward the living.

Contrast judgments also explain why perceptiveness fares no better than other ideals, why it too is subject to moral blindness. The ideal, for James and Nussbaum, is to be "someone on whom nothing is lost," someone who recognizes qualitative distinctions—the special value of the multiplicity of goods available in a situation—and the relevant properties of the situation that make achievement of those goods possible. However, if both the recognition that a certain kind of activity has a special status and the motivation to act on that recognition are dependent on the realization that other activities are base and unworthy of respect, it becomes less clear how someone who possesses the virtue of perceptiveness could also be someone on whom nothing is lost. Maggie's perceptiveness was conditioned by love for Adam and Amerigo and by her commitment to personal integrity, which for Maggie demanded her extraordinary search for constancy in a shattered world. Yet these high and honorable motives produced indifference to the harm to Charlotte's prospects. In James's *The Ambassadors*, Lambert Strether's perceptiveness rests on his ability to see the virtues of both the libertine sensibility of Europe and his blue-blooded New England heritage. Yet his perceptiveness makes him incapable of either the decisive action or the kind of involvement love requires. Nussbaum attributes this to the gulf between "love and ethical attention" that might lead the lover "at times beyond the ethical stance into a world in which ethical judgment does not take place."[22] However, the prevalence of contrast judgments suggests that the blindness associated with love is not restricted to love but afflicts "ethical attention" itself. To the extent that perceptions are guided by contrast judgments, the perceiver cannot "see it all" either; I would want to claim that contrast judgments of the sort described above are not rare, but frame a good deal of our practical reasoning.

If moral judgments are significantly bound up with contrast judgments, this will have important consequences for the capacity of any moral point of view to transcend its limitations and sustain a conception of universal moral agency. Because the intelligibility of moral goods is dependent on not sharing in the experiences held in contempt and on not identifying too closely with them, the arena of mutual interaction with others who represent the outlook in disrepute will be restricted. The demands of others whose sense of what is admirable differs markedly will only evoke from the person of integrity a contemptuous discounting of whatever qualities others might possess. What is more, these losses need not be a source of regret. Judgments of qualitative contrast must endorse the higher value despite the losses that are suffered. Because the assignment of value is the result of a contrastive judgment, one can't eliminate the contrast while sustaining the recognition of the higher value. I therefore fail to see how someone can sustain these qualitative judgments while aspiring to be "someone on whom nothing is lost." Perception will induce its own form of blindness, dependent as it is on judgements of contrast and narrative structure.

Thus, Nussbaum's account of moral perception fails on a number of scores. It fails, first of all, to resolve the tension between concrete ethics and the aspiration to transcend the limits of one's moral point of view. Moral perception functions within the narrow confines of specific, contrastive judgments and has no particular ability to transcend the parochial. It also fails to resolve the tension in her account of moral character between the richness and diversity of goods on one hand, and the integrity of moral character on the other. It is not obvious how we reconcile the diversity of goods with sustained commitment to those goods, if the expression of the appropriate emotion is rejected as a sufficient account of what it means to sustain commitment.

Moreover, although Nussbaum's commentaries on literary works succeed in elevating perceptiveness and imagination to their rightful place alongside other modes of reflection and discourse, they have not demonstrated any superiority, since perceptiveness and virtue seem to result in a moral blindness similar to that which also afflicts theory.

Finally, that judgments of contrast are central to moral judgment in general, and that narrative structure produces irrevocable commitments from the particular, partial perspective of one's own life, provides some philosophical support for the general claim that I argued was illustrated by tragic literature—that a particular form of moral blindness is the product of those very ideals and virtues we think are morally praiseworthy. In both cases, part of the meaning of the judgments themselves is their capacity to subordinate dimensions of experience and inhibit our capacity to recognize when a moral claim is at stake. The implications of this argument for philosophical theories that take virtues and moral character to be the data of moral assessment are serious. The kind of moral blindness that antitheorists argue is endemic to traditional theoretical approaches may be characteristic of virtue ethics as well.

Contrast judgments, then, are one way of explaining the moral blindness that afflicts tragic heroes and heroines, for they are often characters with great enthusiasms and equally magnificent contempt. However, tragic literature is not merely a source of examples for illustrating contrast judgments. In experiencing the plight of these characters, our attention is turned back on ourselves. The strong emotions this genre produces in the spectator or reader are, in part, a product of a more important recognition—that in our own enthusiasms, we may be victimizers. Tragedy harbors the insight that only an incredulity toward our own ideals will mitigate the consequences ensuing from tragic conflict. I will return to this point at the close of the next chapter.

4

A Theoretical Riposte

I argue that moral virtues and ideals, like moral theories, are flawed in that they encourage a kind of moral blindness—the failure to perceive something of value. Consequently, they also fail to advance the aspiration of transcendence, which I argue is part of the very enterprise of morality. However, the premises of my argument thus far do not force us to draw this conclusion; these premises suggest only that moral ideals rest on an opacity—from a moral point of view we cannot see all there is to see. It does not follow that what is missing from our attention has moral value. Intuitively, Charlotte and Iphigenia both have moral value, and discounting their value would appear to be a wrong. Still, what reason do we have, in general, to claim that what is subordinated by contrast judgments possesses a value that deserves recognition? Tragic literature presupposes that the silencing of morally relevant considerations by the protagonist's fateful decision is a serious loss. Yet the author relies heavily on the intuitions of the audience, and a literary work would seem to be the wrong sort of discourse to provide further justification.

This leaves my argument open to a possible objection by Nussbaum. She can respond to the sort of objections I've advanced against her ethics of virtue by arguing, as she does, that literature alone cannot satisfactorily inform our moral perspectives. The issue of what things human beings value should be included in an understanding of what makes a good human life. Without understanding how to answer that question, any attempt to describe judgments as perceptive or blind will be difficult, since these judgments presuppose some notion of what is valuable. While it may be the case that contrast judgments subordinate dimensions of experience that have moral significance, only an assessment of what is excluded in light of a conception of the "good for man" will answer this question one way or the other.

Although literature provides examples of the broad panoply of human experiences—candidates for inclusion in a conception of a good human life—the task of comparing and assessing these alternatives is a specifically philosophical task, according to Nussbaum. The aim of ethical inquiry is to seek "a consistent and shareable answer to the 'how to live' question, one that will capture what is deepest and most basic. . . ."[1]

In this section, I consider Nussbaum's conception of theory in order to evaluate the degree to which it mitigates the objections raised above. On procedural issues in philosophy, Nussbaum is wedded to her own version of reflective equilibrium, which is inspired by Aristotle as well as Rawls. Such an inquiry begins by asking the question, "How should a human being live?" and proceeds by assessing alternative conceptions drawn from literature and history, as well as philosophy, by,

> holding them up against one another and also against the participants' beliefs and feelings, their active sense of life. Nothing is held unrevisable in this process, except the very basic logical idea that statement implies negation, that to assert something is to rule out something else.[2]

What such an inquiry seeks is the best overall fit between a general conception of a good human life, of which moral theories are candidates, and "what lies deepest" in the lives of the agents in question.

Nussbaum argues that philosophical inquiry has the practical aims of "promoting individual clarification and self-understanding" and "moving individuals toward communal attunement." For the agents in question, this means the results must be constrained by "their hopes and fears for themselves, their sense of value, what they think they can live with."[3] Nussbaum is, therefore, committed to a version of internal realism that seeks to develop a coherent set of beliefs from within a particular moral point of view, while demanding of those beliefs that they be broadly shareable and consistent.[4] The aspiration to transcend the parochial is captured by the aspiration that one's moral outlook be broadly shareable—for what Nussbaum intends is that we work outward from our narrow points of view, continually seeking points of agreement with alternative outlooks, modifying our point of view when it is warranted. This requires a method that seeks to assess as wide a range of general conceptions as possible.

What we will discover in these confrontations between various accounts of what is valuable and significant is a residue that will constitute "what we most deeply consider worth saving."[5] This conception of philosophical method is called "perceptive equilibrium," in contrast to reflective equilibrium, because it takes more seriously than Rawls and Daniels do the particularity of the judgments to be attributed to the agents in question. Thus, Nussbaum's account of philosophical method promises to rectify the limitations of reflective equilibrium, discussed in Chapter One, because it was in the generalization from particularity to general principle that I found reflective equilibrium wanting.

Unlike Rawls and Daniels, Nussbaum will not restrict the initial judgments under consideration to those we can confidently assert and which are absent of emotion and self-interest. Instead, perceptions that arise from "situational immersion," that may be accompanied by "powerful feeling," that may surprise us in their novelty, and about which we may feel "perplexed, difficult, unsafe" are under consideration, as well as are our more reflective judgments.[6] Also, unlike Rawls's version, the procedure does not attempt to generalize from these perceptions and judgments by forming principles that explain or justify them. Rather, it seeks to develop comprehensive accounts of alternative systems of ethical thought (including literary representations), and proceeds to show how these are related to each other and to the perceptions and judgments drawn from the lived experience of the agents. Principles are relegated to a heuristic role. They are convenient ways of summarizing moral relevant properties of concrete commitments. Theories serve to raise patterns of salience that differ from those expressed by the "morality of perception," that emphasize features of a situation other conceptions may not take seriously. Therefore, justification does not proceed by the mutual revision of theory, principles, and considered judgments when these come into conflict.

> Where there is inconsistency or irreconcilable tension—and where this tension corresponds to something that we notice in our own experience and thought (individually and communally)—we aim to revise the overall picture so as to bring it into harmony with itself, preserving, as Aristotle says, "the greatest number and the most basic" of the original judgments and perceptions. There is no rule about how to do this. Individuals simply ask what looks deepest, what they can least live without—guided by their sense of life, and by their standing interest in consistency and in community.[7]

The demands of community (expressed by the aspiration that certain properties be widely shared) require that we sometimes move toward shared perceptions, by actively transforming our particular perceptions and judgments. Such transformations require the kind of reflectiveness appropriate to the consideration of alternative theories. Theory asks us to provisionally and—for heuristic reasons—temporarily stand back from our commitments, in order to consider, without the usual investments, different patterns of salience. This makes alien points of view more accessible. Moral theory helps to systematize the activity of comparing and assessing competing points of view, in a way that captures points of agreement among all the various perspectives. A perception or judgment that survives the confrontation with diverse theories will be evidence that the perceptions or judgments in question are a relatively fixed point across a wide range of human experience. The justification of a perception or judgment is accomplished by demonstrating its relative fixity and scope. We seek to preserve those commitments that look "deepest," what one can "least live without." However, the demands of community often require that we seek to transcend our limited points of view. Thus, moral reflection is constrained by the aspiration to move toward perceptions and judgments that are broadly shareable.

Despite assigning a significant role for theory, Nussbaum insists that particularity receives priority in her methodology. Thus, she attempts to mediate the dispute between theorists and antitheorists by adopting a specific picture of how generality and particularity work to form a comprehensive moral point of view. However, it is not clear that this wedding of situational responsiveness and general understanding will hang together, for it is uncertain whether the comparison of alternative moral points of view will succeed in identifying judgments or perceptions that are both broadly shareable and responsive to particular situations. It is not obvious how a judgment or perception can be responsive to particularity and broadly shareable as well.

Nussbaum uses the word "particularity" to refer to "concrete, situational judgments" in situations that possess at least one of the following properties:

(a) Novelty—The relevant properties or their configurations are appearing for the first time.
(b) Uniqueness—The relevant properties or their configuration are not common to other situations and may be, in principle, nonrepeatable.

(c) Complexity—The number of relevant features and their configurations are too large to be manageable by a general description.[8]

The distinctive feature of Nussbaum's ethics is the concern that agents be
responsive to situations exhibiting these features. Can perceptions or judgments that identify these properties be broadly shareable across a wide
range of human experience? I think the answer must be no, at least for
the property of uniqueness. For a property to be unique to a situation (or
uniquely salient in a situation), it is by definition not common to other
situations, and thus not present across a wide range of human experience.
Since perceptions and judgments that pick out properties are individuated
by their content, i.e., by the properties they identify as salient, the perceptions and judgments will not be present across a wide range of experience either. There is no reason to think that a unique property could be
identified as salient by a wide range of theoretical perspectives, for if it
were, it would not be unique.

The properties of novelty and complexity, on the other hand, are not
logically incompatible with widely shared perceptions. We cannot rule
out the possibility that some set of moral theories will be responsive to
novel or complex situations. However, what clearly will make a difference when assessing the importance of moral theories to this process of
justification is the degree of systematicity between the circumstances that
demand a moral response on one hand, and the kinds of moral judgments
that can be plausibly argued to be appropriate responses to those circumstances on the other. As I argued in Chapter One, given the premise
(which Nussbaum accepts) that contingency and unpredictability pervade
social reality, moral norms must respond to nonideal circumstances.
Theory will only be relevant if there is sufficient systematicity between
these nonideal circumstances to which morality is a response, and if there
are broadly shareable moral perceptions across a wide range of experience. The contingency thesis gives us some reason to be skeptical of
the shareability of these perceptions of vulnerability and, hence, their
potential for accommodation within perceptive equilibrium. However,
Nussbaum argues that there is indeed such systematicity.

Nonrelative Virtues

In "Non-Relative Virtues: An Aristotelian Approach," Nussbaum de-
fends the position, attributed to Aristotle, that a virtue ethic offers trans-
cultural norms that can be justified according to universal standards of

human reason, and that refer to "features of humanness that lie beneath all local traditions and are there to be seen whether or not they are in fact recognized in local traditions."[9] If this is the case, then the aspiration to transcend the limitations of a moral perspective can be satisfied, and charges of moral blindness with respect to certain moral ideals will be mitigated by this account of human nature that explains our capacity for shared perceptions.

Nussbaum begins by arguing that there are "spheres of experience," or "grounding experiences," in which all human beings have to make choices. One can ask what it means to act well or badly within each separate sphere. Consequently, we must have some sense of what counts as human flourishing within each sphere. The recognition that there are stable dispositions to act in these spheres allows us to roughly fix the reference of virtue words. For instance, all human beings fear death and injury. Consequently, all human beings must have some conception of the appropriate response to the fear of death and injury—a response referred to as courage. Similarly, all human beings experience bodily appetites and their pleasures, and so all must have some conception of moderation; all must distribute limited resources, and thus must have some conception of justice, etc.

Merely by fixing the reference of the virtue word, Nussbaum argues that we have a "thin" or "nominal" definition of that virtue. Any disposition that counts as responding well within that sphere of experience will be the referent of the virtue term. Further specification of the virtue will involve vast disagreement, since every society or tradition will have its own locally defined dispositions. However, because the spheres of experience are common within all of human experience, competing specifications of the virtues will nevertheless be disagreements about the same thing. Every society or tradition will contain some response to that sphere of experience, and it is that to which the virtue word refers.

Progress in ethics consists of "finding the correct fuller specification of a virtue."

> This progress is aided by a perspicuous mapping of the sphere of the grounding experience. When we understand more precisely what problems human beings encounter in their lives with one another, what circumstances they face in which choice of some sort is required, we will have a way of assessing competing responses to those problems, and we will begin to understand what it might be to act well in the face of them.[10]

This way of conceptualizing moral theory is fully immersed in the lived experience of agents, and accommodates the notion that morality is a response to vulnerability and contingency. Nevertheless, it attempts to uncover a systematicity to our moral dispositions, to describe morality as a function of more or less permanent, widely shared features of the human condition. Despite the diversity of moral codes and practices, we can objectively assess them with respect to how well they enhance human functioning within these universally shared spheres of experience.

Such a theory of the virtues supplements perceptive equilibrium because it suggests that the weight given to our perceptions, and the importance of preserving those we can least tolerate, is compatible with our aspiration to transcend the limits of local norms and avoid the moral blindness associated with the tragic understanding of moral ideals. Because as human beings we share similar concerns and respond to similar circumstances, we have the capacity to understand the diversity of what counts as flourishing within these circumstances. This lends coherence to the task of comparing and assessing alternative moral points of view. Human practices that might look utterly alien can be made intelligible, since they share similar aims with more familiar practices.

The obvious objection to this attempt to systematize the virtues is that, even if we grant the demarcation of spheres of experience in a way that accurately describes the experience of many cultures and traditions, it does not mean there will be a single account of that virtue at the end of our inquiry. We are more likely to have a plurality of conflicting, culturally specific accounts. Nussbaum does not grant this objection. She argues that the upshot of such an inquiry will be a small number of competing accounts, all of which will be further specifications of the "nominal" account. However, she arrives at this conclusion only by denying the importance of particularity and the intrinsic value of the virtues she otherwise endorses.

Nussbaum's conception of a virtue is an instrumental one. We are to identify and define virtues in terms of the way they contribute to certain outcomes within independently described spheres of experience. Therefore, virtues, whatever else they may be, are a means of achieving this state of affairs. Although virtues may have intrinsic value, their instrumental value in regulating conduct is what connects them to their respective spheres of experience. For instance, courage is important in ensuring the survival of the community, and what counts as the appropriate regulation of the fear of death or injury is tied to the need for that survival. This functional role that courage plays will be recognizable across a variety of disparate societies and traditions, and the particular accounts will be assessed according to their effectiveness in defending the community. However, courage is also valued for its own sake. It is often praised even when it does not succeed in bringing about desirable consequences. I suspect the reasons for this and the particular ways this intrinsic value is expressed will be less common to all societies, will tend to be unique to particular contexts, and will be more difficult to assess than the instrumental value of courage. This is because the value courage has, over and above its instrumental value in sustaining bonds of association, will be connected to psychological attitudes and social conditions that will vary across cultures, societies, and individuals. These will not be widely shareable, unlike a general description of instrumental value. An objective, systematic account of the instrumental value of the virtues will fail to explain their intrinsic value and the context dependence of their full moral worth. This seems incompatible with the priority of particularity upon which Nussbaum insists elsewhere.

This objection operates under the limiting assumption that we can demarcate spheres of experience in a way that accurately describes the experience of diverse cultures and traditions. However, as Nussbaum recognizes, Foucault and others have attempted to show the cultural variation in the way "grounding experiences" are constructed. Fear of death, the experience of bodily appetites and other desires, the role and function of material resources, and basic assumptions about the nature of social association show such diversity throughout history and across cultures that one can persuasively argue there is no "bedrock of shared experience, and thus no single sphere of choice within which the virtue is the disposition to act well."[11]

Nussbaum grants that "grounding experiences" are subject to wide cultural and historical variation, but this does not prevent us from assessing them from her viewpoint. The fact that the intelligibility and coherence of experience is only fully intelligible from within a particular conceptual framework does not mean that all interpretations are equally valid or incomparable. It simply means that standards of assessment must come from within the conceptual framework in question, or from those elements in the interpretation of experience about which a consensus can be formed, or that are widely shared and intelligible from many points of view. The only burden this imposes on moral evaluation and criticism is a sensitivity, or "inclusive understanding," of the conceptual scheme being criticized. Furthermore, she will claim that, despite the differences in interpretation between cultures, there is a remarkable degree of "attunement, recognition, and overlap" between them as well. This is evidenced by the fact that cross-cultural communication is a ubiquitous feature of life. We converse fruitfully with people from disparate cultures, and read with understanding and empathy writings from distant epochs. Even when substantial differences in conceptualization are discovered, they motivate critical debate rather than obstruct it. Therefore, there is no reason why at the end of inquiry we cannot justifiably say that certain ways of conceptualizing death, bodily appetites, and the other grounding experiences are more "in keeping with the totality of our evidence and with the totality of our wishes for flourishing life than others. . . ."[12]

These responses to relativism do not set aside doubts about the systematicity of the "spheres of experience." Nussbaum's arguments are responding to a version of the incommensurability thesis that is, I argued in Chapter One, typically improperly formulated. This version asserts that there are no permanent, neutral, universal standards of rationality, and consequently no way of rationally assessing competing points of view that presuppose quite different standards of rationality. Nussbaum correctly asserts that permanent, neutral standards need not be in place in order to assess competing points of view. However, I argued in Chapter One that we should think of incommensurability as an empirical phenomenon, a breakdown in the conventions that allow us to communicate. It is not a relation between a conceptual scheme and an assertion logically inadmissible within that conceptual scheme, but is instead evidence of pressure to reform prevailing conceptual structures. Formulated in this way, the issue between Nussbaum and the defender of the incommensurability thesis will have to do with the adequacy of internal resources in re-establishing communicative links that have broken down, and finding a basis for shared moral discourse.

In light of this recharacterization of the incommensurability thesis, one of the internal realist's standard responses to relativism is question-begging. The internal realist claims that there is no reason to think that *at the end of inquiry* a consensus on moral questions cannot be discovered. Placing the criteria for determining the prospects for rational consensus at the end of inquiry is an idealization that asks us to suppose we have all limiting factors such as time, resources, good will, and the pressures of real-life struggles and decision-making under control. Under those circumstances, we might well discover enough commonality with human experience to warrant a rational consensus on moral questions and grounding experiences. However, given the reformulation of the incommensurability thesis motivated by Ramberg's Davidsonian account, it's precisely these limiting factors that are the source of incommensurability. Thus, in order to answer the question about the prospects for agreement, we cannot simply wish these limiting factors away.

What, then, are the obstacles to consensus regarding "grounding experiences," and does Nussbaum's methodology give an adequate account of how they are to be overcome? Ramberg mentions the tendency of linguistic practices to outstrip linguistic conventions, thus requiring interpretation on the part of the interlocutors. Nussbaum rightly argues that interpretation is such a central component of human experience that incommensurability of this sort is a temporary, surmountable phenomenon. However, I have argued that the processes by which we attach significance to beliefs issue in a more serious form of incommensurability, one that raises less tractable obstacles to our capacity to share these beliefs widely. This is especially true of those beliefs attached to what Nussbaum calls "grounding experiences." "Grounding experiences" are the sort of experience that contribute most to the construction of personal and social identity. Beliefs about mortality, the meaning of human life within the larger scheme of things, the economy of desires and the distribution of emotional and material resources to satisfy them, the norms that govern self-respect and moral worth, the attitudes and forms of organization that govern social life, are all central components of any human life. They supply the core beliefs without which we could not see ourselves either as individuals or as members of communities. However, in determining what and who we value, these grounding experiences are expressed in judgments of contrast that play a central role in determining the narrative structure of life. What we take to be important is guided by proximity to or distance from the beginnings, middles, and ends of the stories of which we are part influencing our judgments about what lies deepest and what we can least live without. I concluded in Chapter Two that these narratives are plural without any over-arching teleological structure, and one of the main points in the discussion of narrative in Chapter Three was to show how these narratives close off possibilities in the course of raising new ones.

Within the framework of this temporal emerging and passing away of possibilities, judgments of contrast express the belief that a certain activity or kind of life, often associated with the grounding experiences Nussbaum mentions, is higher and more admirable than others—and that only those who share this belief are worthy of respect. Contrast judgments, therefore, represent largely insurmountable obstacles to the search for agreement on basic judgments and perceptions that is at the heart of the methodology of internal realism.

It is important to reiterate that the source of incommensurability is not the logical incompatibility of two independent, conceptual schemes. Rather, this incommensurability thesis relies on facts about human motivation and how human value is expressed. What makes this form of incommensurability intractable is that it is the very conditions under which we come to share beliefs that give rise to unresolvable conflict. Our identities as persons and as members of communities are bound up with judgments that exclude others.

As a consequence of the constrastive, narrative structure of judgments, Nussbaum's objections are ineffective against this version of the incommensurability thesis. If one has the second-order belief that among one's first-order beliefs there are perceptions, judgments, and beliefs any agent worthy of respect ought to share, and this second-order belief is accompanied by the second-order motivation to have one's beliefs expressed in one's life, then one has a value structure with not only a tendency to pull like-minded individuals together, supporting and enhancing a conception of community, but that also as a condition of the bond requires the exclusion of individuals who don't share those beliefs. To fail to discount incompatible beliefs is tantamount to denying the special force of the beliefs held in esteem, given the above analysis of contrast judgments. And the same conditions will likely hold for the virtues as well as the grounding experiences. Perceptions and judgments are the mechanisms by which dispositions to act respond to circumstances. Given the partiality of perspectives resulting from the contrastive nature of perception and judgments, there is no reason to think that fuller specifications of how the virtues function in context will demonstrate a high degree of regularity for the person of integrity who wishes nothing more than to have her life express only that which is admirable, the moderation of the conformist who seeks to suppress such demands will not be a virtue at all. In societies in which a code of honor is prescribed by local norms, courage takes on a meaning and significance it does not have in societies without such codes.

Thus, the motivating factor behind perceptive equilibrium—the aspiration to articulate shared perceptions—has inherent limitations. In striving to find a convergence of belief, we inevitably make such a convergence impossible because the motivation to share—to express one's beliefs publicly and have them confirmed by others—is precisely what motivates the contrastive judgments that suppress the significance of conflicting values. Moral reflection, if it is a working back and forth between a mitigated, impersonal point of view motivated by the demands of community and those particular perceptions and judgments upon which the intelligibility of one's life depends, will operate within a narrow framework imposed by narrative structure and judgments of contrast. There is no objective point of view, even when construed as a forged consensus on belief, that will adjudicate competing contrast judgments.

One might object that what I have described is an attitude of intolerance that is itself an inappropriate response to differences in conceptualizing the grounding experiences. It is, of course, the case that tolerance is often a virtue and can mitigate the effects of disagreement. However, we cannot be tolerant of everything and remain committed to the view that many aspects of life have special, intrinsically valuable qualities. A life full of many valuable things will inevitably take the shape of a narrative in which the realization of some possibilities will require the concealment of others. Only the very fortunate or the pathologically apathetic will have the luxury of such tolerance.

It also could be argued that, although moral agents are often motivated to express judgments of contrast, it is precisely those motivations to which theory need not succumb. The relatively impersonal point of view that the practice of theorizing promotes mitigates the motivation to have life express one's beliefs. However, the internal realist cannot abstract from these judgments without sacrificing the connection with lived experience, its central component. Because internal realism assigns weight to initial judgments, especially those that are central to the agent's personal and social identity, whatever constraints exist on those judgments are also constraints on the theory. Those judgments for which the motivation to have them expressed in life is strongest are those the methodology demands we take seriously.

Although Nussbaum is correct to point out the success we often achieve in our attempts to forge consensus, the nature of contrast judgments and narrative structure explain this success as well. They presuppose the capacity and motivation of every agent to recognize what has value, and to see oneself as part of a community that shares beliefs and values. Yet it is just when we reach such attunement that we become blind to the goods that are concealed by our possibilities or that contrast with our most deeply held beliefs. The picture of morality I am developing is not one of incessant conflict, but one that oscillates between agreement and conflict.

Consequently, Nussbaum's responses to the threat of incommensurability fail to show why grounding experiences are not subject to enough disagreement to preclude any systematic account of widely shared responses to those experiences. Because the possibility of an adequate theory of moral justification that would establish the components of the good life for man was dependent on such a systematic account, I conclude that Nussbaum's attempt at such a theoretical justification fails.

Internal Realism and Tragedy

The notion that moral ideals can be the source of moral failure raises another difficulty with internal realism related to the credibility of the initial judgments and perceptions from which inquiry begins. The justification for such a starting point is that it places the moral theorist within the lived experience of a particular moral point of view, thus responding to the charge that theory is too abstract and cut off from historical circumstances to offer relevant moral prescriptions. Yet even this historically embedded methodology tends to separate morality from social history.

In starting from within a particular moral perspective, resources for criticism must be drawn from the ideals that define that moral perspective. When we look at the moral world that we actually inhabit, we do find considered judgments and moral perceptions around which substantial agreement might be forged. Within the culture of Western liberal democracies, judgments about freedom of speech and religion, basic rights of self-respect, fairness in distribution of wealth, perceptions of the value of particular persons or communities, and feelings of commitment to them are all legitimate starting points for an inquiry into the nature of the human good at this time and place. Part of what gives the choice of these judgments some initial credibility is the overall conception of the human good in which these judgments and perceptions find their place. But in focusing on an initial, plausible conception of the human good in answer to Nussbaum's initiating question, "What is the good for man?" a good deal of social history is excluded. Existing side by side with these judgments and perceptions that we praise are monstrous acts of cruelty. Assuming that we consider our moral context to include our European heritage, it is not obvious why the attempt to discover the judgments by which we live should not include reference to Auschwitz and the Gulag, as well as Wounded Knee and the slave trade, to mention just a few. Of course, the reason such events are excluded is that, ostensibly, we are seeking "the good," and these events are not plausible candidates for that honor. Are not these events examples of people who have lost their moral bearings, who are no longer following the beacon of human goodness but have chosen instead naked self-interest, a perverse delight in cruelty, or have reverted to some prehistorical instinctual rage against civilization? I doubt it. What is striking about the devil's handiwork is that it often advances under the auspices of more noble motives. Consider the following partial list of apparent contrasts:

Kant's Categorical Imperative	Eichmann's use of that imperative in his own defense
Motherhood (Germany, circa 1938)	Advocates of national socialism
Self-determination	"Ethnic cleansing" in Bosnia/Herzegovina
Family privacy rights	Spousal and child abuse
Advancing civilization	Wounded Knee
Personal responsibility	The decay of America's inner cities

In each case, the phenomenon on the right is given sustenance by the moral good listed on the left. Judgments and perceptions that express the moral good of the items on the left belong on any list of considered judgments. However, I doubt such a list would include a reference to the full history of appeals to that good, hence isolating morality from its history.

Indeed, the evils of our social history are treated as mindless, without rationality, the result of some mass self-deception, a glitch in the software of an otherwise smoothly functioning program. Yet the magnitude of the distortion is too great to be accounted for as a mistake, the result of ignorance, self-deception, or weakness of the will. We should not forget that there are ideas behind these rents in the fabric of morality, and that cruelty has been carried out in the name of these ideas. Thus, we should be suspicious of attempts to separate these ideas from the actions that accompany them, suspicious of a methodology that encourages a kind of blindness, as I think internal realism does.

The motivation behind nonfoundationalism and internal realism is that it avoids appeal to an objective point of view outside the lived experience of moral agents. It seeks a mode of justification that takes its orientation from a particular culture or society, and attempts to show the internal coherence of that point of view while seeking similarities and a basis for general agreement with alternative points of view. Its critical resources are the moral ideals of a particular perspective, in terms of which we measure the realities of social life. I have argued that this internalist approach does not have the conceptual resources to test the credibility of the ideals themselves, the basic judgments and perceptions that are in question. This is in part because incommensurability (understood in terms of judgments of contrast and narrative structure) prevents the articulation of serious rival points of view. It is also because judgments of contrast are obstacles to the interrogation of the beliefs one takes most seriously. Yet if foundationalist theories are suspect for the reasons adumbrated in Chapter One, and nonfoundationalist theories are incapable of criticizing basic beliefs, how do we begin to assess moral judgments?

Here I think a sensitivity to the tragic dimension of morality expressed in tragic literature should play a significant role in moral reflection. Tragedy reminds us that our most fervently held ideals and virtues most worthy of respect can be the source of moral failure. Tragedy leads us to criticize our moral ideals from within the context of their pursuit, without requiring objectivity or an impersonal point of view. Because the circumstances and the protagonist's responses to them lead to moral conflict, the circumstances are themselves self-transcending. The limits of our moral perspectives are expressed within the structure of tragic circumstance, and critical pressure is generated from the failure of our ideals to resolve the conflict. The virtue of tragic literature is that it makes us aware of ourselves as potential victimizers before we see ourselves as victims. As I argue in the next chapter, this may be the most appropriate moral stance in a world in which "virtue itself of vice must pardon beg" (Hamlet).

5

Prophecy and Community

In Chapter Three, the exploration of the role of narrative in moral reflection leads us to consider the tragic vision and the form of moral dilemma it represents. In the course of that exploration, I argue that tragic literature illustrates the notion that moral ideals themselves might be the source of moral failure; that moral blindness may be an integral part of many of our moral judgments. I attempt to give a systematic explanation of this blindness by appealing to judgments of contrast. This places obstacles in the path of any attempt to explain and justify a conception of universal moral agency, because contrast judgments and the consequent moral blindness prevents agents from acquiring a wider perspective from which to view legitimate moral claims. Thus, the problems with theoretical approaches to morality identified in Chapter One persist despite attempts to accommodate the concerns of antitheorists by considering alternative methodologies. However, in response to the troubling claim that our moral ideals might lead to moral failure, one might argue that this tragic conception of ethics points out the futility of moral ideals. The conclusion that moral ideals, values, and qualities of character create the conditions for moral failure would seem to lead directly to moral skepticism, as well as the *reductio ad absurdum* of the claim that tragic literature embodies a moral perspective. By demonstrating the limits of our capacity to respond to pervasive tragic conflict, tragic literature not only leaves us with no guidance at all, but seems to suggest that moral nihilism lies at the end of this road.

Is there a recognizable moral perspective compatible with the notion that good moral character might be a source of moral failure? In this chapter, I argue that Rorty provides us with such a perspective. I also argue that Rorty's work reflects a sustained awareness of the tragic dimension of morality, which he locates within the conflict between public and private life. And, I argue that Rorty's account of our capacity to transcend the limitations of a point of view ultimately stumbles on the contrastive nature of moral judgment, just as Nussbaum's did. He nevertheless points the way to an alternative conception of moral agency that promises to resolve this difficulty. In the process, Rorty adds to our understanding of how literature enhances moral reflection.

Irony and Culture

For Rorty, the capacity to transcend the limits of one's point of view and the capacity to recognize the claim of universal moral agency rest, in part, on the contingency of language, self, and community. All human beings employ a vocabulary that expresses their ultimate hopes and fears, and in which they formulate terms of praise and blame, admiration and contempt. The language of modern science, of democracy and freedom, and the parsing of the human psyche into an essential rational component as well as a separate, less important emotional component are the basic vocabularies of modern Western societies. But these vocabularies are contingent in that there are no essential characteristics more fundamental than those employed in the historically specific vocabularies of diverse cultures, ones that enable us to distinguish what is genuinely human from what is an inferior facsimile. Thus, these vocabularies are final in the sense that there will be no noncircular argumentative recourse when such justifications are confronted with disagreement.[1] There is no fixed human nature underlying our various ways of speaking about human reality that would justify some and disqualify others.

The absence of a fixed human nature on which to rest our justifications is liberating, for it suggests a way of satisfying the aspiration to transcend parochial points of view. The consequence of accepting the contingency of language, self, and community is a recognition of the irony associated with attachment to any final vocabulary. While we might endorse a familiar way of life as our own, we cannot find any *ultimate* justification for this endorsement. Curiosity about other forms of life might lead to doubts about one's own vocabulary that cannot be assuaged by appeal to an underlying human nature. Of course, neither will these doubts suggest the superiority of some other point of view, since all points of view are, although not equivalent, at least equally contingent. Thus, the internalizing of the contingency of language, self, and community is likely to make us more tolerant of other points of view, since we no longer have reason to think our own is grounded in the nature of things. For someone who is familiar with and impressed by a wide range of human practices and is suspicious of deep justifications, an attitude of irony toward one's own final vocabulary is unavoidable. The ironist is a promising embodiment of the transcendence we have been seeking, for she at least manages to recognize the limitations of her own point of view.

The ironist, convinced of the futility of seeking philosophical foundations and having doubts about her own beliefs, cannot discover criteria for determining which representation of reality ought to gain our allegiance. Thus, significant revisions in beliefs will be ". . . dominated by metaphors of making rather than finding, of diversification and novelty rather than convergence to the antecedently present."[2] For the ironist, the process of reflection and inquiry is not one of explanation and justification but of redescription—using words in new ways to expand the way we look at the world.[3] The ironist seeks to get beyond her doubts about her own vocabulary and self-image by creating a new one using the people she encounters—both real and fictive—as grist for her imagination. As long as our language is open to external influence, Rorty seems to argue, we have the capacity to transcend our limited viewpoints and the blindness that accompanies them.

> Nothing can serve as a criticism of a person save another person, or of a culture save an alternative culture—for persons and cultures are, for us, incarnated vocabularies. So our doubts about our own characters or our own culture can be resolved or assuaged only by enlarging our acquaintance.[4]

Thus, Rorty will argue on grounds only partly overlapping those of Nussbaum that literature and literary criticism, rather than philosophy, are the discourses best equipped to aid moral reflection.

> Within a liberal metaphysical culture the disciplines which were charged with penetrating behind the many private appearances to the one general common reality—theology, science, philosophy— were the ones which were expected to bind human beings together, and thus to help eliminate cruelty. Within an ironist culture, by contrast, it is the disciplines which specialize in thick description of the private and idiosyncratic which are assigned this job. In particular,

novels and ethnographies which sensitize one to the pain of those
who do not speak our language must do the job.[5]

This conception of an aestheticized self and community, however, cannot
by itself give an account of universal moral agency because it provides us
with no account of moral obligation. The tendency of irony to separate us
from our final vocabularies would seem to separate us from those commitments that frame our understanding of moral obligation, and there is
no reason to think that literary facility and the redescriptions that flow
from it will tend to draw us toward the moral world. How then is irony
linked to moral obligation in Rorty's work?

Solidarity and Judgments of Contrast

Rorty's account of moral obligation revolves around the notion of "solidarity," a term that contrasts with "objectivity" in that it defines obligation
in terms of the de facto relationships holding a community together—
instead of the neutral, impersonal "view from nowhere" that characterizes
standard moral theories. For Rorty, our capacity for compassion, a respect
for justice, and a sense of duty are the results of a history of specific
human attachments and the institutions in which these relationships are
embedded. Thus, we have obligations to others by virtue of having shared
a relationship, of being part of a group with certain common experiences,
or having a shared final vocabulary. Proceeding from Wilfred Sellar's
notion of "we-intentions," Rorty claims that

> This analysis takes the basic explanatory notion in this area to be
> "one of us"—the notion invoked in locutions like "our sort of people"
> (as opposed to tradesmen and servants), "a comrade in the [radical]
> movement," a "Greek like ourselves" (as opposed to a barbarian), or
> a "fellow Catholic" (as opposed to a Protestant, a Jew, or an atheist).[6]

This sense of solidarity and obligation is contrastive, and suggests
comparison with the way judgments of contrast were described in
Chapter Three. The sense of value attached to one's own group depends,
in part, on the contrast it draws with other sorts of people who, for one
reason or another, are excluded from this group and with whom identification is problematic.[7]

Rorty is driven to this account of obligation because of the inability of
philosophy to identify a more inclusive account. A central part of Rorty's

argument is that philosophy is a history of failed attempts to show that there is a single, rational faculty within all humans, or an objective point of view that underwrites moral conduct by showing why the failure to act on one's obligations is irrational. When we "de-divinize" language, self, and community, we are left with only finite, mortal, contingently existing human beings on whom to depend.

However, support for this analysis of obligations in terms of "we-intentions" can also be found by the sorts of explanations typically given when moral obligations are in play. Rorty will argue that Europeans who aided the Jews during the German occupation were more likely to give as the reason for their acts of heroism that they shared certain parochial features with the victims—residents of the same city or village, members of the same profession, parents of children—rather than an obligation to aid all humans. Rorty's point is that we in fact feel more strongly obligated when we share a special relationship with the person to whom we are obligated.

This account of obligation runs against the grain of our Christian heritage and the Enlightenment, from which we have acquired very strong intuitions that moral obligations are owed to all humans, and that the moral vocabulary has force independently of particular times and places. Rorty's identification of moral obligation with attachments to specific groups has led to charges of relativism, and moral as well as political conservativism. If loyalty to one's social institutions and conformity to group norms represents the limits of morality and obligation, then these norms and practices are shielded against criticism; they encourage moral blindness. Important human needs that require articulation outside these norms and practices may not be recognized, and political change, far from transforming social norms, must remain wedded to them.[8]

Rorty responds to these charges by arguing that there is nothing other than the limits of our awareness that prevents us from conceptualizing and accepting a wider notion of obligation. Happily, the very set of "we-intentions" that Rorty shares with most of the inhabitants of Western, liberal democratic societies includes the notion that moral obligations extend to all human beings. The very fact that "we" have a history characterized by increasingly inclusive practices and the emergence of institutions like a free press, an independent judiciary, an educational system that aids social mobility, and an extraordinarily wealthy and productive economy that has made our culture more inclusive mitigates, in Rorty's view, the charge that "solidarity" entails a pernicious form of moral blindness incapable of recognizing human need beyond local boundaries. Although the social bond is explained in terms of "we-intentions," happily our "we-intentions" include the notion that all human beings are moral agents. Thus, worries about moral blindness are unwarranted. This is not to say that the "we-intentions" of those who share this Enlightenment heritage are not in contrast. Clearly, they mark a contrast with those who do not take as seriously as we do the ideals of democracy and freedom. There are some ideas and ways of living that are proscribed by that heritage, and we should not presume a "duty to justify everything" or "pretend an impossible tolerance" given that we must begin from where we are. The particular virtues of the lifestyles of Teutonic Knights or Trobriand Islanders may escape us, and our sensitivity toward their needs may be limited. Furthermore, it may be impossible to conceptualize the point of radical political revolution given the relative success of liberal, democratic institutions in advancing freedom and equality. For Rorty's mild ethnocentrism, this means only that some ideas are so unfamiliar it is not obvious how they can be made more familiar. The proscription, the meaning of the contrast built into our "we-intentions," is simply a prediction about the sorts of ideas that can be rewoven with ideas we already have, not a rigid, conceptual net that limits our moral sensibilities.

Thus, the issue in Rorty's attack on traditional moral theory is not about the implications of "ethnocentrism" on our cultural practices, for the habits of contemporary life are largely unaffected by philosophical argument. Rather, it is the explanation of those practices that is at issue, so Rorty argues. Metaphysical constructs, human nature, a built-in rational faculty—these concepts simply do not explain our capacity for moral obligation, nor are they needed for its defense. Only a contingent historical account is required to explain liberal democracy, and only the will to continue those practices is required for their defense.

Rorty's romanticism also helps him rebut this charge of parochialism and conservatism. It will be the capacity of language users to use words in new ways, to redescribe the familiar in new terms that will aid the reweaving of the web of belief and explain social and moral change. Interpretation is, to a significant degree, a matter of spinning off metaphors that will hopefully reshape the hearer's perceptions of similarity and difference.[9] The ironist and her redescriptions will make us see the world in new ways and will make the unfamiliar seem familiar, and thus will continually extend the reference of "we." The Christian and Enlightenment heritage extending full moral standing to all persons is advanced by linguistic experiments that progressively allow us to perceive more and more similarities within our differences.

Public Virtue/Private Idiosyncracy

The obvious question to ask about the foregoing view is this: Why do linguistic innovation and an attitude of irony toward one's own final vocabulary have a tendency to reinforce solidarity rather than undermine it? There is nothing inherently inclusive about metaphor or poesy. Linguistic innovation, instead of making similarities more salient, might just as easily enable us to see differences where we had previously seen similarities, thereby making the familiar seem unfamiliar. Furthermore, the view that the wordsmith has some special capacity to expand our sense of obligation has an elitist ring to it, as if only writers are capable of genuine moral judgment. Moreover, the potential link between the aestheticization of politics and fascism has been noticed by more than one commentator on the emergence of fascism in Germany.[10]

Rorty recognizes that the connection between aesthetic sensibility and solidarity is thin.

> Irony, as I have defined it, results from awareness of the power of redescription. But most people do not want to be redescribed. They want to be taken on their own terms—taken seriously just as they are and just as they talk. The ironist tells them that the language they speak is up for grabs by her and her kind. There is something potentially very cruel about that claim. For the best way to cause people long-lasting pain is to humiliate them by making the things that seemed most important to them look futile, obsolete, and powerless.[11]

Consequently, Rorty argues, liberal society rests on maintaining a sharp boundary between the public and private arenas of life. For purposes of public discourse, in which the potential for intersubjective agreement is primary, the liberal ironist will constrain her capacity to redescribe others by her sensitivity to the humiliation her words might cause. For private purposes, when questions of the suffering of others and duties to the community are not relevant, self-creation is all that matters. Thus, a sense of solidarity with the institutions of democracy must always constrain intellectual and artistic projects, making the tradition of social criticism from Hegel through Foucault largely irrelevant for purposes of public policy and moral practice, in Rorty's view.[12] Critics of the ideals of democracy and freedom are engaged in the private pursuit of radical autonomy rather than useful political discourse.

Similarly, traditional philosophy that perceives itself carrying out the Kantian project of placing other disciplines in their proper place in the hierarchy of inquiry has a negative impact on culture. In presupposing that inquiry cannot legitimately proceed without securing epistemological foundations, philosophy closes off certain kinds of inquiry that lack the appropriate epistemological credentials—roughly everything that does not emulate scientific methodology—and diminishes the resources available for redescription.

Philosophy, in becoming less scientific and more political and artistic, will stop seeking a shared human essence and will proceed to defend cosmopolitanism by extending our historically shaped "we-intentions." A methodology of proceeding from agreed-upon criteria is replaced by a process of making the unfamiliar seem familiar through redescription. In the context of philosophy, redescription involves sketching what Rorty calls a "liberal utopia"—an attempt to imagine what an ideally inclusive version of liberalism would look like once appeals to philosophical foundations have been left behind. Rorty's ideal liberal society is one that "has no purpose except freedom, no goal except a willingness to see how such encounters go, and abide by the outcome."[13] Such a society would understand the founders and preservers of society as poets and revolutionaries. Our language, conscience, morality, and hopes would be recognized as literalizations of accidentally produced metaphors—those that help us extend the reference of "we" by helping us see differences as unimportant when compared with those similarities having to do with being potential victims of pain and humiliation.

In his sketch of a liberal utopia, Rorty has proposed a solution to the problem of accounting for universal moral agency without appealing to philosophical foundations. The historically conditioned "we-intentions" of liberal societies share an abhorrence of cruelty, and this sense of solidarity with others is extended to unfamiliar others by our capacity for linguistic innovation. The inevitable conflicts that arise between our historically conditioned concern for others and the heterogeneous goods we pursue as individuals are mitigated by our consigning the pursuit of autonomy to the private realm, and our refusing to insist that our idiosyncratic pursuits receive intersubjective support.

The difficulty with Rorty's liberal utopia has to do with the instability of the distinction between public and private. It must be the case that conflict between final vocabularies either is adjudicated as a matter of public debate, or understood by the parties of the debate as inappropriate for adjudication in the public arena. The former option seems unlikely, given the nature of solidarity as Rorty has described it; the latter option misunderstands the significance of final vocabularies. It should be mentioned, first of all, that because "we-intentions" are contrastive, i.e., because the sense of value attached to those intentions depends in part on the contrast they draw with other sorts of people who do not share them, "we-intentions" are resistent to the expansion of intersubjectivity. In cases where these "we-intentions" cannot be widely shared with the larger community, they must be viewed as legitimately pursued only in private, in ways that do not disrupt the intersubjectivity of the larger community. However much depends on how this distinction between public and private is drawn, for there is considerable ambiguity in the way Rorty employs the term "private."

A good example supporting Rorty's parsing of the public and private domains is religious freedoms in the United States. Religious beliefs are a matter of personal choice. The separation of church and state is designed to insure the protection of alternative religious viewpoints, in part by minimizing the opportunities for religious conflict in the public arena. However, it is important to point out how unstable this separation is. For example, Catholics insist on criminalizing abortion, Native Americans object to development on their traditional burial grounds, Christian Scientists run afoul of laws against child endangerment by refusing medical treatment, and religious fundamentalists block the institutionalization of gay rights. The boundary between public and private easily erodes.

Moreover, a great deal of what Rorty would want to count as social progress has resulted from forcibly exposing privately held final vocabularies to public ridicule. One could argue that, in the 19th century, the treatment of African-Americans and women as property was a private matter, and belief in the superiority of white males a final vocabulary that enjoyed remarkable intersubjective agreement, even among its victims, as Fanon and Friedan have shown.

Rorty is not committed to the view that the private should never become public. In fact, persuading the public that a private vision is relevant to public life is what those "poets and revolutionaries" whose idiosyncratic expressions gain popularity do. Nor can it be a matter of principle or prediction whether a private vision is worthy of public acceptance. Nevertheless, the above examples illustrate two points I wish to make. First, if the emerging autonomy of women and African-Americans counts as the transformation of a private vision into an object of intersubjective consensus, why not hold out that possibility for any radical critique of society, including those such as Foucault or Heidegger, that Rorty wants to dismiss as a private search for radical autonomy? The reason for excluding ironist theory from public debate cannot rest solely on the absence of potential for intersubjective agreement, since history is full of examples of radical ideas becoming commonplace. Second, the above examples point to something that Rorty leaves out of his account—namely, that the desire for one's deepest beliefs to be expressed in one's public life is not a trivial matter. It is, in fact, one of the motives for holding those beliefs.

Expressivism

In Rorty's conception of liberalism, solidarity is sustained to the extent the citizens (especially including the intellectual elite) succeed in privatizing their final vocabularies. Anyone in pursuit of a private ideal in a public context for which intersubjective agreement is absent risks damaging the consensus-forming resources of society by imposing an idiosyncratic set of beliefs. However, I think this view of the public/ private distinction fails to take seriously the notion that our most deeply held beliefs are the sort of thing we cannot intelligibly want to be excluded from public expression.

Many of our actions acquire value by virtue of the outcome they help bring about. We care little for the action itself, and will place value on alternative actions if they brought about the same outcome. However, some of our projects involve actions that have a different teleological structure (perhaps best described by Hegel) in which the point of the action is to give expression to something—to an idea, a capacity that one has, or a desire that one suffers. Works of art, social and religious rituals, and actions that demonstrate qualities of character have this teleological structure. In these cases, the action has value not only by virtue of the state of affairs brought about, but also because the action expresses the idea, capacity, or desire in question. Expressions of value, however, are social phenomena. If an expression is to communicate something, it must be expressed to someone in one context or another. The value of the action is in part a function of how well it expresses the idea in question. It is against the resistance of the social world that actions have significance and are judged, and thus it matters to whom the idea is expressed, what form that expression takes, and how it was received.

The social character of expressions is even more evident when the ideas, capacities, or desires in question are central to a person's identity. This is because our identities as individuals are realized through actions that are part of the public world, shaped by public institutions. How we are viewed publicly influences how we see ourselves. As MacIntyre argues, the fact that as individuals we are subject to description by others imposes rather strict identity conditions on us.[14] To hold beliefs that are not encouraged or are actively discouraged by society can itself be a source of humiliation. Moreover, we often tend not to want to see our separate selves as the ultimate authorities on value, but instead defer to socially constituted standards to evaluate our actions. Only by recognizing our own limited resources for self-understanding can we make sense of distinctions between satisfying desires and achieving genuine happiness, or between actions that achieve some end or other and those that are true accomplishments to guide our judgments. To not accept the authority of others on these matters is to risk losing control over how others view us— it is to risk being irrelevant, performing actions of no consequence. Even a staunch defender of romantic individualism such as Nietzsche took very seriously the impact of his writings on his future readers and heirs.[15] Thus, we are inevitably pulled toward a public world.

If the significance of an action is seen against the background of socially established standards, a final vocabulary can only be final if the person using it can find herself either within social practices that employ that vocabulary, or in opposition to social practices from which she is alienated. Only then will her attempts at self-creation have the significance to qualify as final, as worth holding on to despite the absence of argumentative recourse. No genuine opposition to a set of social practices can be safely domiciled within the private realm, given that the significance of one's beliefs is subject to some degree of public assessment. Even in opposition, it is the resistance of these standards that give the actions their significance. Thus, we can make sense of a search for private autonomy only by making reference to its attempts at public expression.

The point of these remarks is to emphasize the degree to which, for any agent, the public expression of her deepest beliefs, desires, and capacities will have value.[16] The importance of public expression confronts the ironist and the liberal ironist with different problems. Consider the ironist (or any linguistic innovator) whose words threaten the prevailing intersubjective agreement for which she has no concern to preserve. The ironist will wish to avoid complicity with the prevailing vocabulary to which she is opposed. Yet projects of linguistic innovation find expression through participation in a system of material relationships—in schools, publishing houses, bookstores, professional organizations, and media phenomena—which are constituted publicly. By participating in the prevailing language game embedded in these relationships, she participates in those very material relations for which her ironist tendencies express con-tempt. Such is the irony of the radical form of autonomy that the ironist seeks. It is, therefore, impossible for the ironist to sustain a claim to radi-cal autonomy or privacy, however much she may claim this as an ideal.

The liberal ironist who endorses the prevailing consensus while har-boring privately idiosyncratic beliefs faces a different problem. She need not resist complicity with these material relationships embodying the prevailing consensus. However, she must decline to put into action the very words in terms of which she expresses some dimension of her final vocabulary, in the interests of sustaining that consensus. If it is the case that private judgments, especially those that lie close to an individual's identity, are contrastive in the way specified in Chapter Three, the liberal ironist risks a private contempt for her public vocabulary, and vice versa. This is exacerbated by her substantial commitments to the above-men-tioned material relationships in which she participates, for her public actions themselves become the object of her own private contempt. While the ironist, when forced to participate in public life, may feel some guilt associated with her complicity in public discourse, she need not define herself in opposition to her own deeply held beliefs. The liberal ironist has no such luxury. To the extent that her expression of private beliefs engages material relationships, she will not only be complicitous with that for which she has a private contempt, she will be contemptuous of some other part of herself that she endorses as well—her social identity. This suggests an open invitation to self-hatred. We have numerous reports of talented 19th-century female writers toiling away in private, striving to publish under pseudonyms while maintaining the public persona of the dutiful wife. Linguistic innovators are often forced under coercive condi-tions to separate public from private, but I fail to see why this ought to be the preferred self-description.

The Claim of History Revisited

I take these remarks to show that the linguistic innovation central to the notion of self-creation as Rorty conceptualizes it cannot be safely domiciled within a private realm. Consequently, conflicts between final vocabularies cannot be mitigated by consigning them to the private realm, thus threatening part of Rorty's conception of how we transcend the limits of a moral point of view. This still leaves open the possibility that irony and redescription have some application to the resolution of conflicts within public discourse.

Rorty is skeptical that irony and redescription play a central role in the public sphere, because they tend to disrupt institutionalized forms of normal discourse.

> But even if I am right in thinking that a liberal culture whose public rhetoric is nominalist and historicist is both possible and desirable, I cannot go on to claim that there could or ought to be a culture whose public rhetoric is *ironist*. I cannot imagine a culture which socialized its youth in such a way as to make them continually dubious about their own process of socialization. Irony seems inherently a private matter.[17]

Nevertheless, he insists that linguistic innovation explains cultural change.

> Revolutionary achievements in the arts, in the sciences, and in moral and political thought typically occur when somebody realizes that two or more of our vocabularies are interfering with each other, and proceeds to invent a new vocabulary to replace both. . . . It [a vocabulary] is a tool for doing something which could not have been envisaged prior to the development of a particular set of descriptions, those which it itself helps to provide.[18]

How do we see these two quite different accounts of the role of linguistic innovation as compatible? If moral change is to be accomplished in the direction of expanded obligations to others, it will have to be accounted for by explaining how abnormal discourse, characterized by intractable moral disputes, can be transformed into normal discourse and carried out within agreed-upon conventions. The question remains: Why will linguistic accidents containing no inherent teleology point us in the direction of greater solidarity?

For Rorty, the emergence of all the great cultural transformations is simply a flight of poetic fancy advanced by those who are beyond the pale of reason.

> But once we figure out how to use the vocabularies of these movements, we can tell a story of progress, showing how the literalization of certain metaphors served the purpose of making possible all the good things that have recently happened. Furthermore, we can now view all these good things as particular instances of some more general good, the overall end which the movement served.[19]

The transformation of abnormal discourse into normal discourse is a matter of retrospectively telling a story about how we came to be the people we are, by employing terms from the new vocabulary. Public rhetoric, the final vocabulary that is used to justify prevailing social practices, is not ironist and does not self-consciously employ the resources of linguistic innovation. Poets and revolutionaries, on the other hand, don't seek intersubjectivity. What nudges these accidental collisions of incompatible vocabularies toward an expanded sense of obligation in "our" case is the historical legacy of liberalism which Rorty claims is increasingly inclusive.

> The right way to take the slogan "We have obligations to human beings simply as such" is as a means of reminding ourselves to keep trying to expand our sense of "us" as far as we can. . . . If one reads that slogan the right way, one will give "we" as concrete and historically specific a sense as possible: it will mean something like "we twentieth-century liberals" or "we heirs to the historical contingencies which have created more and more cosmopolitan, more and more democratic political institutions".[20]

Thus, the capacity to transcend the limits of one's vocabulary depends upon finding a role for linguistic innovation that can only be accommodated within the orbit of intersubjectivity, by a retrospective historical narrative. Rorty's solution to the problem of conflicting final vocabularies engendered by linguistic innovation is a historical story, in which our increasing knowledge of the consequences of contingent events gives a new vocabulary increasing credibility. This narrative will also explain how contrastive "we-intentions" are compatible with the aspiration to transcend. The "we" referred to here are those who have internalized a Christian ethic and have benefited from institutions that have their source in the Enlightenment—institutions like a free press, an independent judiciary, an educational system that aids social mobility, and an extraordinarily wealthy and productive economy.

Unfortunately, Rorty's appeal to a historical narrative that defines who "we" are will run up against the historical-narrative problems explicated in Chapter Two. We have to decide which events or historical practices will be included in that narrative, and any history including the Enlightenment and post-Enlightenment will yield an ambiguous legacy. A story about the increasingly inclusive social practices of the West will not mention the slave trade, the fate of the American Indian, endemic racism and sexism, Auschwitz, colonialization and imperialism, Vietnam, the demonization of communism in the Third World, etc. The presence of conflicting histories will be unlikely to resolve the problem of conflicting vocabularies, since our perception of the past is to be heavily influenced by perceptions of the present and anticipations of the future. Lack of agreement about how things turned out precludes intersubjective agreement on a new vocabulary that is supposed to explain the events in question. Thus, the reference of "we" threatens to split into competing camps separated by competing narratives.

We can, of course, acknowledge the flaws in our imperfect social institutions without condemning the ideals and accomplishments that make up the history of the West. Against the received notion that the poet and revolutionary are alienated, Rorty claims:

> One can substitute for this the idea that the poet and the revolutionary are protesting in the name of the society itself against those aspects of the society which are unfaithful to its own self-image.[21]

However, when we try to become specific about what counts as a moral or political ideal that would enjoy intersubjective agreement we come up with words like "freedom," "democracy," "technological progress," "prosperity," etc. These are commendable terms of praise when understood in abstraction, but are as empty of specific content as terms like "reason," "human nature," and "truth," which Rorty would like to expunge from the philosophical lexicon, in part because they do not explain anything. If our attachments are best explained in parochial terms, as Rorty suggests, then these general terms of praise with which Rorty describes the Enlightenment tradition will hardly anchor our sense of solidarity.

In fact, when we look closely at Rorty's own social and political ideals, we find commitments to "we-intentions" that are more locally defined than "heirs of the Enlightenment." On questions of policy, Rorty advocates a version of social democracy that is probably well to the left of mainstream political thinking. Moreover, his utopian vision of a poeticized culture, in which the freedom to pursue idiosyncratic fantasies is the highest ideal, is hardly everyone's vision of an ideal—even in the intellectual culture that is Rorty's audience. The point here is that Rorty's use of the terms "us" or "we liberals" is not univocal. It variously refers to anyone who identifies with the Enlightenment tradition, or to social democrats, or to Rorty's personal vision of a liberal utopia. The domain over which the term "solidarity" ranges is fragmented and contested, not as monolithic as Rorty sometimes describes it.

Thus, the appeal to generally accepted laudatory terms will not help us sort out the question of which self-image our culture should be striving to live up to. Moreover, Rorty's account is not helped by our invoking the institutions he praises. As commendable as an independent judiciary is, the tradition of possessive individualism is equally salient and supported by said judiciary; our prosperity is unthinkable without the rapacious business practices and coercive media that make such prosperity possible.

It is, therefore, difficult, given the conceptual resources Rorty makes available, to give an account of the Enlightenment tradition as a historically constituted collection of "we-intentions." Whatever solidarity is, it is not as massive or monolithic as that. If "we-intentions" can only be given content when we invoke the narrative histories of specific groups who are similarly affected by that history, then our "we-intentions" point to something significantly smaller and more parochial than "heirs of the Enlightenment." Consequently, the capacity to transcend the limitations of one's moral perspective cannot be explained in terms of an obligation to extend the reference of "we," since that reference is thoroughly ambiguous. In fact, the very notion of solidarity would seem to be appropriately applied only to small-group identities.

"solidarity"

If "heirs of the Enlightenment" does not adequately characterize the historical legacy that explains the capacity of linguistic innovation to extend our conception of moral agency, perhaps a more locally defined sense of community will help. Feminism represents perhaps the most important recent attempt by Western liberal democracies to extend the reference of "we." Yet in Rorty's view, feminism will only succeed if it resists assimilation into normal discourse.

In his Tanner lecture entitled "Pragmatism and Feminism," Rorty criticizes universalist moral philosophy for positing that a purely rational agent could, under ideal conditions at any point in time, imagine all possible moral identities.[22] This idea leads to the assumption that the currently available language of human rights provides all the conceptual space required for the redress of sexual discrimination, once we have discovered through hard, intellectual labor the intrinsic properties of what it means to be human. Invoking the work of Catharine MacKinnon, among others, Rorty argues that injustices toward women might be so built into our cultural practices, legal framework, and the very vocabulary we use to spell out what it means to have human rights that these injustices can only be recognized when women learn to speak *as* women. Advancing women's rights under the banner of human rights forces women to occupy slightly modified traditional roles, since what it means to be human has traditionally been defined by men in terms of male characteristics. The problem is not that men are incapable of clear thinking or that women have a uniquely feminine style of reasoning unavailable to men. Rather, it is that constructing the identity of a collective entity without historical precedent requires the participation of those who are accountable to that entity —whose loyalties and commitments are directed toward that community. Divided loyalties are ineffective when self-definition is at stake.

This creates an obstacle for the feminist: This new voice cannot proceed to prosecute its case from premises shared with the larger culture, as it will have no historical antecedents and therefore no standards of rational acceptability. What we have been calling "abnormal discourse" will sound merely crazy. Thus, it will be engaged in neither explanation, argument, nor an interpretation or updating of historical practices, but will be more appropriately described as prophecy. Like the early Christians and the Nazis, this prophetic voice will be ". . . trying to actualize hitherto undreamt-of possibilities by putting new linguistic and other practices into play, and erecting new social constructs."[23]

Just like the ironist described above, the prophet uses linguistic innovation as her tool, because what matters to this radical breed of feminist is that she gain "semantic authority" over descriptions that apply to her. Finding an identity as a woman involves making her claim to be a woman central to making the choices that she makes; for this she needs to forget those descriptions of herself that define her solely in terms of her relationships to men. To seek "equal rights" will not suffice, because that would be to seek something that men already have. This demands of women that they describe themselves in terms of those categories already devised for them. Thus, to achieve this authority she may have to become isolated from the rest of culture, as only that separation will facilitate the kind of experimentation required to create a new social reality.

> To get such authority you have to hear your own statements as part of a shared practice. Otherwise you yourself will never know whether they are more than ravings, never know whether you are a heroine or a maniac. People in search of such authority need to band together and form clubs, exclusive clubs. For if you want to work out a story about who you are—put together a moral identity—which decreases the importance of your relationships to one

set of people and increases the importance of your relationships to another set, the physical absence of the first set of people may be just what you need.[24]

This process of social change, which results from the attempt of a group to gain semantic authority over their social identity, requires the linguistic innovation of prophecy. In Rorty's Davidson-inspired account of language, these changes in belief are not motivated by reasons, because they are not regulated by a rule-governed social practice. Whatever motivates such change can only be characterized as a cause of the change, not a reason to change. Consequently, philosophy will have very little to say about such a process, because the paradigmatic activity of the philosopher is to uncover the rules that guide social practice. Only when the goals of a practice are firmly in place, so that the activities constituting the practice can be understood as leading toward realization of that goal, can we talk about reasons and criteria; this involves the formation of a new, concrete practice, whereby innovation becomes normal discourse within a small group.

It is important to note, however, that this distinction between normal and revolutionary discourse is unstable at best. Rorty is dangerously close to asserting that there is a sharp distinction between reason on one hand and imagination and emotion on the other—the same assertion he accuses traditional philosophy of making. Rorty conceives of the courage, emotional bonding, and redescriptions of social reality that cement the solidarity of small social groups as utterly distinct from a practice that operates within the parameters of agreed-upon standards and criteria. Commendatory terms like "rationality" and "justification" are reserved for normal discourse, but surely there is confusion here. The process of identifying and explaining the ways in which a dominant discourse excludes certain ideas from serious consideration involves the use of standard canons of rationality: a commitment to plausibility and intelligibility constraints, consistency, etc. Creating conceptual space is not simply a matter of naming hitherto unrecognized phenomena, but of showing the similarities and differences between new and old concepts, and attempting to predict the consequences (including logical consequences) of adopting new self-descriptions. Notions like "explanation," "criteria," "justification," and "argument," which Rorty consigns to normal discourse, play a role in describing similarities and differences and in predicting consequences.

No doubt, linguistic innovation is important in easing the creation of social identities. The emergence of terms like "date rape," for instance, has called attention to phenomena that formerly went unreported and unrecognized. However, as Nancy Fraser points out in her response to Rorty's paper, such redescriptions are not so much the emanations of a literary sensibility that has induced changes in meaning as they are the products of consciousness-raising that involved "the invention of a new discursive practice."[25] What secures a collective social identity has to do with changing the norms that govern interaction between interlocutors as well as creating what Fraser calls a "counterpublic sphere"—networks of bookstores, festivals, and other public fora that engage a full range of practical reasoning skills not reducible to the poetic. There is something right about pointing to the prophetic dimension of such a movement. Something is being created *ex nihilo,* but I doubt that a contrast between reason and prophecy will properly characterize the formation of social identity.

More important for my purposes here is that the judgments of separatist feminism are contrast judgments. They acquire their meaning through conscious opposition to those who are not included within the group. Through Rorty, we get a clearer picture of why the acquisition and maintenance of a social identity might require these contrast judgments: They enable their proponents to resist the imposition of a social identity and the helplessness of a life lived on someone else's terms. Yet given Rorty's definition of moral progress as the extension of historically shaped "we-intentions" that tend toward the inclusion of diverse others, he will have to explain how the linguistic innovations of radical feminism can be made available and familiar to the larger social and political context in which they operate.

Unfortunately, Rorty fails to say anything enlightening about this process—in part because his view of social change pulls in opposing directions. Rorty advocates that we understand the causes of significant changes in vocabulary as "constellations of random factors that have made some things subjects of conversation for us, others not...."[26] Often he characterizes such changes as the result of "blind, contingent, and mechanical forces," as if they were independent of human agency altogether.[27] Yet on the other hand, Rorty will argue that linguistic innovation is the result of "having hit upon a tool that happened to work better for certain purposes than any previous tool."[28] This latter quotation seems much more appropriate for the phenomenon of social change, because it suggests that behind the linguistic tools there are actual human beings consciously fashioning a new social reality. However, none of this explains why the dominant discourse would so readily give up its hegemony, why normal discourse would be open to the incursions of a new vocabulary, especially if the solidarity of that dominant discourse is contrastive as well.

Needed to supplement marginalized groups' account of prophecy and linguistic innovation is an account of how the very categories of belief that count as normal discourse are undermined in this process of social change. Simply pointing to the availability of a new vocabulary and the aspirations of a marginalized group will not explain why those aspirations and vocabulary come to be viewed as normal discourse. Semantics, after all, can be pushed around endlessly without result. The trajectory from "niggers" to "coloreds" to "Negroes" to "Blacks" to "African-Americans" has not done very much to alleviate the plight of most members of this marginalized community. As a society, we have gradually come to associate the word "person" with "African-American," while increasingly coming to see African-Americans as irresponsible "people" as undeserving as before. Somehow, our judgments escape our linguistic innovation.[29]

Thus, Rorty's account of transcendence is inadequate. In Rorty's own view, the existence of small solidarities is crucial to the sort of autonomy he thinks liberalism helps us achieve. Yet the importance of the public expression of one's beliefs as an element of that autonomy can not avoid threatening the solidarity of the larger community. Moreover, the conceptual resources seem to be unavailable to explain how these small solidarities can be linked to a more inclusive sense of community, if we take the notion of contrastive "we-intentions" seriously.

The difficulty is that "we-intentions" are contrastive and resistent to intersubjective agreement; linguistic innovation does not explain how such resistance can be overcome in order to promote an increasingly inclusive moral point of view. This makes any large-scale solidarity an inappropriate starting point for giving an account of transcendence, even if we mean by "account" an attempt to imagine novel possibilities.

Rereading Rorty

My interpretation of Rorty thus far has treated him as a historicist, in the sense that moral obligations are understood only as products of culture and history, and justifications are constrained by interests and context. The notion of "solidarity" names the fact that the social bond is constituted by other concrete human beings who share historically shaped "we-intentions." Although this standard reading of Rorty is a plausible rendering of his texts, there is a dimension to some of his work, especially parts of *Contingency, Irony, and Solidarity,* that does not fit comfortably within the historicist framework and that provides intimations of a different kind of argument.

There is, after all, something odd about Rorty's liberal utopia: It is without optimism. Not only do current conditions fail to approximate Rorty's ideal liberal culture, Rorty claims we have no good reason to think they ever will. Although he writes in the spirit of "playful jouissance," in the words of one commentator, his texts are peppered with some rather dark sayings suggesting that whatever optimism he harbors is tempered by an overwhelming sense of the contingency of everything. In his discussion of the character O'Brien in Orwell's *1984*, Rorty writes

> I do not think that we liberals *can* now imagine a future of "human dignity, freedom and peace." That is, we cannot tell ourselves a story about how to get from the actual present to such a future. . . . Sometimes things prove to be just as bad as they first looked. Orwell helped us to formulate a pessimistic description of the political situation which forty years of further experience have only confirmed. This bad news remains the great intransigent fact of contemporary political speculation, the one that blocks all the liberal scenarios. . . . I think that the fantasy of endless torture—the suggestion that the future is "a boot stamping on a human face—forever" is essential to *1984*. . . . He [O'Brien] is not saying that the nature of man or power or history insures that boot will grind down forever, but rather that it just *happens* that it will. . . . As a matter of sheer contingent fact—as contingent as a comet or a virus—that is what the future is going to be.[30]

The sharp, stylistic contrast between the lighthearted rhetoric of Rorty's liberalism and these intimations of hopelessness locate the tragic dimension in Rorty's thought. For Rorty, liberalism may wake from its good intentions to discover, like Hamlet, that bodies now litter the historical stage. The thought that there is no very general reason for thinking that the future will be like the past, that whatever moral progress has been made will as likely as not end with the next roll of the dice, is not a comforting one.

When Rorty argues that there is nothing in the nature of humankind or history that should lead us to think that liberal, democratic institutions are indelibly written in the book of history, he disconnects the prophetic voice from the teleology in which it found aid and comfort in Marx and Hegel. If history has no meaning that serves to justify a utopian vision as a further specification of its inner logic, social hope is then an article of faith rather than a reasonable expectation. Thus Rorty's utopia is perhaps an abstraction, without connection to life as we know it.

Moreover, this vision of a thoroughly aestheticized culture has a dark side. In Rorty's comments on Nabokov and Orwell, which immediately precede the chapter entitled "Solidarity," there is a common theme—the cruel aesthete who pursues a personal ideal at the expense of others. Both these authors have created characters of imagination and perception who employ these virtues in the service of humiliation and cruelty. Similarly, as I noted earlier, in the discussion of ironist theorists like Nietzsche, Derrida, Foucault, and Heidegger, Rorty argues that their work should be understood as the pursuit of a radical form of personal autonomy that, if taken seriously as social commentary, would threaten the intersubjectivity on which social reality depends. Rorty continually berates the Marxists for forecasting,

> a new kind of being—someone on whose body "power" has inscribed nothing, someone who will burst the bounds of all the vocabularies used to describe the old, tattered, palimpsests.[31]

What ties these criticisms of theory to the fictional characters is a claim to the effect that moral failure is the result of the obsessive pursuit of personal and/or social ideals. Both Nabokov's Humbert Humbert and Orwell's O'Brien not only find enjoyment and satisfaction in the abject degradation of another person, they find integrity and a peculiar form of all-consuming piety in it. Orwell and Nabokov describe a kind of moral blindness that comes from seeking a condition of purity or perfection with regard to some idiosyncratic personal ideal. Rorty finds a similar blindness in the narratives of declining civilization told by Heidegger and Foucault, and the passionate calls for ideological purity from the Marxists. This anxiety about obsession that lurks beneath the surface of the book suggests that Rorty's playful jouissance rests on an abyss, that his utopian vision is spoken in irony, that *Contingency, Irony, and Solidarity* is an instance of liberal irony. These troublesome characters are all citizens of Rorty's utopia who produce "tingles," rather than timeless truths, to fascinate our imaginations.

Thus, a central feature of Rorty's work is the recognition that not only theory but ideals—his own ideals—may be dangerous. This antiperfectionism feeds into my earlier discussion of tragedy. Rorty's ironic stance toward even his own moral ideals resonates with that conception of tragedy revealing the questionable character of our deepest commitments. Therefore, the questions that arose as the result of our discussions of tragedy arise in connection with Rorty's utopia as well. How do we reconcile idealism and skepticism with the requirements of successful action? What sort of person and what personal characteristics can best harbor both the unconditional commitment to moral ideals and the knowledge that these very ideals might lead to moral failure?

To answer these questions, we need to begin by providing a better understanding of what concepts will help explain the corruption of moral ideals. The recognition that corruption is built into the structure of our world, and that morality is a part of that structure, will shape our attempts at moral reflection at both a practical and philosophical level. This is because it forces us to ask how it is that our best intentions are distorted when they encounter the resistance of the world. It is here that we confront the absolute boundaries of human action, the things over which our actions have no control—our mortality and the "blind impress" of the past that has shaped each of us. Rorty writes that it is our attempts to cope with these boundaries that form the background against which we acquire a moral conscience.[32] Any attempt to answer the questions of what action to take or what sort of life to lead are framed by our limited future and our completed past, and are therefore not to be separated from emotions that are our only means of coping with these boundaries—rage, anxiety, compassion, and guilt, to name just a few. Including these emotions within the causes of our moral perspectives will, therefore, invoke a vocabulary of psychological terms like "obsession," "compulsion," and "paranoia," not traditionally thought to be part of the moral vocabulary. Such an orientation toward understanding the sources of our commitments would help to provide a conceptual framework for explaining how these commitments can sometimes turn against us. It may be much more important for us as moral beings to learn to recognize the causes of corruption and evil than to imagine ideal utilitarian observers or paragons of virtue.

This seems to be, in part, Rorty's motivation for choosing *Lolita* and *1984* as examples of literature that carry a moral message. Literature such as *Lolita*—which explores the very thin line between love and obsession, degradation and refinement—provides us with a rich source of examples from which these sorts of recognitions might flow. As Rorty suggests, almost anything can become the source of an unconditional attachment, a fact that literature recognizes more explicitly and with greater frequency than philosophy.[33]

At the level of social and political thought, a similar shift in orientation is suggested by the claim that corruption is built into the fabric of our moral world. We might take seriously a suggestion by Judith Shklar that the dominant tendency in philosophy, which sees justice as the datum of analysis and injustice as a secondary phenomenon, be reversed. Shklar argues that injustice is the central and ineliminatable feature of the world because "we simply cannot know enough about men or events to fulfill the demands of justice."[34] Faith in the effectiveness of norms leads to a potentially deceptive intellectual self-assurance. Replacing this faith with a sustained focus on injustice might illuminate phenomena neglected by the more traditional model—the many faces of victimization and "the many ways in which we all learn to live with each other's injustices." Moreover, placing the focus not on the recognition of goodness but on the recognition of evil, injustice, cruelty, etc. seems better suited to the complex intentionality of moral conduct. We seldom consciously seek "the good" (when this good is something more than our ordinary desires) unless our aspirations are placed in question. This perspective, drawn from the dark side of Rorty's utopia, suggests that we should first view ourselves as potential victimizers rather than potential victims. Discovering the components of "the good life" in order to measure the cost of evil may be less fruitful than ferreting out the injustices, small and large, that regularly seep into our experience. Skepticism toward moral ideals need not lead us away from moral considerations, but can deepen our understanding of moral failure.

In the end, however, this cannot be the whole of moral reflection. In order to recognize failure we need some sense of what counts as success, and this seems to reintroduce worries about how to characterize moral ideals in the face of the inevitable corruption that the tragic vision expresses. Irony is not skepticism. The ironist must be able to endorse the vocabulary about which she is ironic. Thus, it is the interplay between skepticism and idealism that Rorty is trying to capture with his notion of irony. We can look at our ideals with appreciation or despair, but if it is with despair, how do we construct a sense of community out of the limited resources despair makes available? One of the leitmotifs of Rorty's corpus is the importance of social hope, and for good reason. What is at issue here is once again the unraveling of moral and social identity, the silencing of a final vocabulary that Rorty describes as a kind of humiliation. A political culture subjected to constant skepticism would be as incapable of coherent action as Winston, the character in *1984* who is the subject of O'Brien's torture. Rorty, therefore, declines to endorse any form of extreme skepticism with respect to moral and political questions. Where, then, is the source of social hope once we have internalized the recognition of radical contingency and rejected the appeals to a glorious past?

I think a provisional answer lies in Rorty's claim that the defining disposition of a liberal is "one who thinks cruelty is the worst thing we do."[35] This claim connects his liberal, utopian dream with an ethical stance appropriate for a world pervaded by contingency, because the capacity to recognize cruelty is compatible with both the endorsement of a particular sociopolitical arrangement and the recognition that the arrangement may produce evil. In Rorty's view, it is our capacity to suffer pain and humiliation that is the only plausible candidate for something that ties all of humanity together. It cuts across all other similarities and differences.[36]

Attention to our potential for cruelty maintains a degree of critical distance from the constrastive "we-intentions" that generate moral blindness out of particular versions of solidarity—but *only* a degree, because I don't think our capacity to experience pain is a universal that simply transcends our cultural experience. This is especially so if we include humiliation within the concept of pain, for what will count as humiliation will differ from culture to culture and from person to person. The capacity to experience pain and humiliation is about the best we can do to identify similarities among human beings that will make a difference from a moral perspective. Human beings tend to share more beliefs about human suffering than we do about courage, honor, justice, etc. Thus, "avoid cruelty" is the closest thing to a moral principle that Rorty is willing to countenance.

In this reading of Rorty, the function of a utopian vision is to keep our attention focused on the need for a moral practice that sustains our sense of social hope.[37] However, the relationship between moral practice understood as the avoidance of cruelty and Rorty's utopian vision is not teleological. Such a moral practice will not help us realize this utopia. Rather, the intuition that cruelty is the worst thing we do reinforces that sense of social hope by reinforcing the notion that recognizing the needs and vulnerabilities of others will help us confront the contingency of the human condition. "Avoid cruelty" is a minimalist ethic and a frank acknowledgment of our finitude.

The contrast between this way of reading Rorty and the more standard version is a contrast between different conceptions of solidarity as well as between the kinds of arguments required for its support. The argument for his historicist approach and the notion of solidarity it supports is primarily a negative one. It follows from the contingency of language, self, and community that there is nothing deeper than history that will explain human practices, nothing but shared practices that secures the social bond, and no alternative but an ethnocentric starting point from which to pursue inquiry. The nature of this ethnocentrism guides the practices of social cooperation. I have been arguing that our intuitions regarding the capacity to transcend the limitations of a parochial point of view could not be accounted for by this sort of argument, despite the appeal to linguistic innovation and a substantive private realm.[38] On the other hand, if we place less emphasis on Rorty's historicism and ethnocentrism and more on the tragic dimension of his work, especially in *Contingency, Irony, and Solidarity,* we find the notion of solidarity gaining support from the assertion that cruelty is the worst thing we do. This assertion expresses the view that only the recognition of our dependence on concrete others will sustain our capacity to cooperate in the face of vulnerability and threat. To achieve this solidarity, we need not be concerned with defining what "we" are, but concern ourselves instead with assessing mutual needs.

This interpretation of Rorty also has the virtue of making sense of Rorty's closing comments summarizing his book. Rorty writes:

> The self-doubt [of Western culture] seems to me the characteristic mark of the first epoch in human history in which large numbers of people have become able to separate the question "Do you believe and desire what we believe and desire?" from the question "Are you suffering?" In my jargon, this is the ability to distinguish the question of whether you and I share the same final vocabulary from the question of whether you are in pain. Distinguishing these questions makes it possible to distinguish public from private questions, questions about pain from questions about the point of human life, the domain of the liberal from the domain of the ironist. It thus makes it possible for a single person to be both.[39]

I believe Rorty is correct in distinguishing these questions but wrong in thinking that this is a thesis about "our" history or about maintaining the split between public and private life. It is, instead, a thesis about social hope in a fractured community.

Despite this reinterpretation of solidarity, difficulties persist. As I tried to show in Chapter Three, moral perception is conditioned by contrast judgments, and it is not obvious why the recognition of our capacity for cruelty would be an exception. However, it is worth noting that there is a strong current of antiperfectionism running through Rorty's work that is less prevalent in Nussbaum's. For Nussbaum, moral perception has to do with the recognition of quality, which immediately invokes a distinction between higher and lower goods. This invites the sort of contrast judgment that I argued is the source of moral blindness in the literary examples discussed in Chapter Three. Although this dimension is not absent in Rorty, it is strongly tempered by his worries about obsession and the cautionary tone he adopts with respect to moral ideals. There is an important distinction to be drawn between moral perception that emerges from an ironic attitude toward ideals, and moral perception that rests on a perspective endorsing the notion that at the end of inquiry there is something like a univocal account of human goodness.

This alternative reading of Rorty raises the basic philosophical conundrum of justification, as well as a puzzle about belief acquisition. In the standard reading of Rorty, the notion of an obligation is cashed out in terms of solidarity. "We-intentions" form the basis of our understanding of to whom obligations are owed and what those obligations are. In my rereading of Rorty, the situation is exactly reversed. It is on the basis of an obligation to avoid cruelty that we gain a sense of community. This seems counterintuitive, especially in light of the conception of ethics that I have been referring to as "concrete ethics." It seems to ignore those obligations arising from participation in the institutions and practices of a community and a shared way of life. How did we acquire such an obligation, and why should we think it is compelling?

Of course, this would not seem counterintuitive to a Kantian. A Kantian would argue that obligations are, indeed, more fundamental than a shared history of moral practice, at least for purposes of justification, but would proceed to ground this obligation in a conception of human freedom or rationality incompatible with the contingency of language, self, and community and thus unavailable to Rorty or any antitheorist.

How, then, do we make sense of an obligation that is derivable from neither a particular history nor from facts about human rationality; that is not embedded in a history, underlying history, or outside history? How do we answer the question "In virtue of what do we have obligations?" In the following chapters I supply at least a provisional answer to these questions.

Part Two

The Postmodern Alternative

Introduction

The foregoing chapters attempt to delineate and assess a conception of morality that eschews appeals to objective standpoints and universal principles and denies the priority of general principles while emphasizing the importance of novel, unique, and particular components of moral experience that also asserts the contingency of moral experience and the partial incommensurability of moral discourse. It follows from this meta-theoretical position that practical moral reasoning begins from within the experience of particular groups of agents and requires an understanding of one's immediate social world and how one fits into that world, an understanding that cannot be adequately articulated by a theoretical discourse—even one of the nonfoundationalist variety. Moral obligation and responsibility are, therefore, at least initially characterized in terms of local norms and concrete relations with familiar others, which must be articulated in particularistic terms not widely shared across communities or traditions.

This characterization of moral reflection leads us to question whether an account of universal moral agency can be generated out of these resources, for it is not immediately obvious how we are to understand obligations to those who do not share a tradition or who owe allegiance to other communities. MacIntyre, Nussbaum, and Rorty propose solutions to this difficulty. They offer alternative views on how the resources of narrative can help fill in the gap between the details of a particular way of life, and a conception of how that life can be transformed through criticism to sustain the ideal of universal moral agency. However, I have argued that in each case the specification of a moral point of view itself seems to require that certain features of moral experience go unrepresented. This,

I have also argued, renders ineffective the attempts to generate a conception of universal moral agency from the resources of "concrete ethics" and narrative structure.

Nevertheless, in assessing the proposed solutions to this problem, we gain a more extensive understanding of the problem of incommensurability. MacIntyre's appeal to the teleological structure of narrative history as a source of obligation yields either a blind adherence to a single tradition or conflicting, multiple narratives, each of which can claim to yield only a partial perspective on history. This renders invisible the moral claims falling beneath that level of recognition. Nussbaum uses the descriptive powers of literary works to explicate a kind of moral perceptiveness that is sensitive to the needs of others. However, this virtue of perceptiveness is based on recognizing the special value that certain goods have—and to recognize that certain goods and aims have a special value involves an implicit contrast with dimensions of experience that do not display that special value. Therefore, it is unclear how this virtue of perceptiveness would be sensitive to the needs of others whose sense of what has value differs significantly, especially when the goods in question are not associated with literary sensibilities. Finally, Rorty appeals to the imaginative resources of figurative language—especially irony and metaphor—to explain how the unfamiliar can be made familiar. Yet in the social and political context, resources for innovation are constrained by the demands of a conception of solidarity that is itself the source of intractable conflict. Moreover, this conception of solidarity requires an ethnocentric starting point characterized in terms of contrastive "we-intentions," which circumscribe social identity precisely because they mark a contrast and exclude those who don't satisfy the conditions of that social identity. Contrast judgments, the expressivism that supports them, and the ambiguities inherent in narrative histories figure prominently in the moral point of view implicit in the antitheory position. All erect obstacles to the sort of understanding that would yield an account of universal moral agency.

At this juncture, I point out an assumption presupposed in each of these attempts to defend concrete ethics that explains this inability to account for universal moral agency. Each author discussed here assumes that moral reflection and inquiry is subject to the hermeneutic circle, and thus presupposes that the general conclusions one finds upon reflection are in some sense "understood" from the very beginning as a condition of their intelligibility. Agents come to moral reflection with a history of involvements and projections of meaning grounded in their situations, which helps determine the perspective from which they will evaluate their choices. However reasonable such an assumption might be in certain contexts, I argue that its effects on moral reflection are to codify the moral blindness with which I have saddled concrete ethics. On this view, intelligibility requires the reiteration of those initial assumptions that orient inquiry and give significance to the questions posed. Although these initial assumptions can be revised through the process of inquiry and reflection, I argue that the resources for critique that this assumption makes available to us are inadequate with respect to the issue of transcending the limitations of one's moral point of view.

The nonfoundationalist approaches to justification, as described in Chapter One, require that theoretical principles be consistent with the norms, values, and ideals of particular groups of moral agents. Consistency in these cases is understood in terms of a process of mutual testing and assessment, in which judgments are assigned initial credibility, principles are modified to accommodate these credible judgments, and these judgments are modified in light of justified principles. Justification is, therefore, dependent upon the reiteration of some portion of the initial set of judgments; namely, those that survive the process of mutual testing. It is important to note that the primary constraints on theoretical principles are these initial judgments of credibility. Arbitrariness is only avoided, and justification accomplished, by preserving a commitment to at least some of these judgments.

MacIntyre, Nussbaum, and Rorty attempt to protect this picture of reflection from overly rationalistic interpretations, making it more responsive to the particularity of moral experience. Yet despite the significant differences between them, they share the presupposition that moral reflection requires a process of sustaining and extending the meaning and significance of historically constituted practices, suitably modified by confrontation with particularity. Each asserts that moral judgments are framed by a preunderstanding of one's immediate social reality, although the nature of that reality is characterized differently in each case. We begin reflection already engaged in this reality. Regardless of what possibilities are projected as courses of action, their intelligibility will depend on sustaining our connections to this preunderstanding of who we are, in part by modifying that reality to reflect this sense of who we are. As I note in the discussion of expressivism earlier in this chapter, bringing social reality into conformity with our sense of who we are is an important component of this intelligibility. Moral reflection is, therefore, bound and limited by the question of social identity, for this question frames both the initial assumptions and the conclusion. Once again, the intelligibility of moral reflection, in this view, requires the reiteration of those initial assumptions that survive this process of assessment.

The consequences of those assumptions regarding the question of how to characterize the aspiration to transcend the limits of a moral point of view are significant, because it means this aspiration must proceed from a description of who or what one is. Therefore, moral reflection, even as reformed by the antitheorists, never escapes the picture of inquiry beginning from a description of a state of affairs to which actions and beliefs should conform. In order to know what one should do, one must know what and who one is. That is, one must project those possibilities conforming to one's pre-understanding of one's immediate social world. Thus, prescriptions are limited by our capacity for self-representation.

In Chapter One, I argue that normative ethical theories typically presuppose an analogy with science as if morality were a representation or description of a "world" independent of the inquirer. The antitheorists object to this alleged independence, as reflective moral agents are caught up in the phenomena they are investigating. Nevertheless, the antitheorists think of moral reflection as, in part, a description of the social entity of which one is a part, the nature and boundaries of which must be specified and respecified through the course of inquiry. The disagreement between theorists who are also nonfoundationalists and philosophers who tend toward the antitheory position is primarily about the extent to which this pre-understanding can be articulated, and the kinds of discourse most appropriate for that articulation. There is, however, a basic agreement among nonfoundationalists and the antitheorists discussed thus far that this pre-understanding constrains the intelligibility of normative judgments.

My worry about this methodology is that if moral reflection is largely a matter of recognizing and articulating one's social identity, there is a kind of moral blindness built into the methodology. It is not obvious that we can represent the needs and interests of the radically "other" simply by articulating and extending the shared beliefs of a particular community. There is no reason to think that the conceptual categories and modes of responsiveness presupposed by that articulation will be up to the task of making sense out of a significantly different moral perspective, given the central role contrast judgments play in moral reflection. As I have tried to make clear in previous chapters, the dominant feature of moral reflection within the context of concrete ethics is the correlation between reflection, circumscribed by the understanding of one's immediate social world, and the persistence of moral blindness. The suspicion that this is more than a mere correlation is impossible to resist.

But what, then, is the alternative? If we must begin reflection from where we are, then some version of "concrete ethics" seems inescapable. If the exploration of our starting point throws up insurmountable obstacles to the recognition of the "other" by generating intractable moral conflict, then it seems we are stuck with this parochialism if we wish to preserve the basic tenets of the antitheory position. Our own historically situated social context is likely to reinforce this parochialism. The persistence of intractable moral and political conflict seems to me to be a salient and rapidly advancing feature of our current cultural condition.

I argue that the intractability of conflict should not lead us to accept the parochialism this position seems to entail. The presumption shared by antitheorists and theorists alike is that the possibility of ethical and political community depends on forging a consensus of shared beliefs, a consensus that will constitute a social identity.

In what follows, I argue that genuine moral judgment, and to a degree political judgment as well, has little to do with social identity, and thus little to do with agreement in belief. Levinas and Lyotard provide us with a general explanation of the correlation between moral blindness and the centrality of the question of self-identity, an explanation that allows us to address the problem of universal moral agency from within the antitheory perspective.

6

Levinas: Ethics without Limit

I include a discussion of some of Emmanuel Levinas's work at this juncture because he provides us with a comprehensive undermining of the
basic assumptions behind concrete ethics and the narrativist approach to
ethics. He demonstrates the limitations of conceptualizing ethics as a set
of obligations determined by norms, institutions, or particular histories,
and shows why the intelligibility of ethics depends on transcendence, thus
providing an alternative account of universal moral agency. Importantly,
he develops his position in a way that is compatible with many of the
assumptions of the antitheory position.

Using an interpretation of Levinas as a vehicle, I argue that morality is
not dependent on our capacity for understanding or representation.
Rather, it is in recognizing the extent to which morality lies beyond our
capacity for comprehension and understanding, in the claim imposed on
each moral agent by the incomprehensibility of suffering, that we sustain
our capacity for moral judgment, especially with respect to the question
of universal moral agency.

Levinas's Critique of the Philosophical Tradition

For Levinas, the dominant trend in Western philosophy is an inquiry
into the process by which an autonomous rational subject explains the
basis for that autonomy by bringing reality under the control of rational
thought. The notion that although the world is external to this autonomous subject, it has meaning only to the extent that it can be brought into
some relation with a unified conception of Being that makes both self and

world instances of rational categories, is the guiding thought of philosophy. The unity of subject and object under the auspices of this subject is, therefore, the aim and measure of philosophy.

This conception of the subject frames the philosophical approach to ethics. Ethics takes up the problem of how this autonomous self is to choose a course of action that is consistent with the canons of rationality established by this unified conception of Being. Ontology is, thus, prior to ethics. Ethics must conform to ontological categories and employ conceptual resources drawn from inquiries into the nature of what exists, and our capacity to understand that nature.

Levinas worries that in this basic philosophical orientation, nothing is truly alien to the autonomous subject—since, as the bearer of rational concepts, it is the measure of all meaning. Such a subject is self-enclosed, unable to grasp phenomena that cannot be represented as instances of rational concepts, thus begging the question of the existence and nature of such phenomena. His concern partly overlaps that of the antitheorists discussed previously, for to the extent that all meaning is reduced to a single horizon of intelligibility, the richness and diversity of reality is diminished, the elements of surprise, novelty, and uniqueness suppressed.

Even more important to Levinas's critique of the philosophical tradition is that it is conceived against the background of the horrific acts of violence and terror staining the history of the very culture that has adopted this autonomous, rational subject as its theoretical justification. Levinas's work compels us to confront the violence that lurks in the notion that some collection of rational concepts or categories will yield a comprehensive understanding of reality. He thus raises the question of the complicity of our civilization's most cherished beliefs in the events of the Holocaust.

> The essential problem is: Can we speak of an absolute commandment after Auschwitz. Can we speak of morality after the failure of morality?[1]

Levinas suggests that the bedrock of our philosophical tradition and culture—the priority of the search for truth over the search for goodness or justice—is in part responsible for the violence of the twentieth century. Recent attempts to mitigate the vices of idealism and rationalism will not set aside these worries. The notion of intentionality, whether it is understood in the terms of Husserl, Heidegger, or Gadamer, will not succeed in illuminating the dimensions of experience excluded by the autonomous subject, or the violence implicit in the comprehension of reality. Intentionality always understands our being affected by the world as presupposing an anticipation of what is grasped, which amounts to a kind of possession of the object prior to understanding. With respect to intentionality, Levinas writes:

> The given enters into a thought which recognizes in it or invests it with its own project, and thus exercises mastery over it. . . . What is realized in and by intentional consciousness offers itself to protention and diverges from itself in retention, so as to be, across the divergency, identified and possessed.[2]

All "consciousness of" is directed toward a range of possibilities in terms of which the object of consciousness is understood as the thing that it is. Yet such a projection requires an initial grasp of the sort of thing that it is. All understanding or interpretation operates within a forestructure of understanding, presuppositions that orient understanding so it is appropriate to the objects in question. Understanding is a matter of finding the appropriate presuppositions on which to base the projection of possibilities, of gathering those possibilities drawn from our own prereflective grasp of how the world is. Thus, a correct understanding is one in which the projection of possibilities coheres with the preunderstanding from which those possibilities were generated. We can see in this recounting of the hermeneutic circle the force of Levinas's objection. We can only be affected by the world in ways that have already been understood. Reality is, in a sense, possessed by the subject prior to its encounter with it. Understanding, in this view, is a form of self-assertion, which according to Levinas fatally misconstrues our capacity for moral judgment.

Levinas views Heidegger's thought as an extension of this trend in Western thought, and often seems to be directly responding to Heidegger's formulation of the problem of ontology. Thus, Levinas's critique of the implicit connections between understanding and possession in the philosophical tradition, and the manner in which this informs our capacity for practical reason, can best be viewed in contrast to Heidegger's work, especially *Being and Time*.

Heidegger's inquiry into the meaning of Being is carried out as an analysis of Being-in-the-World, because it is through *Dasein*—Heidegger's name for the peculiarly human mode of Being-in-the-World—that Being reveals itself. The fundamental characteristic of *Dasein* is the fact that it is the only being for whom Being is an issue.

It is peculiar to this entity that with and through its Being, this Being is disclosed to it. *Understanding of Being is itself a definite characteristic of Dasein's Being.*[3]

Being, for Heidegger, is something that shows itself to *Dasein* through the disclosure of *Dasein's* Being. However, the Being of Dasein is understood in terms of the way it relates to itself, such that its essential characteristic is "mineness." Individual Dasein is constituted by the possibilities on which it chooses to act, decisions that ultimately cannot be delegated or passed on to someone else and thus belong to *Dasein* essentially.

That entity which in its Being has this very Being as an issue, comports itself towards its Being as its ownmost possibility. . . . As modes of Being, *authenticity* and *inauthenticity* . . . are both grounded in the fact that any Dasein whatsoever is characterized by mineness.[4]

By "mineness," Heidegger is referring to the way in which each of us is ultimately responsible for self-fashioning, choosing our possibilities against the background of facticity and throwness. Being reveals itself in the course of *Dasein* appropriating its own possibilities. The comprehension of one's own possibilities, the autonomy of action, and the comprehension of Being are interrelated, central features of authentic *Dasein*. In less technical language, the comprehension of reality that each of us has as individuals is informed by the process of actualizing certain possibilities for ourselves, and excluding others, in light of our prereflective understanding of the situations in which we find ourselves.

Levinas objects to Heidegger's formulation because it reduces reality to what can be appropriated for *Dasein's* use. In fact, Levinas sees Heidegger's work as an instance of traditional philosophical procedure that defines knowledge and understanding as a process of assimilation, whereby particular appearances of things are brought under the scope of general principles and concepts.

Levinas calls this approach to meaning and understanding "the rediscovery of the Same in the other," because it assumes that the networks of identifications already at work in our cognitive activities are sufficient for explaining our openness to reality. We find echoes of Levinas's characterization of the philosophical tradition in the approach to philosophical justification discussed in my earlier chapters. Levinas is, in effect, arguing that the philosophical tradition has assumed that intelligibility requires the reiteration of the initial assumptions that orient the inquiry in question and give significance to the questions posed.

Levinas, however, argues that this basic orientation fails to explain our openness to novelty and the givenness of phenomena.

Against this "egology," as he calls it, he argues that we find ourselves always confronted by something that escapes the grasp of our concepts and undermines the autonomy of our actions—the "Other"—that Levinas will ultimately argue is my moral relationship with another person. Ontology must admit the existence of a dimension of experience inaccessible to the cognitive discourse of ontology. Although the meaning of our own existence, our very subjectivity, is "grounded" in this relationship with the Other, we cannot approach this relationship by attempting to understand the nature of the Other—it is utterly beyond comprehension. Levinas will argue that only ethical language can express this transcendence, and any understanding of reality must emerge from within the acceptance of a radical responsibility for the Other. The priority of ontology to ethics, characteristic of the main currents of the philosophical tradition, is thereby reversed. Ethics is not just a branch of philosophy but is indeed first philosophy: "Morality thus presides over the work of truth."[5]

The Social Relation—Self and Other

In asserting the priority of ethics and in grounding the comprehension of reality in the social relation, Levinas obviously intends a sharp break with the philosophical tradition; his rather enigmatic pronouncements regarding the scope of our moral responsibility toward others suggest a radical revision of our philosophical understanding of social reality. The contrast can be most clearly brought out once again by comparison with Heidegger. For Heidegger, *Dasein* is always already Being-With. The world we confront is already occupied by equipment pointing to the interests and goals we share with other people. We inhabit a publicly shared world of interrelated roles available to us to the extent that we understand these interrelationships and master the norms associated with them. The social relation is constituted by this preunderstanding that the self has of other people. Essentially, for Heidegger, the self understands the other as another self.

Heidegger's analysis of social relations is firmly rooted in the situatedness of *Dasein* and, at least to that extent, shares its basic orientation with what I have been calling concrete ethics. Yet this Being-With is interpreted by Heidegger in terms of the loss of authenticity. In the mode of everyday existence, *Dasein* simply takes up those possibilities made available by its throwness and, understanding them in the manner in which the anonymous "they" understands, acts on them in thoroughly conventional ways. However, the call of conscience summons individual *Dasein* back from its lostness in the "they" to the solitary task of an authentic retrieval of its past and projection of its own possibilities in the future. As Being-toward-death, individual Dasein confronts its ultimate demise with an ineluctable concern for the meaning that one's life has as a whole. The one possibility that cannot be transferred to another, that cannot be understood anonymously, and that summons me to invest my life with special significance and take responsibility for my existence, is death. To live authentically is to live resolutely within the recognition of one's finitude. My own possibilities are understood in terms of a possibility that in principle cannot be shared. Thus, what we might call self-actualization is a solitary condition. The social relation, if not abandoned, at least plays no role in the process of self-actualization.

For Levinas, on the other hand, the social relation is not constituted by common interests or a shared understanding; autonomy is not understood as a willful separation from this social context. Although we do encounter others in a context of norms, equipment, and an implicit understanding of goals and purposes, there is a deeper aspect to this relation that cannot be understood as a product of these social phenomena. Rather, underlying these social phenomena is an *unmediated* relation between the absolute alterity of the other person and the utter passivity of the self. The concrete, naked presence of another human face, the recognition of otherness—without regard for distinguishing characteristics such as beauty, talent, social role, etc. that would bring the Other into the orbit of a shared understanding—is the foundation of social reality. This relation of self and Other is neither a union of two separate entities nor a separation between two previously joined entities. Contact is not secured by what is shared nor by some process of mediation that links separate entities despite their differences. It is otherness itself, the absolute difference between the self and Other that links self and Other. The Other is what I myself am not; it is precisely this not-being-me that secures my relation with the Other.

Levinas articulates this relationship of alterity in a number of different ways because he argues that it is the very foundation of subjectivity— our openness to the world, the givenness of entities in the world, and the relation of the self to its experiences are all structured by alterity.

Ultimately, he will argue that alterity must be given an ethical interpretation. To see why this is the case, we must first look at these other dimensions of subjectivity.

One way that Levinas explicates this seemingly paradoxical relationship between self and Other is by showing how the erotic relationship is structured by it. *Eros* is not merely an example of a relation that is dependent on alterity, but one that fundamentally defines the relationship between subject and Other. In *eros,* the lover and the beloved desire to be united into one being. This desire can never be satisfied because such a unity is impossible. The lover can never possess the beloved without destroying the basis of the love that exists between them—the freedom and agency of the beloved. It is this failure of possessiveness that makes erotic desire obsessive and inexhaustible. Thus, eros demonstrates that the alterity of the other person is absolute. Even love cannot compromise the otherness of the beloved.

> The relationship does not *ipso facto* neutralize alterity but preserves it. The pathos of voluptuousness lies in the fact of being two. The other as other is not here an object that becomes ours or becomes us; to the contrary, it withdraws into its mystery.[6]

Otherness is only revealed by its hiddenness. It is an unknown that yields nothing of itself except its otherness, which, in denying satiation to the lover, sustains the obsessional desires of erotic love. Sexual difference is the very quality of difference, never yielding its otherness, and thus revealing the irreducible pluralism of reality. It is a relationship that transcends knowledge, that can be recognized only as a mystery.

The significance of Levinas's discussion of social relations as a relationship built on alterity is that it allows us to conceptualize social relations without intermediaries. Unlike Heidegger's notion of Being-with, which makes social relations dependent on mediating terms like everydayness, the ready-to-hand of equipment, or the goals and social roles that constitute facticity, in Levinas's view there is no "third term" that explains how self and Other are related through a shared conception of social reality. Thus, Levinas promises an account that will explain the basis of social relations in the absence of a shared understanding. His discussion of eros is helpful in clarifying the apparently paradoxical notion of a relationship of proximity that is sustained by alterity without mediation. However, it is not yet obvious why *eros* should be taken as the exemplar of social relations in general, nor has my account of Levinas's work made clear why the intimacy of the face-to-face relation must be given an ethical interpretation. In fact, Levinas's remarkable assertion is not merely that this face-to-face relation must have ethical meaning but that its ethical meaning "grounds" subjectivity and cognition, that ethics is prior to truth. The argument for this claim is a rather circuitous one that can be made intelligible only through Levinas's account of the temporality of the passive subject.

Time and the Passive Subject

For Levinas, our openness to the world and our capacity for self-relation are structured by alterity. However, Levinas's account of subjectivity is not based on a theory of intentionality but rather on a nonintentional "experience" of temporality. Traditionally, the experience of time has been understood as a synthesis of protentions and retentions, anticipations of a future linked to memories of the past, all of which are anchored by a subject that experiences itself as the bearer of these moments in the present. These moments of past, present, and future can be made the object of intentional acts that treat all moments as occurring simultaneously with those of the subject. The future is an anticipation of things to come from the point of view of the present. The past is a memory of what once happened represented in the current understanding of a subject, presented as a theme in one's recollection. Yet for Levinas, this notion of time cannot account for the fact that when we encounter another person, we do not meet as contemporaries. The time of the Other is outside the domain of my temporality.

Once again, Levinas will appeal to eros to bring to light the dependence of temporality on alterity. What is significant about eros in connection with time is that in eros, the subject and the Other are confronted with the fact that the beloved—the Other—has its own future. The lover can never possess the beloved because the beloved is always beyond comprehension and always more than what the lover can predict or project. Voluptuousness faces an absolute future that is more than the subject's own future. Thus, the Other makes available to the subject the mystery, unpredictability, and surprise that characterizes our experience of the future. ". . . Love seeks what does not have the structure of an existent, the infinitely future, what is to be engendered."[7]

Levinas refers to the relation between a subject and the future as "fecundity." Because eros produces offspring, the fecundity of time lies in its capacity for infinite renewal. The child represents possibilities forever closed to the parent, thus establishing a relationship with a time wholly unrelated to that of the parent. Eros pardons the subject, releases the subject from the present, by generating a new beginning beyond anything the present offers. Thus, time, conceptualized as the promise of the future, flows from the Other. Despite the fact that a good deal of human activity is occupied with choosing among possibilities already made available by the past, a conception limited to those possibilities misses the sense in which the future is opened up by the possibility of novelty and surprise. The future is not a projection of the subject's powers and capacities but is a subjection to the other, renews without limit, and is therefore an infinite future.[8]

The alterity of the future is made concrete in Levinas's account of death. Unlike Heidegger, who thought of death as the possibility that makes all possibilities available to a finite subject, Levinas views death as the erosion of subjectivity. The future is not something generated by my resolute projection as a being-toward-death. Instead, death is an unknown that comes at me from outside, overwhelming my capacity to act and understand. Death is beyond the range of my possibilities, not a horizon but an alien presence, an utter mystery that comes too soon and unexpectedly. Yet it reveals to me that:

> We are in relation with something that is absolutely other, something bearing alterity not as a provisional determination we can assimilate through enjoyment, but as something whose very existence is made of alterity.[9]

Levinas's account of the future, analyzed through the phenomena of procreation and death, casts doubt on the notion that the future is primarily constituted by possibilities to be appropriated by the subject. This sense of passivity toward the Other that presents itself out of a future that is not mine is deepened by an account of the alterity of the past. Just as the alterity of the Other opens us up to an infinite future beyond our projections, alterity reveals an infinite past beyond memory. The Other presents herself out of a past that is also her own, not mine, and therefore can never be an object of recognition. The past of the Other, as well as the past of the subject, is something that in principle can never be reassembled in memory; despite our best recollections, the past goes by irrevocably. There is a dimension to the past that is opaque to consciousness, for although memory involves bringing the past to presence, this activity of "making present" misses the dimension of time that is irreversible. Despite the fact that we remember episodes from the past, the time that transpired is not recoverable. It is irretrievably lost to consciousness.[10] This dimension of the past that cannot be recovered by consciousness is referred to as the immemorial.

The immemorial never enters experience as the object of an intentional act. Yet Levinas will argue that this thoroughly passive dimension of human existence that can neither be possessed as an object of knowledge by the subject of experience nor controlled by an act of will—nevertheless, it conditions my experience of the world. Although it cannot become an object of knowledge, there are events in one's experience that give rise to intimations of this unrepresented past, that signify this passivity at the heart of subjectivity. The passage of time visited upon the body through the aging process is one such trace of an irrevocable past.

> This duration remains free from the sway of the will, absolutely outside all activity of the ego, and exactly like the ageing process which is probably the perfect model of passive synthesis, a lapse of time no act of remembrance, reconstructing the past, could possibly reverse.[11]

We typically think of time as an active synthesis of moments by a subject who forms a history out of a successive series of "nows" by projecting a future out of its comprehension of the past. The discussion of narrative structure in Chapter Two presupposed this conception of time, but for Levinas this active synthesis is conditioned by a passivity unaffected by any intentional act. The past is not only retained in memory but lapses without the possibility of recovery, passively born rather than experienced.

Thus, we in effect live within two temporal frames—that of retention and protention, giving the illusion of synchrony and simultaneity, and the passive duration of diachronic time that leaves its traces but can never be fully represented. Behind the synthesizing consciousness lies the alterity of an unrepresentable past and an unpredictable future recognizable only by its trace, which Levinas will argue is ultimately the face of the Other.[12]

Thus, time for Levinas is not merely part of the architecture of consciousness, not merely the manner in which objects and events are distributed for consciousness. Time is a dimension that transcends experience and comprehension, beyond being but not the achievement of the social relation; it is only the encounter with the Other that brings into proximity the infinity of past and future.

Thus far, the notion of alterity has been concretely exhibited in a variety of ways. Otherness was discovered in the erotic relation, in the utter mystery of death, in the irretrievable passage of time immemorial, and in the fecundity of the future. Moreover, Levinas has argued that our very openness toward the world and our self-relatedness is "grounded" in this alterity, since the present moment that gathers retentions and protentions to itself is shown to lack subsistence. The pure duration of the immemorial and the utter mystery of the future is discontinuous with that which can be remembered and projected. Yet even if Levinas is correct about the discontinuity of time and the pervasiveness of the relationship with alterity in these concrete experiences, it is not obvious how the givenness of entities is generated by this relationship with alterity. How is the givenness of phenomena generated by that which cannot be described or represented? The notion of grounding here must be understood atypically, since it is not obvious what to make of the claim that phenomena are rationally grounded in something wholly inaccessible to cognition.

The givenness of entities cannot be understood independently of our sensuous immersion in material reality, which in turn must be explained in terms of a relationship with alterity. Levinas understands the sensuous as at bottom a nourishing medium, a medium in which we eat, drink, and gather sustenance. Yet it is the source of nourishment because our capacity for sustenance by sensuous material is conditioned by alterity; that is to say, the objectifying distance required by perception and cognition is grounded in a deeper immersion in the physical world, made possible by proximity. Our immersion in the physical world of sensation and sensuousness—the sense in which we are always "touching" the world without the mediation of thematic recognition—is explained in terms of the way alterity brings the world into proximity. Levinas's account of alterity in *eros*, fecundity, and the immemorial were characterized in each case by an inability of the subject to escape from immersion in sensuousness. Despite the distance of unfamiliarity created by the utter mystery of death, the erotic relation, and the aging process of diachronic time, the trace of the Other reveals the perpetual enclosure of sensuousness in which the human subject is enveloped. Sensuousness cannot be understood as an intentional act, as a correlate of the *noesis/noema* framework, because no sharp demarcation between the sensation and the sensed can be drawn. Prior to the intentional activity that carves the world up into meanings, we are enveloped in a world of sensation graspable only belatedly by cognition, but nevertheless in proximity—in unmediated contact.

The passivity of the immemorial is essential for understanding this unmediated contact. The time of sensation is diachronic, passing without anticipation, independent of memory, utterly surprising in its effects, and

recognizable only belatedly. The fact that we are fully exposed and without the power to suspend or distance ourselves from sensuousness is the
opaque background of sensory experience. Alterity sustains our contact
with the world. Before the world of objects is ready-to-hand, it nourishes
us, sustaining both life and interest.

The Priority of the Ethical Relation

The discussion of Levinas's views on time and eros clarifies the sense in
which subjectivity is grounded in the social relation, for it is our encounter
with others that gives rise to the meaning of time as not our own—as the
infinite future of fecundity and the immemorial past. However, Levinas
argues that all the senses of alterity explicated thus far ultimately take on
ethical meaning, although the foregoing has not shown why the ethical
relation in particular takes priority over other sorts of social relations. The
claim that ethics is prior to truth can be captured in three claims that have
yet to be explicated. (1) The primary trace of the Other is the human face;
(2) the proximity of this face must be understood as an ethical imperative
that imposes a responsibility of infinite dimensions on the subject; and (3)
this moral responsibility grounds subjectivity.

Alterity is made concrete in the face of another human. Although we
often perceive other persons as fellow humans who occupy roles, perform
functions, and satisfy mutual needs within social reality, and although we
can give physical or aesthetic descriptions of others, these are all ways of
looking at another person as an instance of our understanding, as modifi-
cations of ourselves, as actors within the networks of conventions and
norms that constitute a shared social identity. Levinas argues that these
descriptions do not exhaust human relationships. Despite the similarities
we share with others, the face of the Other also expresses something completely alien, other than me and other than all others. It expresses itself as
radical singularity and absolute alterity. It is the face, after all, that indicates the concrete presence of another person, in which the individual
becomes visible, where sensuality is expressed, where diachronic time
most evidently ravages the body, the indicator of our inner states but also
the harbinger of mystery, the locus of inscrutability in which the expectation of understanding is disappointed.

As an expression of absolute alterity and radical singularity, the Other
cannot be grasped by familiar categories and is beyond my capacity for
assimilation or comprehension. The face of the Other confronts me as the

face of a stranger who disrupts my ordinary ways of experiencing the world. Like Levinas's other characterizations of alterity, the face of the Other is the trace of a bond that has already occurred in diachronic time prior to my initiative or comprehension. It is part of the facticity of my existence that I find myself obligated to others, the product of a past that cannot be reconstructed. The face of the Other does not signify the Other's identity but is rather a trace of an inaccessible past.

The meaning of this face and the nature of the disruptive bond is irreducibly ethical. In this inscrutable human face I recognize an appeal, and respond with a physical sensitivity to the claims revealed by the presence of another person. This moral obligation is imposed by way of a command, the content of which is that you are not allowed to kill me; you must accord me a place and the means necessary to live as a human. Prior to any action I might take, I am thoroughly exposed to the Other as moral claimant, and vulnerable to its demands.

> The proximity of the other is the face's meaning. . . . Prior to any particular expression and beneath all particular expressions, which cover over and protect with an immediately adopted face or countenance, there is the nakedness and destitution of the expression as such, that is to say extreme exposure, defenselessness, vulnerability itself.[13]

This suggests that the very fact of another person's existence makes me responsible for my situation and that of the Other person beyond what I can or could have willed or predicted. I am responsible without limit for what occurred before my time and after my death. Thus, I am hostage to the Other; not master of the situation but vulnerable and possibly persecuted. This obligation, according to Levinas, is the basis for all ethics.

Levinas argues that moral obligation is not merely something added on to our experience as a set of values acquired through socialization, nor is it the upshot a process of reasoning or a calculation of interests. We do not comprehend the world about us and then discover that in order to live together we must honor moral obligations. The recognition of obligation is a product of the mere proximity of another person. We find ourselves in a world in which we are already obligated prior to an agreement or contract.[14]

In the face of the Other, all of Levinas's characterizations of alterity come together. The trace of the Other characterized as diachronic time and appearing as the process of aging is understood more fundamentally as the face of the Other. And the passivity of diachronic time, essential to a sensuousness that conditions our cognitive activity, is understood more fundamentally as an accusation, an infinite responsibility that imposes an obligation on me. Thus responsibility is constitutive of subjectivity.

> The consciousness is affected, then, before forming an image of what is coming to it, affected in spite of itself. In these traits we recognize a persecution; being called into question prior to questioning, responsibility over and beyond the logos of response.[15]

When confronted with the vulnerability of the Other, the self-interested, dominating consciousness is placed in question and the Other appears not as an instance of my capacity for understanding but as a genuine Other, incomprehensible to the structures of rational thought. The result of my own constitution being called into question is that I become fearful for the Other. Yet this concern is not a concern added onto or limited by my other concerns. In the face of the Other, I am infinitely responsible beyond all the qualifications and limitations we would normally place on responsibility. This simple confrontation between the self and the Other (without introducing a third or fourth other to complicate matters) implies an unlimited concern for the Other without regard for oneself.

> Responsibility for the Other, for the naked face of the first individual to come along. A responsibility that goes beyond what I may or may not have done to the Other or whatever acts I may or may not have committed, as if I were devoted to the other man before being devoted to myself. Or more exactly, as if I had to answer for the other's death even before *being*. A guiltless responsibility, whereby I am none the less open to an accusation of which no alibi, spatial or temporal, could clear me.[16]

This is an exceedingly strange argument, for nothing that has been said up to this point would appear to entail this burden of responsibility. Although Levinas's phenomenology of time has uncovered the inexorable stream of diachronic time manifested in human corporeality, nothing in this analysis demands that subjectivity's dependence on a time before and after the time of the subject be understood in terms of the bond of an infinite moral responsibility.

Method or Grace?

Among the many meanings of alterity, it is not yet obvious why the ethical interpretation is forced on us. This simply raises the question of whether demonstration is the point of Levinas's analysis. Levinas's way of proceeding usually suggests a transcendental argument in which the conditions of subjectivity are systematically laid out according to the disclosedness of the phenomenon in question. However, as a series of deductions, Levinas's arguments seldom demonstrate the logical steps required for that sort of necessity. Moreover, to rely solely on such a systematic approach to demonstrating the necessity of ethics would appear to be incompatible with Levinas's project. To express a meaning that transcends all experience, that is other than Being, Levinas must indicate a presence that is neither a phenomenon nor a product of cognition. It must, by definition, resist logical or intuitive demonstration. Levinas seeks to discover the ethical imperative prior to the emergence of a constituted world—an irrecoverable past. Thus, any attempt to systematically represent ethics as the origin of subjectivity will necessarily be self-refuting. Of course, the refusal to produce a systematic demonstration of alterity begs the question of why we should be compelled by these controversial and highly questionable claims. The issue of how one philosophically justifies an implication of something inherently nondemonstrable has increasingly come to preoccupy Levinas, especially in *Otherwise Than Being or Beyond Essence*. It is an issue of enormous complexity that cannot receive adequate treatment here. However, in the course of showing the significance of Levinas's work on this question of universal moral agency, it is incumbent to say something about why we ought to be convinced by Levinas although this will fall short of a comprehensive defense.

In fact, Levinas does not thoroughly abandon conceptual analysis, for one could argue that he is engaged in the process of spelling out the implications of the concept of infinity. Conscious experience presupposes a relation to something not given as a phenomenon—a relation to the irreducibly Other that cannot be constituted or comprehended by the subject, available only by virtue of the traces it leaves behind in experience. Yet this Other is not "nothing," not a mere absence posited by dialectical necessity nor a limit concept that invokes skepticism. The idea of the Other does not correspond to its object because the object *surpasses* or *overflows* our capacity for representation. This means consciousness is a relationship with the infinite, for the idea of the infinite is an idea of an object that cannot be represented by finite consciousness. The Other resists incorporation into an intelligible horizon, cannot be reduced to a mere instance of a concept or category but rather exceeds our rational categories and is thus without limit. There are, therefore, rational grounds for identifying the Other with the infinite.

The consequences of this identification are extraordinary for Levinas's argument, especially when coupled with the claim that opens *Totality and Infinity*—that the relation between I and the Other is best characterized as a *desire* with infinite dimensions. The first section of *Totality and Infinity* is entitled "Desire for the Invisible." The section begins with the comment that:

> "The true life is absent." But we are in the world. Metaphysics arises and is maintained in this alibi. It is turned toward the "elsewhere" and the "otherwise" and the "other." For in the most general form it has assumed in the history of thought it appears as a movement going forth from a world that is familiar to us . . . toward an alien outside-of-oneself, toward a yonder.[17]

That metaphysics has sought a perspective transcending the familiar is not a surprising or novel thesis. Neither is the thesis that humankind seeks a meaning beyond the human. What is important in Levinas's characterization is that the "yonder" desired can never be glimpsed, let alone occupied. It can in principle never become familiar, despite our enthusiastic attentiveness.

> The metaphysical desire does not long to return, for it is desire for a land not of our birth, for a land foreign to every nature, which has not been our fatherland and to which we shall never betake ourselves. . . . The metaphysical desire has another intention; it desires beyond everything that can simply complete it. It is like goodness— the Desired does not fulfill it, but deepens it.[18]

The relationship between I and the Other is not only a relationship with the infinite but is best characterized as a desire. Because it is a relationship with the infinite, it has the structure of a desire. The infinite Other can never be grasped without being destroyed, just as the object of desire can never be possessed without extinguishing that desire. Proximity only increases the sense of absence at the heart of desire. Thus, it is the distance of what is sought in metaphysical desire, the invisibility of what is aimed at, its infinite dimension that nourishes and sustains that desire.

As a characterization of the religious or philosophical impulse, this notion of metaphysical desire is not implausible. It is precisely the deepening of the mystery of God or nature at which religion and philosophy respectively aim. However, Levinas adds a significant twist to this desire for transcendence; it does not take us beyond the human at all. Levinas argues that the most fundamental characterization of metaphysical desire is something thoroughly human—the ethical relation to the Other.

The fundamental question on which this chapter turns is, "Why must transcendence take on an ethical interpretation?" Even if Levinas has established the significance of alterity, why does it impose a moral obligation on me?

The capacity to act without considering one's self-interest is implicit in the subjection of consciousness to alterity. Recall that, for Levinas, cognition as it is commonly understood is a matter of making reality conform to the networks of identification already constitutive of the self. He shows that it is as passive subject, open to the immemorial, the fecundity of the future, and sensuousness, that we experience reality by resisting the identification of the self with reality. To give of oneself, to give one's life or sustenance without expectation of reward, is the most profound expression of this resistance to a possessive, grasping ego. For Levinas, the meaning of the ethical relation is that it exsists in this capacity to transcend any moment, to resist any completion, to oppose what is with a future of infinite renewal and a past of infinite obligation. To resist naked self-interest is the practical expression of the resistance to the discovery of the Same in the Other. To the extent that my experience of reality is conditioned by my actions, I only fully experience reality through the ethical relation.

The burden of ethics, then, is to express in our conduct this capacity for resistance and transcendence, which ultimately boils down to acting on the value of love without reward. When we act independently of our self-interest, when we give without expectation of return, the human capacity for transcendence is given expression in concrete human experience. Ethics, although not dependent on religious faith, is akin to it—a gratuitous appeal.

The ethical event of "expiation for another" is the concrete situation designated by the verb *to not-be*. It is by the condition of the hostage that there can be pity, compassion, pardon and proximity in the world—even the little that there is.[19]

Once the centrality of preserving the capacity for transcendence is acknowledged, and the relation with the Other understood as a relation to the infinite, Levinas's claims regarding the burden of infinite responsibility become more plausible. The disruptive force of metaphysical desire places exorbitant constraints on my capacity to satisfy ordinary desires. I cannot limit in advance the claims the Other makes on me by invoking my understanding of it in specifying excusing conditions that limit responsibility. The Other's nature and my own responsibility for questioning will always exceed that understanding.

The face of the Other calls into question not the existence of the subject but the very right to say "I," because I must perpetually keep open the question of what justifies my existence in the face of this burdensome responsibility.

> My being-in-the-world or my "place in the sun", my being at home, have these not also been the usurpation of spaces belonging to the other man whom I have already oppressed or starved, or driven out into a third world; are they not acts of repulsing, excluding, exiling, stripping, killing?[20]

The very meaning of "beyond being" is to ask myself if my mere existence prior to any action I've taken has denied something to someone else. This question of one's right to be appeals to no law or principle but simply to the infinite dimensions of one's responsibility. The Other is never given in experience but is a perpetual questioning, and as such there can be no limit to the scope of responsibility.

Moreover, it is the infinite claim of responsibility that constitutes me as a *unique* individual. The shock provoked by the face of the Other is that I have been delivered to the Other prior to my agreement in an infinite past, that the source of obligation has already passed away, the recognition of responsibility belated. Being accused in the immemorial past by the Other guarantees that one is not just one person among others. For me to accept *infinite* responsibility for the other is to do what no one else can do in my place.

> In the face of the other man I am inescapably responsible and consequently the unique and chosen one. By this freedom, humanity in me (*moi*)—that is, humanity as me—signifies, in spite of its

ontological contingence of finitude and mortality, the anteriority and uniqueness of the non-*interchangeable*.[21]

I am the only one summoned because only I can accept this responsibility despite my innocence. Such an extreme responsibility cannot be demanded of another without a gross injustice. Thus, I am irreplaceable and unique as one summoned and elected. Moreover, because only this infinite responsibility will individuate me, I can only be fully constituted as a subject of experience through the acceptance of this responsibility.

One way of understanding Levinas's argument is that it has primarily a metaethical significance. It shows how ethics is possible, shows why, if I'm committed to following the logic of the infinite, I cannot avoid the burden of obligation, for any attempt to limit responsibility will be arbitrary. Yet Levinas clearly intends more than this, for he argues that we are already seized by this infinite responsibility prior to cognition, prior to choosing possibilities or courses of action, not as a possibility but as something accomplished. Moreover, he claims that we find ourselves in a sensuous medium, the immediacy of which presupposes the ethical relation as if we could not imagine perceiving objects in the world without acknowledging the ethical relation. This move to ground subjectivity in the appeal for support of the Other, in the face that betokens an infinite responsibility, is less than compelling, it is not obvious why the specifically ethical interpretation of alterity *must* condition our openness to the world and our self-relation. More importantly, as one of Levinas's recent interviewers put it "... if the commandment is absolute, how can people act unethically?" Levinas's response, in part, is as follows:

It is in the human being that a rupture is produced with being's own law, with the law of being. The law of evil is the law of being. Evil is, in this sense, very powerful. Consequently, it is the unique force. Authority is a paradox. Both authority and morality are paradoxes.[22]

It is central to Levinas's view that Being which discloses itself to be known is dominated by the struggle for survival in an economy of needs and satisfactions that often degenerates into a Hobbesian world of all against all. The comprehension of being results in a totalizing system in which the synthesizing consciousness seeks a unity that establishes the other as one's own, thereby obscuring our dependence on alterity and submerging ethics in egoism.

But to be human is to be capable of a response to such a condition—to "be" otherwise than being.

There is a moment where the idea of freedom prevails—it is a moment of generosity. Here there is a moment where someone plays without winning. That is Charity. . . . It is gratuitous, a gratuitous act.[23]

At this point the attempt to view Levinas's argument as a transcendental argument breaks down. Such a moment cannot have a logically rigorous rationale, for the sort of necessity involved in logic would be a form of coercion inimical to the gratuitous character of ethics. "The face is not a force. It is an authority. Authority is often without force."[24]

Levinas concludes "Desire for the Invisible" with the following:

Demented pretension to the invisible, when the acute experience of the human in the twentieth century teaches that the thoughts of men are borne by needs which explain society and history, that hunger and fear can prevail over every human resistance and every freedom! There is no question of doubting this human misery, this dominion the things and the wicked exercise over man, this animality. But to be a man is to know that this is so. Freedom consists in knowing that freedom is in peril. But to know or to be conscious is to have time to avoid and forestall the instant of inhumanity. It is this perpetual postponing of the hour of treason—infinitesimal difference between man and non-man—that implies the disinterestedness of goodness, the desire of the absolutely other or nobility, the dimension of metaphysics.[25]

In this passage the disinterestedness of genuine moral conduct is implied by the awareness of humanity's peril. In recognizing the hegemony of hunger and fear—and thus in the absence of any meaningful conceptualization of a state of goodness—I must also recognize that ethics places extraordinary demands on me. If hunger and fear can prevail over every human resistance and every freedom, if we are continually threatened by the hegemony of evil, then at the moment of confrontation and summons the possibility of ethics rests solely on my shoulders, for I cannot depend on the natural responses of others.

Passages such as this suggest that Levinas's argument proceeds from two directions. On the one hand, Levinas proceeds as a phenomenologist seeking to ground subjectivity in our sensuous contact with the world, which ultimately rests on the various dimensions of alterity explicated above. On the other hand, he proceeds from observations concerning human history "after Auschwitz," noting the hegemony of evil, the perpetual peril of humanity, and both the infinite desire for the good and the invisibility of ethics in human history. This suggests a different kind of argument drawing its persuasive force from a perspicuous characterization of the human condition. It may be that these two approaches, from the standpoint of methodology, never join. Ultimately, for Levinas, ethics demands that we dispense with theory and simply respond to human need. The priority of the ethical relation is not something that can be logically demonstrated any more than the priority of truth can be argued for without circularity. Rather, the priority of ethics is something to be simply acknowledged, a gratuitous appeal.

It might, therefore, be prudent to take the vocabulary of "priority" and "ground" as a misleading holdover from the phenomenological background of Levinas's intellectual biography. Ethics as the locus of ultimate concern is not to be deduced by philosophical argument, but held out as the stakes of human history and admired for its significance in the face of its scarcity.

To be human is to act on the possibility of goodness while recognizing the alterity of goodness in the face of the hegemony of evil, to uphold its claim despite the pervasiveness of hunger and fear. Paradoxically, to "postpone the hour of treason" against humanity, we must acknowledge how genuinely alien and unfamiliar goodness is. Ethics begins with the recognition that "the true life is absent," as represented in the logical gap between "ought" statements and "is" statements. Yet it also requires the recognition that the "true life" is forever beyond our reach, that our humanity is always imperiled, for only this recognition preserves our capacity to resist complicity with the dominion of evil. Levinas's thought thus hovers between skepticism and idealism, because in his view the tension between the invisibility of ethics and the excellence of ethics defines what it means to be human. It is no accident that at the pinnacle of human progress we seek, but cannot find the antidote to human violence. It is just this tension between our desire for peace and our incapacity to conceptualize it that situates the gratuitous appeal of ethics.

For my purposes here, what Levinas achieves is a glimpse of what ethics must be like if it is to escape the pitfalls of both abstract universalism and concrete ethics. Levinasian ethics is noneschatological, finding freedom only in the resistance offered by this gratuitous appeal. Only a moral point of view that allows grace to guide its judgments can protect itself from the debilitating effects of contrast judgments and expressivism.

None of this sounds very plausible if we think of Levinas as providing a justification for some particular set of moral principles or an answer to the moral skeptic. However, as Steven Smith notes in commenting on Levinas's methodology,

> Ethics is only an "optics" by a very strained analogy, for ethics does not present an object to vision or intuition, or demonstrate the conclusion of an argument, but rather makes a gratuitous *appeal*. The value of the human is always refutable. Ethics cannot vanquish its sceptic, Cain, who does not obey "the gleam of exteriority" in the Other's face.[26]

For Levinas, ethics is fundamentally a gift born by pure resistance to the hegemony of the ego, and only derivatively a set of principles or guidelines to follow. However, what Levinas must demonstrate is that ethics can signify the extreme alterity of the Other without reduction to a mere concept. For Levinas, ideas are ultimately not traced to their ground but rather advance toward their superlative; only such a progression demonstrates the capacity for transcendence that Levinas seeks. Thus, the proximity of the Other becomes responsibility for the Other, which in turn becomes substitution for the Other. What Levinas needs to show is not that I must be committed to a moral point of view due to threat of irrationality or disloyalty. Rather, he must show that I cannot remain oriented toward the Other while rejecting its claim that ethical relations can impose this *infinite* obligation on me, and hence deserve the claim to be "beyond being." In short, he must show that ethics is the sort of thing to which our attachment can plausibly be construed as a metaphysical desire resisting the tendency to draw boundaries that fall back on comprehension and understanding. I return to Levinas's conception of ethics in the next chapter in order to fill out the conception of moral obligation at work here. However, I widen the inquiry here by placing it more firmly in a sociohistorical context.

One obstacle to sustaining the infinite appeal of the Other is the presence of "the third man," the "neighbor of my neighbor." The introduction of other people divides my responsibility, cancels the asymmetry of one-for-the-other, and raises questions of distributive justice and social organization that the face-to-face relation cannot address and that seems to require the calculation and balancing of interests inimical to ethics as Levinas has construed it. I now turn to Lyotard's attempt to employ Levinas in the context of the social condition of postmodernity.

7

Welcome Stranger:
Toward a Postmodern Ethics

The work of Emmanuel Levinas promises a moral point of view that explains the capacity to recognize the needs and interests of the radically Other. Levinas, however, understands this capacity in terms of the obligation imposed by the presence of another person, without sufficiently clarifying how such a relationship is related to the larger social and political context involving multiple relationships and conflicting obligations. Jean-Francois Lyotard explicitly takes up this issue, placing it in the context of the social conditions of postmodernity. In the process, I shall argue, Lyotard provides us with an explanatory framework for understanding the correlation between moral blindness and the question of social identity, and suggests a promising approach to the problem of universal moral agency in the social and political sphere.

Lyotard advocates an antitheory position that denies the relevance of self-representation for purposes of moral reflection, insisting instead on a sharp distinction between descriptive and prescriptive discourse.[1] I argue that in preserving this distinction, Lyotard's conception of "justice without criteria" avoids the problems of concrete ethics, and yields a notion of obligation and a conception of universal moral agency without appeal to foundations or solidarity.

The Condition of Postmodernity

In his influential work *The Postmodern Condition: A Report on Knowledge*, Lyotard claims that the grand historical narratives around which

161

Western Civilization has been organized since the Enlightenment have lost their credibility.[2] The popular Enlightenment narratives that anticipated unlimited prosperity and political freedom for all through the practical application of scientific knowledge have failed to deliver on their promise. Furthermore, the philosophical accounts traceable to Kant and Hegel "such as the dialectics of Spirit, the hermeneutics of meaning, the emancipation of the rational or working subject, or the creation of wealth" that gave legitimacy to these ideas by telling a sweeping historical narrative about how history will progress have lost their credibility, and no longer govern our lives.[3] This condition of "incredulity toward metanarratives" Lyotard calls "postmodernism".[4]

In the wake of their breakdown, and accelerated by advances in communication technologies that have resulted in making knowledge a commodity, traditional sources of value such as "nation-states, parties, professions, institutions, and historical traditions" no longer function as reservoirs of the cumulation of knowledge, and are "losing their attraction."[5] Consequently, the social bond is no longer constituted by those traditional sources of value, but instead is constituted by the fabric of relations established by the locations one occupies within circuits of communication as receivers, senders, and referents of messages. The language game is the minimum bond upon which society rests, and is the unit of social analysis.

The Archipelago

Given this change in the nature of the subject of knowledge, Lyotard analyzes relationships between members of a group in terms of the pragmatics of their utterances—the perlocutionary effects of language in use.[6] The dominant insight in Lyotard's conception of language is that utterances tend to group themselves around an implicit goal or purpose, which along with the strategies for achieving this goal constitutes a "genre" or language game.[7] Social reality is likened, by Lyotard, to an "archipelago"; autonomous "islands" of utterances, each congealed around strategic and constitutive norms that govern intelligibility.[8] Lyotard's vision of social reality is that of a fractured world composed of numerous incommensurable language games, each with their own goals and rules that govern discourse and action.

This picture of social reality as an "archipelago" of autonomous language games leads to a significantly transformed conception of social identity. Instead of viewing the social bond as a shared identity in terms of which conflicts can be resolved through the forging of consensus, "otherness," in Lyotard's view, appears to be a constitutive feature of the social bond. Language games are a source of intractable conflict, competing for hegemony in an "agon" of incompatible goals.

What is interesting is that a by-product of successful linguistic representation is almost invariably the suppression of something else that cannot be represented in the successful idiom. Such conflict Lyotard dubs a "differend," defined as follows.

> As distinguished from a litigation, a differend would be a case of conflict, between (at least) two parties, that cannot be equitably resolved for lack of a rule of judgment applicable to both arguments. . . . Damages result from an injury which is inflicted upon the rules of a genre of discourse but which is reparable according to those rules. A wrong results from the fact that the rules of the genre of discourse by which one judges are not those of the judged genre or genres of discourse.[9]

A "wrong" in Lyotard's specialized use of the term is a damage, the occurrence of which the agent cannot prove for lack of the appropriate idiom in which to express it.

Lyotard is apparently committed to the view that differends are a component in all language, and thus take a multiplicity of forms. This claim is insufficiently defended in Lyotard's work, but this will not concern me here. He continually returns to a single example of a differend that he takes to be especially pernicious, and which will cast considerable light on the problem of representing the needs and interests of the radically Other. The source of this differend is the inappropriate application of the cognitive or descriptive language game to situations that demand prescriptive phrase regimes.[10] Lyotard will argue that this confusion of the descriptive with the prescriptive is characteristic of the ethical genre, and is the source of the differend to which ethics continually succumbs.

Perhaps the central element in Lyotard's recent work is his defense of the Kantian notion that a statement of obligation (which includes a prescriptive) must be, in some sense or other, disconnected from the cognitive capacities through which we understand the world. This claim was prominent in Levinas's view of ethics, and Lyotard attempts to translate both the work of Kant and Levinas into his preferred idiom of pragmatics. Lyotard makes the familiar point that a prescription cannot be deduced from a description. Yet he also claims that the attempt to

perform such a deduction issues in a form of blindness that he explicates
by translating Kant's notion of a transcendental illusion into the language
of pragmatics.[11]

> The fact that two million people are unemployed in a country does
> not explain that the unemployment must be remedied. For this to
> take place, a minor premise must be understood or presupposed;
> namely, the prescription that all those who can work ought to work.
> The blindness or transcendental illusion resides in the pretension to
> found the good or the just upon the true, or what ought to be upon
> what is.[12]

A prescription to take a particular action presupposes a suppressed
premise—in this case, that all those who can work should work—which
would require for its justification a model of a just society, the existence of
which cannot be confirmed or verified according to the regime of cognitive
phrases. Lyotard's central claim, most clearly articulated in an article entitled "Levinas' Logic," is that a certain subset of prescriptions—namely
"demands, pleas, orders, wishes, prohibitions"—differ from other forms of
speech acts such that any attempt to make the satisfaction of this class of
prescriptions dependent on these other speech acts undermines the
action-guiding force of the prescription.[13] I will call this class of prescriptions "Lyotardian prescriptions," for reasons that will be apparent shortly.

Three features of this subclass of prescriptions support its autonomous
status. First is that a "Lyotardian prescription" only requires of the
addressee that he or she bring about a state of affairs—that the command
or request be executed. Thus, there is an asymmetrical relationship
between addressor and addressee, for only the addressee is receiving a
directive. However, if the addressee feels compelled to comment on the
prescription, to form denotative statements in order to evaluate the extent
to which it satisfies truth conditions, for instance, he or she would place
the prescription in a commentary that transforms it into a quotation or
report of itself. In the process, the addressee becomes an addressor, someone compelled to argue or analyze rather than act. This transformation
will neutralize the action-guiding force of the prescriptive (the sense that
what is called for is the immediate satisfaction of the prescription), for the
conditions that would satisfy the commentary are no longer simply that
of bringing about a state of affairs. Any attempt to make these prescriptions subject to the satisfaction of truth conditions will require a second
discourse with the first as its referent, a discourse that must now sort out

questions of reality and truth, etc. In the terminology of Lyotard's pragmatics, the addressee of the prescription becomes an addressor—someone who is no longer immediately obligated. According to Lyotard, this
cancels the asymmetry between addressor and addressee in a prescription, thus sustaining the privilege of the subject of knowledge. Second, the
primary function of prescriptives is referential rather than denotative.
They usually do not serve as a symbol for or a name of something.
Instead, prescriptives refer to an immediate situation. The force of the
prescription depends on it being appropriate to the current perlocutionary situation, for it is the perlocutionary situation itself that indicates the
prescription can be executed, that disambiguates the references in the
statement, thereby preserving its prescriptive force. Thus, "close the door"
has prescriptive force to the extent "the door" is understood as "the door
of which I am speaking and of which you know; this one here. . . ."[14]
Commands typically are action-guiding only to the extent they make
reference to the current situation.

Third, these prescriptions refer to a state of affairs that does not yet
exist; once the prescribed state of affairs is brought about, the statement
loses all prescriptive force. Once the door is closed, "close the door" is no
longer action-guiding. Thus, prescriptives are "never true in the sense of
conforming to that of which they speak, for they either anticipate when
the reference is not correct or they must not be correct when the reference is."[15] There is nothing literally "in reality" at the time of utterance to
which the prescriptive conforms. Members of this particular class of
prescriptives can only have the value of a prescriptive at the time of their
utterance.

Clearly, not all prescriptive utterances will satisfy these conditions.
Normative statements like "people should avoid cruelty to animals" or
general prescriptions like "we should exercise more often" do not have the
immediacy of the prescriptions that interest Lyotard, which is why I treat
"Lyotardian prescriptions" as a subclass. Normative statements are, in fact,
not prescriptions at all in Lyotard's view, a point I will discuss next.

The properties of this subclass of prescriptives suggest that according
to the internal rules of prescriptives, they have their own authority. Their
action-guiding force is independent of any further discourse or commentary that would have the original prescriptive as its referent. Furthermore,
this analysis suggests that any attempt to determine their authority by
submitting them to a second-order discourse will undermine their action-
guiding force. Importantly, not all prescriptives have this sort of autonomy, for some are intended to invite commentary—especially those that

appeal to a general code or institution, the authority of which might be
derived from past statements. However, general norms cannot have the
status of a genuine prescription.

> Injustice cannot be detected by any constant signs; on the contrary,
> to have recourse to the constancy of would-be clear signs, to the arti-
> cles of the code, to established institutions, recourse to the *letter* as
> that which allows the just to be separated from the unjust—that is
> unjust. The criterion [of justice] "exists" but cannot be the object of
> omni-temporal discourse.[16]

For Lyotard, any prescription transcribed into a meta-language quoting
that prescription "passes under the legislation of truth functions and loses
the remarkable properties that it had in the natural language."[17]

What is the case for this subclass of prescriptives is the case *a fortiori*
for the prescriptive that imposes an obligation. It follows from the nature
of prescriptions that when the source of the obligation (the addressor) and
the meaning of the law in question become objects of discussion, when
the prescription is quoted within a discourse with stakes other than that
of satisfying the prescription, it loses its power to obligate.[18]

With this analysis of prescription, Lyotard has rendered some of
Levinas's views on obligation into the language of pragmatics. In the
course of this translation, we are given additional reasons for endorsing
Levinas's view that ethics is opposed to the realm of cognitive discourse.
Evidence for the immediacy of the ethical relation is found by Lyotard in
the distinctive rules that govern the language game of prescription. It is
the immediacy of the ethical relation—prior to any commentary or quotation—that accounts for its action-guiding force. Moreover, in describing
the distinctive qualities of prescriptions, Lyotard comes to the same
remarkable conclusion as Levinas. The addressor of a prescription must
be unknown—what he ironically calls the "Unnameable."

Lyotard's analysis of prescriptives is relevant to the issues under
discussion in this book. Although the issue is more complex than I have
indicated thus far, I want to claim that a moral point of view primarily
concerned with understanding one's immediate social world, as is the
case with concrete ethics, requires the assimilation of prescriptives to
descriptives. Placing the addressee of a prescription in the addressor role
by introducing a commentary on the source of obligation makes ethics
dependent on the subject that must grasp his own nature and make social
reality known before acting. As I have been arguing, this dependence on

self-representation is an obstacle to the attribution of universal moral agency. If Lyotard is right, then he provides us with at least the beginnings of a general framework for understanding the failure of concrete ethics to provide an account of universal moral agency—in canceling the immediacy of the ethical relation through commentary.[19]

Lyotard and Levinas seem to be in agreement at least on the question of the immediacy of moral obligation. But whereas Levinas is addressing a metaethical question about the meaning of ethics that conditions what we ordinarily take to be ethical discourse, Lyotard would appear to be taking a more radical step outside any ethical discourse at all. Lyotard is suggesting that any discourse questioning authority or seeking to define the source of an obligation is no longer obligating. Lyotard draws a stark and unbreachable barrier between ethical *discourse* and action-guidedness that seems incapable of explaining why we engage in the practice of giving reasons for our actions at all.[20] In the absence of any concern for justification, what are the constraints on moral conduct? Is anything permitted as long as the call of conscience is purified of descriptive elements? Even if we were to accept the claim that there is a certain immediacy to the call of conscience, one wonders why, despite the temporary suspension of action-guidedness, it cannot be in force once understanding has been achieved. Why do an understanding of the source and reasons for a moral claim not strengthen the obligation? Lyotard seems to claim that the recognition to which I am obligated is independent of the question of who authorizes the obligation and why I am so obligated.

However, Lyotard's point is not that these questions are uninteresting or irrelevant but that they cannot be answered by a commentary. When I, as the addressee of an obligation, engage in discourse about the obligation, something essential to the claimant, the addressor, is lost. I now become the addressor and the role of claimant disappears. "The I effaces the you."[21] Lyotard refers to this as a kind of blindness.

> The blindness is in putting yourself in the place of the other, in saying *I* in his or her place, in neutralizing his or her transcendence.[22]

The transcendence of the Other—the infinite dimension of the obligation in Levinas's terms—is neutralized when obligation is subject to discourse. The otherness of the Other is canceled, although the villain for Lyotard is not just ontology but any language game that need quote the prescription (i.e. mention within a commentary). With respect to this question of preserving the "otherness" of the Other, we would do well to keep in mind that morality, for Kant, was a matter of treating others as the bearer of independent ends, never as a means to our own ends. A similar notion is at work here, albeit with a significant twist, for the implication is that I cannot engage in cognitive discourse or commentary without interposing my own ends, a result that Kant would not have welcomed.

There is, however, a suggestion that this unfortunate impasse between the cognitive and prescriptive can be resolved. This is because as much as Levinas and Lyotard agree on the nature of obligation, Lyotard is less inclined to view the Same and the Other as permanent metaphysical categories. The conflating of descriptive and prescriptive discourse, and the consequent loss of the power to obligate, gives rise to a differend that precludes a clear statement of what it means to treat someone as an end. Yet differends always leave the door open to resolution.

> The differend is the unstable state and instant of language wherein something which must be able to be put into phrases cannot yet be. This state includes silence, which is a negative phrase, but it also calls upon phrases which are in principle possible. This state is signaled by what one ordinarily calls feeling: One cannot find the words: etc. A lot of searching must be done to find new rules for forming and linking phrases that are able to express the differend disclosed by the feeling. . . .[23]

How does one work through a differend without commentary? The same questions that arose with respect to Levinas in the previous chapter arise with Lyotard's position. What sort of accessibility and understanding is involved? How can we come to recognize as a moral claim something that cannot be meaningfully expressed within current linguistic practice? To make clear the difficulty with the practice of giving reasons and the role of the understanding in neutralizing the otherness of the Other, we need to pursue what Lyotard thinks of the practice of justification in general.

Lyotard assigns the problem of authority to the normative phrase regime. With this discussion of norms, Lyotard's conception of the social and political realm begins to emerge. In the course of this discussion, Lyotard's connection to my conclusions regarding narrative, expressivism, and contrast judgments will also be clarified.

It is through the appeal to moral and social norms that we typically justify our actions and our social institutions. However, although normative discourse refers to codes and conventions that are not immediately obligating, the normative phrase is not descriptive because its aim is not truth but justice. Nevertheless, it shares one feature with descriptions: It quotes the prescriptive phrase, thereby functioning as a meta-language with the following form: *It is a norm decreed by (y) that "(x) ought to carry out such and such an action. . . ."*[24] In the normative phrase, the threat constituted by the absence of authority in the prescriptive is "normalized" and forms the basis of community.

> The normative, excluded as it is from the ethical, leads into the polit-
> ical. It constitutes a community of addressees of the prescriptive,
> who qua addressees of the normative, are advised that they are, if
> not necessarily equal before the law, at least all subject to the law.[25]

Thus, the role of the normative is to subject heterogeneous phrases to a system of permissions and prohibitions guided by the aim of justice. It accomplishes this task, in Lyotard's terminology, by the "fusion of the addressee of the prescriptive with the addressee of the normative."[26] The person who is obligated is also subject to the law.

However, like all such attempts to reduce the heterogeneity of phrase regimes, this attempt to answer the question of authority by appeal to the normative phrase is unstable and is itself the source of differends. The difficulty arises because the question of authority and legitimacy can only be answered by the normative phrase if (y), the legislator of the law, in fact has the authority to prescribe to (x), the person subject to the law and thus obligated. However, the mere linking of these two phrases does not establish such an authority because of the differences in the two phrase regimes. Normative phrases are like performatives in that their formulation entails their legitimacy. The phrase universe is centered on the addressor instance, which functions as a legislator. Yet as I noted previously, the question of authority is left open in the prescriptive phrase. Therefore, it is not obvious why the addressee of the prescription is obligated by the addressor of the norm.

There are a number of solutions to this problem, the most familiar to us being that of a constitutional democracy formulated on the Republican principle of autonomy. Under the Republican constitution ". . . the addressor of the norm, y, and the addressee of the prescription, x, are the same . . . the obligated one is able to promulgate the law that obligates him or her."[27] The names (x) and (y) are thus designated by a collective "we" (as in "French citizens"), which masks the fact that the constituents of this "we" take different elements of the phrase universe in order to be central. The authority of the normative phrase is unstable because the phrase

regimes each maintain their distinct characteristics. "You ought to" cannot
be derived from "I declare," in part because although the prescriptive
would situate (x) and (y) on the addressee instance, the normative would
situate (x) and (y) on the addressor instance as a metaprescriptive
comment on the prescription, once again undermining the distinctive
characteristics of an obligation. In other words, prescriptives obligate
immediately, while normative phrases obligate by mediating the prescriptive with the assertion of authority. Because the two phrase regimes
function differently, any attempt to join them is continually threatened.
Employing the pronoun "we" merely creates the transcendental illusion
that the one who speaks the law and the one to whom the law applies are
identical. On these grounds, the notion of a social contract to which citizens have implicitly agreed and must recognize as binding is not credible.
The source of the illusion is that "I" and "you" will be deployed in particular contexts in which the persistence of a "we" cannot be maintained.

> It is not surprising that, in the "currentness" or "actuality" of obliga-
> tion, the we that reputedly unites obligee and legislator is threat-
> ened with being split.[28]

The implication is that collective identities are always threatened with
disruption by the peculiar nature of prescriptives that obligate immediately and need not take the question of collective identities seriously. It is
evident, then, that Lyotard wants to redescribe Kant's distinction between
merely acting in accordance with a moral principle, in this case a norm,
and acting out of a genuinely moral motive—in this case, the immediate
response to particularity.

The question of authority is not solved merely by invoking the normative phrase. However, in the course of history Lyotard argues that, in fact,
it is the deployment of the narrative genre that reinforces the authority of
normative discourse by imposing its own stakes and strategies. In the
battle over the hegemony of phrases, it turns out that the narrative genre
is most effective in covering over the differends and perpetuating the illusion of the collective "we," a claim that Lyotard was presupposing in his
account of the postmodern condition.

There are, in fact, two kinds of narratives that Lyotard describes, which
link on the question of authority in the following way. As I said before,
the normative phrase generates a phrase universe in which the addressee
is the addressee of the prescriptive phrase. Yet it also has, as its addressee,
any third party (z) that must deal with (y)'s authority.

The gap between the normative prefix and the prescription creates the gap between the community of the obligated and whatever is outside this community but which should also be made aware of the law.[29]

The identification of (x) and (y) as constituents of a collective "we" in contrast to (z) is dependent on (x) and (y) being designated by a proper name, e.g. "the French." This contrast tends to take two forms, each of which constitute the linking of the normative phrase with the narrative genre.

In the first case, it is assumed that (z) can be included within this collective "we"—that all addressees of the normative can be addressees of the prescriptive. This requires that the proper name be absorbed into the idea of humanity, a process that Lyotard describes through an explication of the "Declaration of the Rights of Man of 1789." This form of narrative takes up the questions of "What ought we to be?" and "What must we do to be that?" by placing them within the context of a redemptive future, thus transforming the stories of particular cultures and nations into the story of man—"the great story of history which has as its end the extinction of names (particularisms)."[30] Such a teleological narrative covers up the differend by transforming the particularity of the past in light of an anticipated future.[31]

On the one hand, narrative recounts a differend or differends and imposes an end on it or them, a completion which is also its own term. . . . Wherever in diegetic time it stops, its term makes sense and retroactively organizes the recounted events. The narrative function is redeeming in itself. . . . On the other hand, the unleashing . . . of the now is domesticated by the recurrence of the before/after. . . . It "swallows up" the event and the differends carried along by the event. Narratives drive the event back to the border.[32]

Retrospective accounts of the past and projections of the future that form the basis of a story about human progress prevent the articulation of human events that find no place in this story, and also suppress the immediacy of obligation silently intimated by the differend.

In the second case, mythic narrative (z) is treated as irrevocably other and eliminable. The name of the nation, tribe, or clan is continually repeated in narratives of origin that Lyotard explicates through an analysis of Cashinahua legends, although the Aryan myth employed by the Nazis serves as an example *in extremis*.[33] The distinction characteristic of this mode of narrative organization is its repetitive, circular self-affirmation. It marks the community of addressors (storytellers), addressees (listeners), and referents (heroes) as exclusive and as substitutable. The narrator has the authority to tell the story because it was told to him and because he, as bearer of the name given to him by that social group, has been named as a referent in accordance with the story. There is no original speaker nor final word because preceding narrations are not incorporated into the story in light of a redemptive future. In this case, the question of what one ought to be never arises explicitly because its answer is given by the name. "We ought to be what we are, which is Cashinahua."[34] Once again, the claims of the Other are extinguished, this time by the circular rhythm of the narrative that cements the collective identity through the story, and the names that authorize its telling.

Thus, Lyotard explains the social bond in terms of the linking of pre- scriptive and normative phrases to the narrative genre. He provides a comprehensive philosophical background for many of the themes devel- oped in the previous chapters—namely, that moral assessment under- stood as concrete ethics presupposes an understanding of one's social identity as a constraint, and that the formulation of these identity condi- tions exacerbates the problem of moral blindness. Both of the narrative types identified above presuppose a principle of identity, for both depend upon the identification of the addressor of the norm and the addressee of the prescription. Moreover, each narrative type employs its own princi- ple of identity. The discourse that begins by explicitly formulating the question "What ought we to be?" assigns value to each element of the phrase universes that link onto this question, by virtue of their contribu- tion to the metanarrative of a universal subject—Man—in the process of self-understanding.

In the mythic narrative, the answer to the question "What ought we to be?" is presupposed in the transmission of the name across elements of the phrase universe. The principle of identity here is the repetitive self- affirmation of the community constituted by the infinite substitutability of exclusively those story tellers, listeners, and heroes who bear the name of the tribe.

This notion of social identity is connected to my earlier discussion of the conflicts over solidarity and expressivism, in that it is precisely the presupposition of a social identity that is the source of differends both in the normative phrase and in the two types of narrative phrases. In the normative phrase, the identification of the addressor of the norm and the addressee of the prescription that is characteristic of the normative phrase

silences the distinctive voice of the prescriptive phrase, thereby neutralizing the immediacy of obligation. The notion of identity, as employed
in the two narrative types in question, are the source of differends as well.
The discourse that absorbs the proper name into the idea of humanity
creates an "insoluble differend about the legitimacy of authority."

> Thereafter, it will no longer be known whether the law thereby
> declared is French or human, whether the war conducted in the
> name of rights is one of conquest or liberation, whether the violence
> exerted under the title of freedom is repressive or pedagogical (pro-
> gressive), whether the nations which are not French ought to
> become French or to become human. . . .[35]

The difficulty with this form of narrative is that the search for something
characterizing "humanity" as a whole and as an aim inescapably identifies
"I" with humanity. Lyotard expresses this when he claims that the identification of (x) and (y) in terms of a collective "we" simply assumes that (z)
is subject to the norm in question.

Mythic narratives, on the other hand, are in their insularity a source of
conflict because the names and narratives of one community exclude the
names and narratives of the other.

> It is thus a litigation over the names of times, places, and persons,
> over the sense and referents attached to those names (This place,
> this woman, this child is not yours).[36]

The effects of these conflicts that have their source in the mechanisms
sustaining social identity (and especially the gap between prescriptives
and genres that employ a metalanguage with the prescriptive as referent)
create a dilemma for someone who, within the context of a particular conception of justice, wishes to allege a wrong. Recall that in Lyotard's sense
of this term, a wrong is a damage for which the victim has no recourse in
the prevailing idiom. To the extent the victim employs the prevailing
idiom, whether that be cognitive, normative, or narrative, the obligation
created by the claim to have been wronged disappears. However, to
decline to speak in the prevailing idiom is to appear arbitrary and without
reason. Thus, the obligation cannot be expressed. As Lyotard puts it:

> This is the case if the victim is deprived of life, or of all his or her
> liberties, or of the freedom to make his or her ideas or opinions pub-

lic, or simply of the right to testify to the damage, or even more simply if the testifying phrase is itself deprived of authority. . . . In all these cases, to the privation constituted by the damage there is added the impossibility of bringing it to the knowledge of others, and notably to the knowledge of a tribunal. Should the victim seek to bypass this impossibility and testify anyway to the wrong done to him or her, he or she comes up against the following argumentation: either the damages you complain about never took place, and your testimony is false; or else they took place, and since you are able to testify to them, it is not a wrong that has been done to you, but merely a damage, and your testimony is still false.[37]

Moral blindness is a product of a differend that emerges within the conflict between the prevailing idioms authorized by norms and a prescriptive that cannot be articulated in those idioms. Given this characterization of moral blindness and the role that the problem of social identity plays in this blindness, the strong family resemblance between the differend and the contrast judgments discussed in Chapter Three is evident. With respect to both contrast judgments and differends, the moral judgments required to sustain a moral point of view themselves result in an incapacity to recognize a potential moral claim. Plus, in both cases, forms of internal justification and criticism that would presuppose the authority of the prevailing idiom are inadequate vehicles for the representation of what is excluded, thus raising the problem of how this limitation can be recognized and transcended. Finally, and crucially for my argument regarding the inability of concrete ethics to generate a conception of universal moral agency, Lyotard's notion of the differend explains the correlation between moral blindness and the problem of social identity. The demand that moral reflection begin from an account of social identity places moral reflection in the domain of a metalanguage that fails to represent certain essential features of an obligation. When obligations are dependent on the question of who or what one is, the action-guiding features of the prescription are suspended.[38]

My aim in reconstructing Lyotard's rather unfamiliar formulations in this context is to provide a larger explanatory framework from which to address the problems raised by concrete ethics. Recall that the results of earlier chapters were that the contrastive nature of the social bond seems incompatible with any characterization of universal moral agency that begins from within concrete ethics. This renders obscure the notion of obligation toward the "other," questioning any account of a critical standpoint from which to identify the limitations of a moral point of view and casting doubt on the conception of community built on shared beliefs. Thus far, I've attempted to map this problem, developed in previous chapters, onto Lyotard's conception of social reality. This will enable me to address the problem of social identity and the Other from within Lyotard's framework. However, although Lyotard's characterization of pragmatics and the postmodern condition seem to explain the phenomena in question, his account of obligation and prescription have not been sufficiently clarified to resolve the difficulties raised by concrete ethics. The foregoing would suggest that the antidote to the moral blindness implicit in the differends between phrase regimes would be to respect the immediacy of the ethical relation along the lines of Levinas. However, it is not at all clear what that means outside of the face-to-face relation of one to another that Levinas describes.

A Call for Justice without Criteria

For Lyotard, justice consists both of recognizing and respecting the diversity and heterogeneity of genres and phrase regimes that constitute social reality, and of respecting the differend by resisting the tendencies of genres to "cover over the abyss" of heterogeneity that permeates language. Such a conception of justice, if intelligible and consistent with the antitheory position, promises to solve the problem of exclusion associated with contrast judgments because respect for what is excluded by these judgments would be prescribed. This would suggest a solution to the problem of universal moral agency based on respect for difference and heterogeneity.

However, there are a number of difficulties with this proposed solution. The first is that it is unclear how something like a language game or a particular idiom can have "rights," or what claim it has to be understood on its own terms. From where does the authority come for this prescription to respect the integrity of language games, especially since Lyotard has already rejected the possibility of metaprescriptive rules that would adjudicate conflicts arising from differends?[39] If Lyotard is to answer this, he must find a way of bridging the abyss between the various genres without covering up their differences. He must show why this respect for difference is justified without grounding it merely in the fact that language games possess distinct characteristics.

The second problem is related to the first. Because a differend is defined as an instance in which something must be but cannot yet be phrased, Lyotard must show what kind of intelligibility this inarticulate-ness has, such that we can recognize in it the demands of an obligation.

Finally, ethics and politics involve collective action. Yet Lyotard's position seems to cut off any attempt to describe types of interaction to which our actions ought to conform. Not only would such a description inevitably raise questions about the source and specific nature of the prescription, but the form of community described would be an illusion on Lyotard's grounds.

I've already discussed the importance Lyotard attaches to narrative as a dominant genre. In fact, Lyotard's answer to these questions concerning the authority of prescriptions and norms cannot be understood without focusing attention once again on historical narrative. It is evident that the problems of social identity and the necessity of preserving the immediacy of obligations within the call for justice are closely bound up with our understanding of history and the role it plays within moral reflection.

Lyotard makes the general accusation that attempts at grand theoretical syntheses have been made implausible by history.

> The names which are those of "our history" oppose counterexamples to their claim.—Everything is real is rational, everything rational is real: "Auschwitz" refutes the speculative doctrine. This crime at least, which is real, is not rational.—Everything proletarian is communist, everything communist is proletarian: "Berlin 1953, Budapest 1956, Czechoslovakia 1968, Poland 1980" (I could mention others) refute the doctrine of historical materialism: the workers rose up against the Party.—Everything democratic is by and for the people, and vice versa: "May 1968" refutes the doctrine of parliamentary liberalism . . . the "crises of 1911 and 1929" refute the doctrine of economic liberalism. And "the crises of 1974–79" refute the post-Keynesian revision of that doctrine. The passages promised by the great doctrinal syntheses end in bloody impasses. Whence the sorrow of the spectators in this bloody end of the twentieth century.[40]

These events give evidence for the claim that the Enlightenment meta-narratives are no longer credible. What has undermined their credibility is the failure to recognize the yawning chasm separating theory from lived experience. Lyotard explicates this chasm using Kant's distinction between concepts and Ideas of Reason.

For Kant, judgments regarding the application of concepts can be made according to the rules of the cognitive faculty because there are ante-

cedently available, universally valid, *a priori* categories that subsume
particular experiences of objects. The referents are part of the causal
mechanisms that make up phenomenal reality and can be confirmed
through empirical evidence. Ideas of Reason, on the other hand, such as
Freedom, Immortality, or God, require judgments that are not simply a
matter of subsuming intuitions under a concept, because their referents
are not subject to causal laws and their empirical existence can never be
established. Thus, judgments that employ Ideas of Reason are reflective
judgments [they must discover their universal rule in the object them-
selves] that function regulatively, since the Idea in question can never be
established as part of phenomenal reality. Most historical events can be
empirically determined, and thus judged according to the rules governing
the cognitive faculty. However, the totality of a series of historical
events—the ultimate end to which they are directed and the beginning
(both essential to narrative history)—are not given to the intuition.
Notions such as "freedom" or a "Republican civil order," so much at issue
during the French Revolution, were Ideas of Reason, not possible objects
of knowledge, in Kant's judgment. The confusion between a historically
existent community and the Idea of a Republican social contract was a
"transcendental illusion," the illusion being the belief that there could be a
direct presentation of the Republican social contract within the causal
regularities that govern nature. The consequence of this illusion can be
seen in the actions of the participants in the French revolution, whose
anticipation of future emancipation and constant disappointment perpet-
uated the cycle of terror and counterrevolutionary violence.

Similarly, for Lyotard, notions such as "communism," "capitalism,"
"democracy," "liberalism," and "emancipation" are similar to Kant's Ideas
of Reason.[41] Despite the significance of these notions, they do not figure
in the explanation of historical events.[42] To employ them in such a manner is to fall into "transcendental illusion" acting, as Lyotard puts it, as if
the explanations were referring to actual phenomena when they are referring to "as if" phenomena.[43] Such a confusion leads us to lose sight of the
contingency of events, and is a source of tragic errors in history.
Apparently Lyotard thinks that identifying particular communities as the
bearers of the historical destiny expressed by these Ideas encourages the
wanton slaughter that darkens recent history. Nothing is as frightening as
storm troopers bearing the "Truth"—a confusion of the cognitive and narrative phrase regimes.

Of course, Kant did not think that history is utterly bereft of order or
meaning, and Lyotard will follow Kant's conception of the meaning of his-

tory up to a point. The violence of the French Revolution convinced Kant that human history was radically contingent, a realm of disorder and misery. Nevertheless, reason is capable of forming Ideas like "freedom" that allow us to hope for progress.[44] Kant reconciled this seeming contradiction by invoking the "sign of history." If there is moral progress in history, then there must be events in history indicating that man is the cause of his own moral progress. In Kant's judgment, it was the enthusiasm of the spectators of the French Revolution that was an indicator of moral progress. Instead of discovering some particular causal mechanisms or teleological order at work in history and then situating events within that order, Kant advocated that we proceed "as if" there were such an order, while recognizing that no such order could be empirically confirmed. The Idea of freedom—that human beings are themselves the authors of causal effects in the world—licenses an analogy with mechanical causality without licensing a determinant judgment regarding historical existence.[45] The appearance of such events would allow us to retrospectively apply this inference of progress to the past, thus providing a kind of historical explanation. However, these events would not be the cause of such progress nor an example of it. They would be an indicator of progress—a sign of history.[46] Importantly, for Kant, we can hypothesize that human beings are subject to the same teleological order as nature, that there is a natural end toward which humanity aims, of which the sign of history is an indicator, thereby giving the sign of history a defeasible but nevertheless universal validity.

Through the device of analogy Kant reconciles the faculty of cognition (the realm of mechanical causality) with the faculty of practical reason (the realm of freedom); or, in Lyotard's terminology, he reconciles the differend between the cognitive and the speculative, narrative genres.

The sign of history is a form of fallibilism, a caution about proceeding with the hubris of science in a domain in which confidence in confirming results is inappropriate, and hubris regarding the historical destiny of ideals breeds violence and human misery. This is an important insight given the tendency of the vigorous pursuit of ideals to yield tragic results, discussed in Part One. Lyotard endorses this fallibilism, and seems to endorse the general notion that the abyss between genres can be preserved and traversed by analogically borrowing the rules and strategies from each other. Thus, Kant's work on judgment provides Lyotard with the general outlines of a model for how judgment can employ elements of various genres without reducing their heterogeneity. Ideas of reason are not reduced to concepts, but partake of the ordered reality of the understanding by means of analogy. The sign of history also provides Lyotard with an example of a reflective judgment not governed by the application of a rule. It allows the articulation of something that is neither grounded in the faculties nor given antecedent to the judgment, thus suggesting a model for the articulation of injustices that are the product of differends.

The Postmodern Sublime

Kant's reflections on the French Revolution are an application of his notion of the sublime—the immediate experience of opposed feelings, e.g. pleasure and pain. It is this capacity to harbor opposed feelings that conditions our judgments regarding the fate of humankind. I will argue that it is Lyotard's transformed conception of the sublime that enables him to render a conception of justice.

For Kant, the Idea of a world, or the infinitely large, or infinitely powerful and destructive, are ideas for which we cannot give examples. They transcend our sensible capacities and are unpresentable except as Ideas in the imagination. This causes us to feel displeasure at the incapacity to represent these Ideas, but also pleasure in our ability to conceive them.[47]

In the historical case, according to Kant, the imagination strives but fails to directly present through an example the Idea of community from the events of the Revolution, in light of the destructiveness of the terror. This produces a recognition of the painful inadequacy of our faculty for presentation *and* pleasure in our capacity to imagine Ideas, such as that of a sense of community, beyond their direct presentation. The sublime is therefore understood as a form of recognition beyond phenomenal experience, one that disrupts the categories of representation through the recognition of its own limitations. However, what enables Kant to reconcile the opposed feelings with this judgment of moral progress in history is the hypothesis of a correspondence between empirical reality and the ends of man, the hypothesis that humanity, like the physical world, shares a natural teleology.[48]

This is the point at which the specificity of the social context in which Lyotard self-consciously writes—the condition of postmodernity—will force a sharp divergence from Kant. Given the breakdown of metanarratives, it is not possible to speak of a single, consummate end to any series of historic events (let alone to humanity in general), for it is characteristic of postmodernity that there are myriad, heterogeneous ends. This produces a rather stunning reversal of the appeal to universality and unity that characterized Kant's use of analogy and his experience of the sublime.

Lyotard's quintessential statement on postmodernism is as follows:

> The postmodern would be that which, in the modern, puts forward the unpresentable in presentation itself: that which denies itself the solace of good forms, the consensus of a taste which would make it possible to share collectively the nostalgia for the unattainable: that which searches for new presentations, not in order to enjoy them but in order to impart a stronger sense of the unpresentable. A postmodern artist or writer is in the position of a philosopher: the text he writes, the work he produces are not in principle governed by preestablished rules. . . . Those rules and categories are what the work of art itself is looking for. The artist and the writer, then, are working without rules in order to formulate the rules of *what will have been done*. Hence the fact that work and the text have the character of an *event*. Hence also they have always come too late for the author or, what amounts to the same thing, their realization (*mise en oeuvre*) always begins too soon. *Postmodern* would have to be understood according to the paradox of the future (*post*) anterior (*modo*).[49]

Built into the postmodern sensibility is a focus on the reflexivity of the process of presentation. The Kantian sublime acknowledges the unpresentable, but substitutes for it a fiction that serves the function of a regulative ideal—the hypothesis of a natural teleology for humankind. By contrast, the postmodern sublime refuses to become nostalgic by invoking the illusion of a redemptive, final end. Instead, the sublime continually makes reference to the impossibility of presenting the unpresentable by refusing to reconcile the opposing feelings. The reflective judgment, which can no longer rely on the analogy with a universal law, must find its own principle without guidance from the presumption of unity or underlying structure.

For Lyotard, this means that judgment (or what Lyotard sometimes calls "paralogy") is, in part, a matter of pointing out the presuppositions in whatever language game is at stake, and petitioning players in the game to adopt new ones. It invents new rules in order to find new ways of bearing witness to what cannot be presented as an object of knowledge. Thus, linkages between genres will be an occasion for invention based on the suggestiveness of the event. History, under postmodern conditions, is the bearing witness to the event that is continually reinterpreted but without the nostalgic yearning for unity or completeness.[50]

This conception of judgment that Lyotard appropriates from Kant and filters through the postmodern condition does address the question of how judgment can bridge the separate, incommensurable, competing genres without permanently occluding their differences. The differences between language games are navigated by analogically borrowing the forms that constitute alternative language games—the "as-if" judgments. Yet in contrast to Kant, there is no end associated with one term of the analogy. Consequently, there is a proliferation of potential forms that can be borrowed, and a multiplicity of ends in terms of which to formulate retrospectively the rules of "what will have been done."

Lyotard is seldom very explicit in rendering these abstract notions into a comprehensible picture of the consequences of this postmodern sensibility. In any case, the aim of his discourse is not to develop a comprehensible picture. However, something like the following is suggested by my reading. In this resolute refusal to impose finality on any discourse, the integrity of the various phrase regimes and genres is preserved because the encroachments among them are mere analogical borrowings. Ethics may employ narrative, but only for the purposes of demonstrating the limitations of a particular prescription; narrative may employ moral prescriptions, but only to demonstrate the limitations of a literary gambit or claim to historical authenticity, etc. The aim of such a conception of judgment is to find the idiom that will give expression to the differends submerged in any form of discourse. The moral weight of this vision apparently is that no idea can bear the burden of murder today if the exoneration it entails will be subverted tomorrow. Thus, the meaning of justice is itself unstable, and the force of any point of view subject to revision as differends become manifest.

> But it is precisely in the attempt to bring an end to *differends*, to transform war into a litigation and pronounce a verdict that will settle the dispute, that a *differend* can manifest itself. It manifests itself by a feeling. Even damages for which reparations have been made can evidently arouse a feeling of irreparable wrong. The purposiveness thus undoes itself, and peace remains an armed state.[51]

Thus, whatever Lyotard means by justice as respect for the heterogeneity of phrases, it is neither an ideal terminus nor a state of political order that can be instituted. The very resolution of the differends that would result from carrying out "justice" by means of judgment would create new differends. Justice itself is a bearing witness to the impossibility of presenting the unpresentable. It is a matter of experiencing simultaneously the pleasure of innovation and the pain of failing to fully codify that innovation within the contours of reality. The enthusiasms we entertain must be tempered by the recognition that they can never be fully reflected within lived experience—happily, this is not an argument against enthusiasm.

There is a difficulty here, however, that casts doubt on the extent to which the postmodern sublime is really a departure from Kant. Although Lyotard claims that the unity of a final end no longer serves as the "guiding thread," as it did for Kant, the disunity suggested by the injunction to bear witness to the impossibility of presenting the unpresentable seems no less a regulative idea—thus preserving the teleological structure of the Kantian sublime. Moreover, the claim that each linguistic production is an event that itself requires a new set of rules to judge it by, rules that were not available antecedently, questions the very distinctions between genres and phrase regimes that form the heart of Lyotard's conception of language. It also questions the conception of justice as the demand to preserve the integrity of these rules. The postmodern sublime suggests it is precisely these rules that cannot be presented. There is a paradox here: If the rules are available antecedently, why are they not the sort of systematic prejudgments Lyotard has rejected? If they are not antecedently available, how can justice enjoin us to preserve their integrity?

Despite Lyotard's continuous praise of the virtues of dissent and conflict, if justice means protecting the integrity of each language game or genre, there is an implicit appeal to unity. The archipelago would contain fixed points on the horizon of all linguistic productions. The social bond would be riddled with conflict at one level, but with insularity and closure at a deeper level at which the phrase regimes specify the rules that govern genres.

Lyotard does not address this problem as directly as one would like, but there are passages in *The Differend* suggesting a resolution of this paradox. Commenting on Kant, Lyotard points out that the faculty of judgment has no object, and thus does not have a unique set of rules that govern judgment. It must borrow its form from the other faculties that can be delimited through critique.

> Furthermore, this is the faculty that has enabled the territories and realms to be delimited, which has established the authority of each

genre on its island. *And this, it was only able to do thanks to the commerce or to the war it fosters between genres* [emphasis has been added].[52]

This passage asserts that the conflict between all the genres itself produces the rules governing them, that this generalized conflict delimits the boundaries between them in a perpetual process of intensification and relaxation. The mere putting into play of language introduces the encroachment of one genre upon another, thus giving rise to differends and the demand for justice. This cannot be antecedently regulated by judgment or discovered through analysis; it is simply the contingent circumstances to which judgment must respond.

This quoted passage makes clear that the purity and integrity of the rules governing genres and phrases is not primordial—nor is it ideal. Lyotard is not calling us to gather once again around the hearth of Being. The very judgment of what would count as integrity and purity must itself be reflective, without recourse to criteria. Thus, the authority or justification of the demand for justice—for preserving the integrity of language games—must, itself, be unpresentable which leaves unresolved how we can be obligated by something that cannot be meaningfully expressed. What is clear at this point is that justice is not preventive medicine. It can only be compensation, coming after the fact and responding to the event of language.

Despite this demonstration of the internal consistency of Lyotard's view of judgments, a number of questions remain. It is still not clear what exactly within the postmodern understanding makes a particular judgment just. By virtue of what does the particularity of a language game have rights? Although Lyotard has argued that the source and authority of a prescription must be unknown in order to maintain the specificity of the prescription, it is still not clear why particularity has such an absolute status. It is not sufficient to claim that differends cause certain claims to go unexpressed, since some account of why the suppressed claims have moral status is required. Furthermore, what is the action-guiding force of such an obligation? To claim that the action-guiding force of an obligation is suspended by a descriptive discourse commenting on the prescription is not to provide an account of the motivations for fulfilling the sort of obligation Lyotard has in mind. Lyotard's tendency to extol the virtues of pluralism notwithstanding, every language game is not equally praiseworthy. Some account of the kinds of discourses that should be fostered or constrained is required. What makes this particularly daunting is that any account of justice consistent with Lyotard's version of postmodernism must carefully avoid the abusive employment of teleological structure and descriptive discourse as a means of articulating the point.

Thus far, Lyotard has focused on the side of the postmodern sublime that takes pleasure in the proliferation of small narratives and the innovations of the paralogical invention of rules. However, the sublime involves the mixing of pleasure with pain; aside from asserting the sublime is a shock and a disturbance to our capacity for representation, very little has been said about that shock and its source. If purity and integrity are neither teleological guides nor a source of respect for justice because, despite their representing the successful litigation of differends, they are also the source of differends, what does provoke a concern for justice?

I argue that these questions regarding Lyotard's conception of justice can only be answered by giving Levinas and his notion of the Other a more prominent role within the postmodern sublime. If the postmodern sublime is a matter of bearing witness to the impossibility of presenting the unpresentable, then a plausible candidate for the "unpresentable" is the Other as articulated by Levinas. Based on this hypothesis, something about the Other to which the sublime makes allusions provokes a sense of justice of the sort Lyotard endorses. Put differently, if the postmodern is "that which, in the modern, puts forward the unpresentable in presentation itself," then postmodern justice puts forward within the attempts to present justice—within the forms and institutions justice presently takes—the absolutely Other. In doing so it is not seeking to fulfill an aim, like integrity or particularity, which can be characterized independently of the Other and its claim on us, but is simply responding to the face-to-face confrontation with the Other. Consequently, whatever value or meaning the particularity or integrity of language games have, the moral claim they exert through the appearance of differends would be by virtue of the obligation the Other imposes in each particular case. If this hypothesis should prove true, then innovation and paralogy receive their "why?" and "wherefore?" from the traces of the Other of which Levinas speaks. Invention and paralogy would "impart a stronger sense of the unpresentable." That is, they would amplify the trace of the Other—make it more salient—within the realm of judgment, without presenting it as a concept under which particular relations can be gathered.

If the unpresentable within the postmodern sublime is the absolutely Other, then the recognition of this Other involves the ethical relation— Levinas's relation of face to face. The radical particularity of the Other's face is just the sort of disruptive force that would create and dissolve differends, disrupting even the particularity of the language games with their rules of strategy and procedure, because this face-to-face relation cannot be represented by norms or rules. Justice, as Lyotard conceives it in terms of paralogical judgment, would in this view be a frantic attempt to represent in terms of innovative strategies what cannot be represented—the ethical relation with the Other intimated with every differend. The aim of paralogy would neither be dissensus nor the integrity of language games, although these indeed might be by-products. Rather, paralogy is provoked by a desire, in principle neither sharable nor satisfiable, for a particular ethical relation. Postmodern justice is the political domain striving to become ethical.

However, if we are to take a postmodern approach to justice seriously, it must promise more than an ineffectual flailing against the limits of representation, a celebratory paean to difference, or the invocation of a quasi-mystical quest for transcendence. As the presentation of a concept of justice, a model or general schema, is ruled out by the presence of heterogeneous ends, we need a stronger characterization of this "desire" for the ethical relation that would clarify the claim the differend makes on us—without reducing otherness to a telos or a simple fact about society to be tolerated. A postmodern theory of ethics and politics must explain how the pain and pleasure of the sublime can provoke in us a moral concern, despite our inability to reduce the source of the obligation to something fully subsumable under rational categories or explicable in terms of a model of a just society.

What, then, are the passages between ethics (understood as the face-to-face relationship with the Other) and justice? How can one acknowledge the authority of a moral command while bearing witness to the impossibility of presenting the unpresentable? To answer this question, we have to look more closely at the nature of obligation.

Between Ethics and Politics: The Incomprehensibility of Suffering

Obligation and responsibility make reference to the past. In obligation we feel the constraint of what has come before, sometimes as the result of an explicitly articulated promise but more often implicitly through a bond taken for granted or presupposed. We feel obligated to our families, communities, nations, and institutions and practices, without having autonomously entered into an agreement. Perhaps more importantly, we sometimes feel compelled to aid people we do not know, to whom we have never spoken, and with whom we have little in common. We feel we already have these obligations as if we acquired them through the mere passage of time. This is what Levinas and Lyotard mean by the unknown source of obligation; it is part of the facticity of existence that we find ourselves obligated.

We can, of course, ask why we should feel so obligated. Part of maturing is acknowledging these obligations and submitting them to a process of justification. To the traditional philosophical theorist, this means submitting these commitments to the tribunal of reason, ultimately seeking the rational principles on which these commitments rest. The anti-theorists discussed in Part One effectively dismiss this notion of a tribunal of reason, but nevertheless advocate a process of justification—one that involves tracing the obligation to its source in a history of concrete relationships supplying intelligibility and meaning to the obligation.

However, as Lyotard points out, such a task suspends the action-guiding force of the obligation pending an answer to the question of justification. Lyotard's discussions of norms and narrative history suggest that in a world-historical context, the question of justification cannot be answered in a way that is compelling enough to reestablish the force of the obligation. However, Levinas's notion of immemorial time suggests a reason for thinking that tracing an obligation's origin cannot succeed in any context.

Recall from the previous chapter that the principle characteristics of diachronic time are its inexorable movement in one direction and the *fait accompli* of its effects that cannot be reversed or represented in memory. We are utterly passive in the face of the passage of diachronic time, which can neither be made the object of an intentional act nor represented in memory, but leaves traces upon the body; namely, the process of aging.

This notion of a temporal continuum incommensurable with the time of lived experience suggests the futility of attempting to reconstruct the history of an obligation. Although we are products of history, it is not merely the history of reported events that shape us. Our lives, characters, and commitments are shaped by the many decisions we make that have never been recounted, secret histories that have never been told of deeds left undone, decisions made in private, whispered conversations, truths not faced, lies never confronted, conspiracies hatched in cabal, mishaps unreported—these are not failures of memory, for they were never known in the first place. The habits and dispositions of individuals as well as the characters of communities and nations are formed from myriad secret histories that can never be recounted because they have never been told. In this sense time is irreversible and irrevocable.

Thus, the feeling of being obligated prior to one's agreement is not a product of inattention that can be corrected by clear-headed analysis. The feeling of belatedness is part of the obligation. Like the postmodern text, obligation is an event that comes too late for its authorization and too soon for its recognition, its origin buried in the darkness of immemorial time.

This, however, does not answer the question that animates this section: What accounts for the peculiar force of the obligation if we cannot identify its source? What gives the command its authority? Why do we find it difficult to discount these constraints even when they conflict with our self-interest? If diachronic time is the time of the Other that never enters my experience, how does it engage my life? In any case, don't we know enough about the past to supply a satisfactory account of obligation despite the secrets the past cannot divulge?

I argue that these questions can be answered by acknowledging the role the human experience of suffering plays in linking the recognition of the transcendence of the Other with the postmodern demand for justice. Suffering plays this role because it serves as a bridge between the known and the unknown, between the concrete human relations available to understanding and description and the utter transcendence of the Other invoked by Levinas. It serves as a passage between the language game of description and the autonomous domain of prescription and obligation.[53]

Clearly, suffering (especially physical suffering) can be an object of cognition and empirical explanation. It is among the most common human experiences, and we have, in most cases, reliable criteria for determining its presence. However, suffering is unique in that some of its features disrupt our self-understanding and the understanding of our immediate social world. This is because it violates much of what we hold in esteem. It respects none of the categories by which we measure ourselves and others, renders everyday tasks and concerns meaningless, and forces us to rethink a good deal of what we take for granted. It can strike the highest or lowest among us; it can neutralize any advantage, destroy any virtue, compromise any power. My point is that suffering renders unimportant the categories, criteria, and dispositions by which we distinguish between self and others. Levinas has an even stronger characterization of the disruption suffering causes.

> For the Kantian "I think" . . . it is as if suffering were not only a *given* refractory to synthesis, but the *way* in which the refusal opposed to the assembling of givens into a meaningful whole is opposed to it: suffering is at once what disturbs order and this disturbance itself.[54]

Suffering is an obstacle to the assemblance of reality into a meaningful whole. It disrupts the everydayness of perceived order, displaying our vulnerability and unmediated exposure to reality.

> The content of suffering merges with the impossibility of detaching oneself from suffering. . . . In suffering there is an absence of all refuge. It is the fact of being directly exposed to being. It is made up of the impossibility of fleeing or retreating.[55]

This inability to retreat is especially true when the suffering is our own, although the suffering of others often provokes a similar obsession when we find we cannot put it out of our mind. Extreme suffering dominates one's life, a constant presence and reference point, a totality that consciousness is incapable of objectifying. Extreme suffering cannot be incorporated as a moment within the stream of conscious life but becomes a sort of shadow "subject" haunting every act of consciousness.

There is, therefore, an implicit duality in the structure of suffering. Suffering is given to consciousness as content, but in suffering consciousness begins to lose its capacity to stand back, reflect upon, and mediate experience. In the inescapability of suffering, we approximate unmediated sensuous contact with the world—vulnerability without reserve, as if suffering were a trace of the Other.

At the same time, suffering makes reference to the nearness of death, "as if despite the entire absence of a dimension of withdrawal that constitutes suffering, it still had some free space for an event. . . ."[56] The proximity of death in suffering reveals to consciousness the fact that an event of absolute otherness can occur. To exist is to maintain a relationship with death as the radically other, to discover as part of existence something inescapable and incomprehensible, a dimension of existence that cannot be shared, owned, or understood but only approached as an utter mystery.[57] Suffering, therefore, is both available to consciousness as something known and understood but nevertheless containing traces of alterity.

This connection between suffering and alterity is deepened by the relation of suffering to the immemorial—the unrepresentable past of diachronic time. Through suffering, lived experience is exposed and made vulnerable to the immemorial. Events that fail to enter the story of history are no less efficacious for going unreported, because they are utterly surprising in their effects. The immemorial is an extraordinary disruption of lived experience, for we are—we must be—blindsided by its effects. Under ordinary circumstances we can safely ignore these effects, telling stories of the past that invoke the comforts of nostalgia and the satisfactions of order and closure. We know enough of our past to tell a coherent story by relating what is known to our hopes for the future. However, suffering denies us this solace, disrupting the play of protention and retention by exposing us to the immemorial. Our various sufferings are events of some significance for which we have no satisfying explanation. How many small decisions—unrecorded and uneventful—did it take to enforce the slave trade, create the gulag, spark world wars, or poison earth and sky? We shall never know. Primo Levi writes with respect to the survivors of the Holocaust,

> We the survivors, are not the true witnesses. . . . We are those who by their prevarications or abilities or good luck did not touch bottom. Those who did so . . . have not returned to tell about it or have returned mute, but they are the "Muslims," the submerged, the complete witnesses, the ones whose deposition would have a general significance. They are the rule, we are the exception.[58]

Much suffering quietly enters the inexorable, mute currents of diachronic time.

Suffering, then, is incomprehensible not because we are in the grip of uncontrollable cosmic forces, but because we are disempowered correspondents able to interview only the saved while trembling at the offspring of events witnessed exclusively by the drowned.

This dimension of suffering cannot be represented. In the idiom of postmodernism, suffering bears witness to the unpresentable. In suffering, as Levinas says, we are exposed to being only because we are confronted by the unknowable. Why only in suffering? Why not in joy or accomplishment? Aren't accomplishments and pleasures the product of secret histories as well? Indeed, but only in suffering is synthesizing consciousness so thoroughly disrupted confronting us with a past we cannot know but that will not recede within the play of protentions and retentions. Suffering is beyond explanation or justification—in its face our stories seem inadequate.

The immemorial and its relation to suffering has enormous consequences for ethics and justice. The immemorial means our sense of obligation cannot stem from tracing a bond back to its origin, for we can no longer hear the originating promise; and the voices of the documented that we do hear are drowned in the silence of the undocumented who appeal to our concern. Those who feel the force of obligation are bound despite history.

This reluctance to identify the source of obligation has positive effects on our sense of it. We can never honestly tell a story that definitively absolves responsibility or disempowers obligation because we can never tell the secret history of "non-events" that inform our present. We can never claim with confidence that we are not perpetuating a clandestine history of cruelty or a hidden strain of callousness that navigates the archipelago alongside our best-informed judgments. To the extent that we are seized by the suffering of another person, an answer to the question of why we should *not* feel responsible and obligated can never be given in good faith.

The recognition that the past can never be filled in, that suffering can never be fully accounted for, amplifies the gratuitous appeal of ethics within the domain of justice and politics. Ethics cannot wait for the explanation or model. It must be impatient with casuistry. Any attempt to limit responsibility by fixing the ethical relation within the boundaries of norms or narratives risks limiting our capacity to recognize the suffering of others.

Thus, the incomprehensibility of suffering explains why the source of obligation must remain a mystery, why our capacity to reason and explain cannot fully articulate the power of obligation, and why the question of justification cannot explain the authority of moral commands. To fill in the addressor instance of an obligation would subject these intimations of the Other to a casuistry that destroys the sense of enormity and incomprehension. Only this sense of enormity and incomprehension sustains our capacity to respond to suffering, for reason alone makes the forgotten eminently forgettable. I do not think a moral perspective that can accommodate the aspiration of transcendence is possible without this sense of enormity.

This constant self-referential invocation of incomprehensibility is what postmodernism brings to the question of justice. The gratuitous appeal of the suffering Other lies hidden in every differend, insinuates itself into every social and political relation, exploding the complacency of understanding. The pluralism and rampant innovation of postmodernism are not goals to be achieved but responses to the shock of the suffering of others, responses that continually demonstrate the limitations of our understanding when we remain open to this appeal. The multiplicity of perspectives postmodernism takes for granted is simply a reflection of the multiplicity of crimes.

Conclusion

What then, is a postmodern conception of ethics? Both Levinas and Lyotard argue that we find ourselves obligated to others without recourse of explanation or justification. Any attempt to supply a justification through theoretical, descriptive, normative, or narrative discourse suspends the force of the obligation pending a compelling account of it. Yet each form of discourse ultimately fails to supply that compelling justification, and, as Lyotard argues in his account of the differend, all discourse has a tendency to suppress obligation. Thus, as Levinas claims, a moral appeal is gratuitous. It asks one to respond without reason. To put the point in Kantian terms, to treat the Other as an end, and not a means requires the recognition that the ends of the Other are never fully accessible. The categorical imperative thus demands that we suspend our ordinary ways of understanding the relationship between oneself and others.

The upshot of Levinas's discussion is that a moral point of view is sustained not by our capacity to justify that point of view but by a desire for transcendence—to go beyond, to respond to mystery, to face the Other. That desire for transcendence is provoked by suffering, for in its incomprehensibility suffering leads us beyond the given, the mundane, and the orderly to seek what is buried in diachronic time—the time of the Other. The incomprehensibility of suffering prevents us from accepting reasons for neglecting the gratuitous appeal, and forestalls the narratives of absolution. This incredulity toward reason has the remarkable implication that we can find no reason not to respond. Our responsibility is without limit.

We can now answer the question: "Is there an account of universal moral agency compatible with the antitheorists' position?" In my judgment, a postmodern ethic provides that account. It may be useful at this point to recapitulate the significance of this question. I argue in the introduction to Part Two that the limitations of concrete ethics were, in part, traceable to the presupposition that the intelligibility of moral reflection depends on the process of sustaining and extending historically constituted social practices. This presupposition makes justification a matter of reiterating modified versions of the basic principles or beliefs from which one begins. Because one begins moral reflection already engaged in one's particular, immediate social world, regardless of what possibilities are projected as courses of action, its intelligibility will depend on a pre-understanding of who one is as a member of this social world. The limitations of this conception of the preconditions for ethics arise because the specification of a particular moral point of view generally requires an implicit contrast with others who do not share that view, thus diminishing the status of the Other. This contrast raises doubts about whether the needs and interests of those who suffer this diminished status can be represented by the moral beliefs, practices, and institutions in question, as well as doubts about the possibility of accounting for universal moral agency from within this point of view.

The moral point of view marking this intersection of Lyotard and Levinas also yields the insight that one begins moral reflection already engaged in one's immediate social world; we do find ourselves obligated without having chosen to take on these burdens. However, postmodernism as I have interpreted it resists the view that sustaining those obligations rests on an understanding of one's social identity. Thus, postmodernism avoids the worries about moral blindness I argued emerge from this concern with social identity. The ethical orientation toward the Other resists the contrast judgments that grow out of our attempts at self-understanding and definition, for it makes the categories and vocabulary through which we praise and condemn irrelevant in expressing concern. The notion of immemorial time and the secret history concealed therein makes availing oneself of a preunderstanding of who one is in relation to a given social world implausible. The self, whether we understand it individually or collectively, is a topography of lost and missing pieces cobbled together by a systematically distorted narrative of the remains. The quest for social identity is just one more vain search for the solace of origins, perpetually contested and itself the source of injustice.

An incredulity toward such a task makes the gratuitous appeal of the ethical relation audible. The limited points of view circumscribed by the contrastive judgments of a shared history or tradition are violated by the shock of recognition accompanying the confrontation with the suffering face of the Other. The acceptance of universality is a willingness to acknowledge that face without reserve, to perpetually transcend the given in order to find the inconspicuous victims. If we seek a moral world, then ethics must be about transcendence. Only then are we responsibly engaged in the effort to sustain a moral point of view.

In articulating this postmodern conception of ethics, I have not strayed from the tragic dimension of ethics. We can never be sure that our attempts to alleviate suffering will not lead to more suffering. This is precisely what makes suffering so difficult to comprehend and disrupts the comforting narratives we tell. This is why ethics must involve constant vigilance and resistance, why we must see ourselves first as potential victimizers. This conception may seem thin and deflationary to some. I have made no attempt to draw practical conclusions from this view because of the impossibility of such inferences. At best, what can be said is that ethics demands of us a willingness to see beyond the given, nurtured by incredulity toward both the orthodox and the Arcadian, and an openness to suffering that refuses to delimit boundaries.

Does postmodernism, then, in the end prescribe a new vision of ethics? Is this new vision not based on a description of the nature of obligation, and shouldn't we therefore consider this a new theory? The complex phenomena of ethics cannot be captured by any single perspective, let alone any formula. Philosophical commentary on ethics, like any form of writing, probably can do no more than articulate a specific moral concern at a particular time and hope this concern spontaneously resonates with the concerns of readers. Lyotard likens the message of any work to a message placed in a bottle and set to sea.[59] Philosophy is at its best when it functions as a "critical watchman," offering resistance to the ossification of language games rather than prescribing set rules. Postmodern ethics nevertheless vigilantly *speaks* as if prescribing.

Appendix

In *The Differend*, Lyotard establishes many of his claims by explicitly appropriating and transforming central argumentative strategies from within the philosophical tradition.[1] In identifying the basic unit of linguistic meaning, Lyotard hearkens back to Descartes—although the result is anything but Cartesian. In the final analysis, what cannot be doubted given "I think" is "there has been a phrase." That is, a meaningful event has occurred that any attempt to doubt would presuppose, since "I doubt there is a phrase" would presuppose precisely what is doubted. What is not Cartesian is that no subject or reality need be taken as logically prior to the fact that "there has been a phrase." Instead, reality and its constituents are bestowed by the phrase in that the phrase attributes reality to a referent. Each phrase sets up a phrase universe consisting of at least one (a) addressor, (b) addressee, (c) referent, and (d) meaning. Questions concerning the nature of reality cannot be addressed independently or prior to a phrase that generates this universe.

> It should be said that addressor and addressee are instances, either marked or unmarked, presented by a phrase. The latter is not a message passing from an addressor to an addressee both of whom are independent of it.[2]

The point of insisting on the priority of the phrase is, of course, to avoid the dualism of subject and object that causes much of the familiar panoply of philosophical conundrums. This is purchased at a cost because the priority of the phrase suggests a thorough linguistification of reality. Such a hypostatization of language is mitigated, however, by the fact that phrases need not be linguistic. Silence can be a phrase; so can "a cat's tail."[3] We might say, then, a phrase is any event that situates the four elements of the phrase universe just listed.

Phrases are necessary; and given any phrase, it is necessary that another phrase be linked to it. Yet which phrases are linked together is a radically contingent matter. Existing with a phrase and phrase universe is a phrase regime—a set of implicit rules determining how the phrase is formed. It is an event that emerges from the presentation of a phrase universe. The significant feature of a phrase regime is its heterogeneity. Each regime presents the phrase universe in a particular way, and cannot typically be translated into or deduced from other phrase regimes. Reasoning, knowing, describing, recounting, questioning, and showing are the examples Lyotard gives.[4] We might also add prescribing, telling a story, telling a joke, etc. With this notion of a phrase regime, Lyotard is very close to speech-act theory, although his view differs in that the speaker's intentions are not at issue.

Despite this heterogeneity, phrase regimes can be linked together in chains that serve a purpose. The purpose of a concatenation of linkages is fixed by a genre that supplies strategies for linking that are appropriate to that purpose. Everything from philosophy and science to auto repair manuals and commercials are genres that impose an end or purpose on heterogeneous phrase regimes. These are the language games that form the social bond according to Lyotard.

> For example, dialogue [a genre] links an ostension (showing) or a definition (describing) onto a question; at stake [the purpose] in it is two parties coming to an agreement about the sense of a referent.[5]

Once again, genres are regulated by their own internal rules which guide the attainment of the end prescribed by the genre. In the case of genre, these are not structural rules but strategic prescriptions which tend to lead toward the prescribed end. There are no general rules for linking genres together. Thus, genres propose rival ways of linking phrase regimes that are in perpetual competition. This will allow Lyotard to argue that there are no grand teleologies, a point which will become important shortly. And it should be emphasized again that no subject, intention, or will is presupposed here.

We believe that we want to persuade, to seduce, to convince, to be upright, to cause to believe, or to cause to question, but this is because a genre of discourse, whether dialectical, erotic, didactic, ethical, rhetorical, or "ironic," imposes its mode of linking onto "our" phrase and onto "us".[6]

To recapitulate briefly, a phrase generates a phrase universe consisting of addressor, addressee, referent, and meaning. Simultaneously, it generates a phrase regime that determines the particular relationships between elements of the phrase universe. Phrase regimes cannot be deduced from or translated into each other, they can only be linked according to strategic prescriptions internal to genres that subordinate the regimes to their purposes. The value of conceptualizing language in this way is twofold. It escapes the conundrum of considering language a medium of representation through which a subject comes to know an object. Moreover, it accounts for the force of language by specifying the displacements visited on the elements of the phrase universe by various language games. This point can be clarified only by looking at specific genres and phrase regimes. It will therefore be helpful to look at what Lyotard calls the "cognitive regime," not only to illustrate how "pragmatics" works but to set the stage for the upcoming discussion of history, in which the cognitive phrase regime plays a significant role.

The point of the cognitive regime is to establish the reality of something. Part of the ends of those genres that employ the cognitive regime (e.g. science and history) is that reality be independent of the addressor and the addressee. That a referent of a phrase is real is suggested by uttering a demonstrative—e.g. "He is here." To establish the truth of this statement, however, independent corroboration is required by phrases designating the same referent. "Here" must refer to the same place and time and "he" to the same person in each case. Because demonstratives depend wholly on context for their meaning, their reference is not fixed. This requires the use of proper names that, like demonstratives, perform a designative function but unlike demonstratives designate the same referent from one phrase to the next. Lyotard, accepting much of Kripke's analysis of proper names as rigid designators, anchors language in the world through proper names.

Networks of quasi-deictics formed by names of "objects" and by names of relations designate "givens" and the relations given between those givens, that is to say, a world. I call it a world because those names, being "rigid", each refer to something even when that something is not there; and because that something is considered to be the same for all phrases which refer to it by its name; and also because each of those names is independent of the phrase universes that refer to it, and in particular of the addressors and addressees presented in those universes.[7]

Thus, establishing the reality of "He is here" requires the addition of proper names: "George Bush is here, in London, on July 18, 1991." Yet this is still not sufficient. An ostensive phrase will also be required to provide an instance in which the cognitive phrase is true. "George Bush is here, in London, on July 18, 1991. Here he is." Still, it might not be the case that this George Bush is the same one inaugurated as President in Washington. Only the validation of a descriptive phrase will provide the warranty for various ostensions of the same referent. Thus, reality is established by the presence of a system of proper names that eliminate demonstratives, coupled with the validation of ostensive and descriptive phrases.[8] The referential system set up by proper names that are "given" by their original dubbings and remain fixed across phrase universes accounts for knowledge without appeal to experience or the subjective "I" of experience. A denotative phrase, then, positions the phrase universe as follows: The addressor in the position of knower, the addressee in the position of giving or refusing assent, and the referent as something that demands to be correctly identified by the statement referring to it.[9]

As I noted earlier, phrase regimes cannot be translated or deduced from each other. Although for Lyotard this is true of all phrase regimes, he is especially concerned with the inability to deduce a prescription from a description. Lyotard's peculiar way of arguing for this familiar point will be important in specifying the sense in which incommensurability reigns at the heart of language.

Notes

Introduction

1. It is important to note that there are two assumptions built into this acceptance of science as the paradigm of inquiry: (1) The success of science entails the accuracy of its representation of reality; and (2) an accurate representation is a sufficient guide to practical action. (1) is called into question by Richard Rorty, among others. See Rorty, "Method, Social Science, and Social Hope" in *Consequences of Pragmatism* (Minneapolis: University of Minnesota Press, 1982). (1) is only tangentially connected to the issues in this dissertation. It receives some limited discussion in Chapter One. (2) will be a central topic of discussion throughout.

2. These terms are notoriously difficult to define. A mention of paradigm cases will have to suffice. The closest thing to a postmodern manifesto is Jean-Francois Lyotard's *The Postmodern Condition: A Report on Knowledge*. The seminal work in what has come to be known as "deconstruction" is Jacques Derrida's *Of Grammatology*. Michel Foucault's work is typically associated with poststructuralism, as is Derrida's. For Foucault's version of poststructuralism, see *The Order of Things*. Rorty has claimed both the mantle of "pragmatism" in *Consequences of Pragmatism*, as well as postmodernism in "Postmodernist Bourgeois Liberalism."

3. This thesis has been attributed to Rorty by his critics. See especially Bernard Williams's review, "Auto-da-fe: Consequences of Pragmatism."

4. For further discussion of the claim that ethics is not sufficiently systematic to require a theory of ethics, see Chapter One.

5. The taxonomic difficulties are substantial because the term "antitheory," as I employ it here, will cut across enormous differences. Part of the purpose of Chapter One is to specify, in some detail, how an antitheory position differs

from simply a theory of a different sort. In the literature there is some prece-
dence for lumping disparate figures together under the antitheory rubric. The
introduction to an anthology by Simpson and Clarke entitled *Anti-Theory
and Moral Conservativism* is the best example, although continental sources
are not included.

6. Readers familiar with the work of Levinas may be surprised to find his work
   described as postmodern. Indeed, his roots are in the phenomenological
   tradition, although his position entails an overcoming of that tradition. In my
   judgment, he belongs in this discussion not only because his work has been
   appropriated by Lyotard, but because in broad outline his conception of ethics
   contributes substantially to a postmodern conception of ethics.

7. I suspect some readers will find the taxonomies in this book rather odd. I
   doubt that admirers of MacIntyre, Nussbaum, or Rorty would think of them as
   analytic philosophers. However, many of the supporting arguments in the
   antitheory literature have been made by philosophers such as Bernard
   Williams and John McDowell, who would surely count as analytic philosophers. Moreover, MacIntyre, Nussbaum, and Rorty are clearly writing in a
   tradition for readers trained in that tradition, although they are trying to
   extend it in ways that radically depart from its methodology. All taxonomies
   risk producing distortions, and one is always faced with making a choice
   about which distortion will do the least harm. In this case, I think it is important to emphasize the point that much of the impetus for the antitheory
   position is coming from thinkers schooled in the rigors of philosophical analysis. The title of the book preserves that point.

8. J. L. Mackie, *Ethics: Inventing Right and Wrong* (New York: Penguin Books,
   1977), p. 83.

9. I have in mind here much of virtue ethics, communitarian political thought,
   religious-based ethical views, and hermeneutics.

10. I encountered this term in Lovibond, *Realism and Imagination in Ethics*, p. 63,
    as a translation of Hegel's use of the word *"Sittlichkeit."* I have not used the
    Hegelian term because I do not want to saddle the position with the baggage
    of Hegel's idealism.

Chapter One

1. The most common criticism of the antitheory position is that a theoretical
   approach that utilizes empirical evidence and employs a nonfoundationalist
   strategy of justification can accommodate the antitheorist's objections. Part
   of my concern in this chapter is to show that certain elements in the antitheory position resist this accommodation. For the best example of this criticism
   see Robert B. Louden, *Morality and Moral Theory*, (New York: Oxford University Press, 1992).

2. I use the word "principle" to refer to any relatively fixed, predetermined policy for guiding action.

3. Bernard Williams, *Ethics and the Limits of Philosophy* (Cambridge: Harvard University Press, 1985), p. 135.

4. Williams, *Ethics and the Limits of Philosophy*, p. 151.

5. Williams, *Ethics and the Limits of Philosophy*, p. 110.

6. The issue of the limits of moral reflection is very much left open by Williams. He does not say enough about what might count as rationality in the context of moral judgments.

7. Richard Rorty, *Philosophical Papers*, vol. 1 (Cambridge: Cambridge University Press, 1991), p. 29.

8. Rorty, *Philosophical Papers*, 1:29.

9. Rorty, *Philosophical Papers*, 1:30. There are extraordinary difficulties in determining who this appeal to "our own group" includes and excludes. I discuss these difficulties in Chapter Five.

10. I don't want to suggest that Rorty and Williams are in agreement on how to characterize the status of objectivity as an ideal. While Williams will agree with Rorty that objectivity is an inappropriate guide for moral and political reflection, Williams will insist on its appropriateness for the pursuit of science and our understanding of human rationality generally. Rorty, on the other hand, will argue that the whole question of our contact with a mind-independent reality is misguided and will argue that intersubjective agreement rather than objectivity is the aim of inquiry. (See Rorty, *Philosophical Papers*, vol. 1, pp. 21–34).

11. As far as I know, John McDowell was the first to use the phrase "uncodifiability thesis," although McDowell attributes the substance of the view to Aristotle. See John McDowell, "Virtue and Reason," in *Monist*, 62, 1979.

12. For this distinction, see especially Rawls's, "The Independence of Moral Theory," *Proceedings and Addresses of the American Philosophical Association*, vol. 48, 1974–75, p. 8.

13. The referent of "we" here is troublesome. Rawls makes it clear that although he is concerned with the judgement of an individual, these considered judgements are widely shared and are reflections of what any reasonable man in modern liberal democracies would say. See John Rawls, *A Theory of Justice* (Cambridge: Harvard University Press, 1971), p. 50.

14. The initial status of these considered moral judgments is a subject of controversy in the literature on reflective equilibrium. Some theorists would be dissatisfied with my characterization, claiming that their epistemic priority requires something stronger, perhaps analogous to observation statements within a scientific theory. However, this would not be in accord with a non-foundationalist strategy of justification, because it suggests intuitionism. My characterization, on the other hand, would seem to be compatible with Rawls's most recent work which has taken a decidedly pragmatist turn. For a useful discussion of the difficulties with the analogy to observation statements see R. B. Brandt "The Science of Man and Wide Reflective Equilibrium" in *Ethics*, January 1990.

15. As it stands, this argument is directed against attempts to force indeterminate moral norms that hold only "for the most part" into precisely rendered discursive statements from which conclusions can be deduced. Because the relationship between principles and considered judgments in reflective equilibrium is not deductive, the objection raised by the uncodifiability thesis would perhaps not be to the point. However, as I show next, the reasons for thinking that morality is not a candidate for codification in a deductive paradigm will also make it a poor candidate for the sort of codification appropriate to reflective equilibrium.

16. By "explanation," McDowell means a "reason-giving" explanation, a description of the beliefs "in light of which we can see how acting in the way explained would have struck the agent as in some way rational." See McDowell, "Virtue and Reason," p. 342.

17. McDowell, "Virtue and Reason," p. 344.

18. Annette Baier, *Postures of the Mind* (Minneapolis: University of Minnesota Press, 1985), p. 217.

19. McDowell, "Virtue and Reason," p. 343.

20. This point is made by Hilary Putnam who also argues that the notion of an exception is conceptually dependent on the presumption in favor of the principle. See "Taking Rules Seriously—A Response to Martha Nussbaum, in *New Literary History*, vol. 15, no. 4, 1983, pp. 193–95.

21. Considered moral judgments can be, but need not be about specific cases. They can be judgments at any level of generality. See Rawls, "The Independence of Moral Theory," p. 8.

22. By extreme cases, I mean those cases in which the presence of certain properties invariably create exceptions. Severe schizophrenia invariably creates an exception to the respect for autonomy principle. With regard to the issue of exceptions, it will, therefore, be useful to distinguish two kinds of generalizations. Weak generalizations support exceptions representing competing morally relevant properties that sometimes create exceptions when present to a sufficient degree. Strong generalizations represent competing morally relevant properties that invariably create exceptions. Ignorance, for instance, is a property often represented by a weak generalization. When we look at cases in which ignorance creates an exception to respect for the capacity of others to make choices, we find very few regularities, and those that we discover are tied to specific situations. We accept the fact that ignorance about the effects of prescription drugs licenses the requirement that we obtain a prescription before purchase, thereby creating an exception to the principle of respect for rational autonomy. But ignorance of the law is not considered an excusing condition. Contracts signed under duress can sometimes be voided, but crimes committed under certain kinds of duress are punishable. What is important about these cases is that when exceptions fail to be action-guiding it is not necessarily because the principle of respect for autonomy is operating. Rather, other morally relevant properties compete for our attention. Crimes committed despite ignorance or duress are punishable at least in part because it would be next to impossible to enforce the law if they were not.

23. For an account of the inadequacies of narrow-reflective equilibrium see Daniels, "Wide Reflective Equilibrium and Theory Acceptance in Ethics," in *Journal of Philosophy*, vol. 76 (1979), p. 259.

24. See Daniels, "Wide Reflective Equilibrium and Theory Acceptance in Ethics," *Journal of Philosophy*, vol. 76, 1979. Also see Rawls, *A Theory of Justice*.

25. Daniels, *Theory Acceptance*, p. 258.

26. See Norman Daniels, "Reflective Equilibrium and Archimedean Points" in *Canadian Journal of Philosophy*, vol. X, no. 1, March 1980, p. 258.

27. Daniels, "Reflective Equilibrium and Archimedean Points," p. 87.

28. See Daniels, "Theory Acceptance," p. 259.

29. See Daniels, "Theory Acceptance," p. 262.

30. Annette Baier, *Postures of the Mind*, pp. 213–16.

31. Baier, *Postures*, p. 218.

32. Baier, *Postures*, p. 222.

33. Richard Rorty, *Contingency, Irony, and Solidarity* (Cambridge: Cambridge University Press, 1989), p. 40.

34. Richard Rorty, *The Consequences of Pragmatism* (Minneapolis: University of Minnesota Press, 1982), p. xxi.

35. Rorty, *Contingency*, p. 5.

36. Rorty, *Contingency*, p. 27.

37. Rorty, *Contingency*, p. 27.

38. Rorty, *Contingency*, p. 32.

39. Rorty, *Contingency*, p. 32.

40. Rorty, *Contingency*, p. 33.

41. Rorty, *Contingency*, p. 37.

42. Rorty, *Contingency*, p. 54.

43. This is a controversial point that receives more detailed discussion in connection with MacIntyre in Chapter Two and Rorty in Chapter Five.

44. Although similar themes emerge from the work of Baier and Rorty, Baier's account of the development of character and personality will not place such an emphasis on idiosyncratic unconscious strategies of adaptation. Following Hume, Baier seems to think that a more or less systematic account of how "moral goods can grow out of natural goods" can be given. See Baier, *Postures*, p. 222.

45. See Hilary Putnam, *Reason, Truth, and History* (Cambridge: Cambridge University Press, 1981), pp. 13–119.

46. See Davidson, "On the Very Idea of a Conceptual Scheme," *Proceedings and Addresses of the APA*, vol. 47, 1974.

47. For a discussion of this point see Bjorn Ramberg, *Donald Davidson's Philosophy of Language* (New York: Basil Blackwell, 1989), pp. 114–37.

48. Alasdair MacIntyre, "Relativism, Power, and Philosophy" in Baynes, Bohman, and McCarthy (eds.) *After Philosophy: End or Transformation* (Cambridge: MIT Press, 1987).

49. MacIntyre, *Relativism, Power, and Philosophy*, p. 405.

50. Most notably, Richard Bernstein holds this view. See *Beyond Objectivism and Relativism* (Philadelphia: University of Pennsylvania Press, 1983).

51. I will discuss both of these claims in Chapters Two, Three, and Four.

52. Ramberg, *Donald Davidson's Philosophy of Language*, pp. 129–30.

53. Ramberg rejects Davidson's implausible claim that knowledge of linguistic conventions does not help explain linguistic practices. For Ramberg, radical interpretation is not a model for all linguistic practice. Ramberg does agree with Davidson that knowing a language (in the sense of being able to employ its conventions) is neither a necessary nor sufficient prior condition for successful communication. See Ramberg, *Donald Davidson's Philosophy of Language*, pp. 98-113.

54. Ramberg, *Donald Davidson's Philosophy of Language*, p. 132.

55. Jean-Francois Lyotard, *The Differend* (Minneapolis: University of Minnesota Press, 1988), p. xii.

56. Lyotard, *The Differend*, p. 9.

57. Williams, *Ethics and the Limits of Philosophy*, p. 103.

58. See my Chapter Seven for a detailed account of this claim.

Chapter Two

1. A social practice, for MacIntyre, is any reasonably complex, cooperative activity in which part of the point of pursuing the activity is the realization of goods internal to it. Internal goods are those that can be described only by reference to the practice. For example, part of the point of engaging in artistic activity, athletic competition, or intellectual labor is the particular satisfactions unique to each practice. This is unlike wealth and fame, which may be desirable but can be achieved through many kinds of activities. See Alasdair MacIntyre, *After Virtue*, (Notre Dame: Notre Dame Press, 1984, 2nd edition), p. 178.

2. MacIntyre, *After Virtue*, p. 220.

3. MacIntyre, *After Virtue*, p. 220.

4. MacIntyre, *After Virtue*, p. 211.

5. Events within a narrative history need not all be related through causal connections. Actions, events, or other elements in the narrative are often significant, not because they lead to a particular outcome but because they fail to cause an expected outcome, or because they are simply interesting given how things turn out. For instance, isolationist sentiment in the United States probably did not causally contribute to Hitler's rise to power in the

Third Reich, but the absence of this particular form of resistance to Hitler is a significant part of the history of that period. Significance, therefore, is not identical to causal influence, although it may be dependent on the causal relationships in the narrative.

6. The circularity here is unavoidable. We attribute significance to, and arrive at descriptions of, events and actions based on our anticipation of ends. Yet the judgment regarding which ends to anticipate is dependent on descriptions of events and actions.

7. MacIntyre, *After Virtue*, p. 215.

8. See Louis Mink, "History and Fiction as Modes of Comprehension," *New Literary History*, vol. 1, 1970. Also see William Dray, "On the Nature and Role of Narrative in Historiography," in *History and Theory* vol. 8, no.1, 1971.

9. W. B. Gallie, *Philosophy and the Historical Understanding*, (New York: Shocken Books, 1964), p. 44.

10. MacIntyre, *After Virtue*, p. 211.

11. MacIntyre, *After Virtue*, pp. 218–19.

12. MacIntyre, *After Virtue*, p. 222.

13. MacIntyre, *After Virtue*, p. 219.

14. MacIntyre, *After Virtue*, p. 221.

15. Alasdair MacIntyre, *Whose Justice? Which Rationality?* (Notre Dame: University of Notre Dame Press, 1988), p. 378.

16. MacIntyre, *Whose Justice?*, p. 141.

17. MacIntyre, *Whose Justice?*, p. 133. This notion that part of the justification of a belief is the political authority that supports it is suggested often by MacIntyre; it seems not to matter that such political authority may be coercive. One of MacIntyre's chief complaints about modernism is its inability to unite conviction and rational justification. Unfortunately, this unity is a double-edged sword. While we might welcome conviction based on rational justification, the contrary is less inviting, although MacIntyre seems unconcerned with the implications. The notion that political authority and inquiry into the good life are intimately related runs the risk of effacing the distinction between rational persuasion and coercion. For the claim that part of the justification of a belief is the political authority that supports it, see MacIntyre, *Whose Justice?*, pgs. 153,166. For the suggestion that coercive political authority may be justified, see page 162.

18. MacIntyre, *Whose Justice?*, p. 362.

19. MacIntyre, *Whose Justice?*, p. 365.

20. MacIntyre, *Whose Justice?*, p. 365. Although in *Whose Justice?* MacIntyre does not state explicitly the requirement that the explanation be the "best explanation," he does so elsewhere, and he certainly requires this condition if the view of rational change of belief is to be plausible. See *After Virtue*, page 270, and "The Relationship of Philosophy to its Past," *Philosophy in History*, ed. R. Rorty, J.B. Schneewind, and Q. Skinner (New York: Cambridge University Press, 1984), p. 44.

21. Charles Taylor, "Rationality," in Hollis and Lukes's *Rationality and Relativism* (Cambridge: MIT Press, 1982), pp. 95–96.

22. David B. Wong, "Three Kinds of Incommensurability," *Relativism: Interpretation and Confrontation*, edited by Michael Krausz (Notre Dame: Notre Dame Press, 1989), p. 153.

23. See Arthur Danto, *Narration and Knowledge* (New York: Columbia University Press, 1985), ch. 8.

24. For instance, we might describe a particular person as taking a leave from his job, writing a book, or engaged in a romantic misadventure. Which of these is significant depends on the kind of story one wishes to tell, its thematic content, and ending. For this point, see Danto, page 168f.

25. MacIntyre, *Whose Justice?*, p. 374.

26. MacIntyre, *Whose Justice?*, p. 382.

27. MacIntyre, *Whose Justice?*, p. 368.

28. MacIntyre, *Whose Justice?*, p. 395.

29. MacIntyre, *Whose Justice?*, pp. 370–71.

30. I don't wish to preclude the possibility that dedicated admirers of alien traditions may succeed in "going native," becoming resocialized into that alternative belief system. However, this would not satisfy MacIntyre's constraint on rational change in belief, which requires the recognition of the superiority of the alien tradition from within the standards of one's own tradition. In this case, a judgment of superiority would be "whiggish"—wholly from within that successor standpoint's assumptions about what is significant and important.

Chapter Three

1. For a discussion of this dominant view and its limitations see Thomas Nagel, "Moral Luck," in his *Mortal Questions* (Cambridge: Cambridge University Press, 1979). Also see Bernard Williams, *Moral Luck: Philosophical Papers 1973–1980* (Cambridge: Cambridge University Press, 1981).

2. Martha Nussbaum, *The Fragility of Goodness: Luck and Ethics in Greek Tragedy and Philosophy* (Cambridge: Cambridge University Press, 1986), p. 4.

3. For a comprehensive discussion of noncommensurability, see Martha Nussbaum, *Love's Knowledge: Essays on Philosophy and Literature* (New York: Oxford University Press, 1990), pp. 106–124.

4. By "intrinsic" I mean desired for its own sake, and thus I intend to appeal to the standard distinction between an intrinsic good and an instrumental good. I am not referring to the distinction between things that have their value "in themselves" independently of context such as Kant's good will, and things that derive their value from some other source. For a discussion of this distinction, see Christine M. Korsgaard, "Two Distinctions In Goodness," *The Philosophical Review* vol. 92, no.2, April 1983.

5. Nussbaum's account of noncommensurability focuses especially on the absence of a common standard of measurement that would allow the ranking of various goods. Noncommensurability is an instance of the more general incommensurability thesis described in Chapter One.

6. Nussbaum, *Fragility*, p. 50.

7. This is an important point, for if Agamemnon is not a person of good character, the tragedy of his circumstances is diminished. I have some doubts about this positive judgment of Agamemnon's character. Not only is he a rather unsavory character in much of Greek literature, I'm not convinced of his sincerity in the play in question. However, for the sake of argument, it is worth granting Nussbaum this point.

8. Nussbaum, *Fragility*, p. 34.

9. Martha Nussbaum, *Love's Knowledge: Essays on Philosophy and Literature* (New York: Oxford University Press, 1990), p. 60.

10. Nussbaum, *Love's Knowledge*, p. 148.

11. Nussbaum, *Love's Knowledge*, p. 154.

12. For this point, see Richard Wollheim, "Flawed Crystals: James's *The Golden Bowl* and the Plausibility of Literature as Moral Philosophy" in *New Literary History*, vol. 15, Autumn 1983.

13. Mary Ann Caws, "Moral-Reading, or Self-Containment with a Flaw," *New Literary History* vol. 15, no. 1: p. 211.

14. Nussbaum, *Love's Knowledge*, p. 136.

15. This conclusion presupposes that Agamemnon is sincere about his commitment to piety. As I noted earlier, I have some doubts about this. However, even if his commitment is to personal honor or the glory of Greece, part of what it means to value something is silencing competing claims.

16. I am not competent or widely read enough to judge whether this is a universal theme in tragic literature. I do think it is a common and persistent theme. Certainly in Sophocles's *Antigone*, both Antigone and Creon are committed to moral ideals that are the source of their moral failure—I have in mind Creon's commitment to civic duty, and Antigone's reverence for the honored dead. One could argue that Hamlet's moral indignation and sense of justice is the direct cause of the bloodbath that ensues upon his return to Denmark. Finally, even James's (and Nussbaum's) principal virtue—perceptiveness— has its limitations, for in James's *The Ambassadors*, Strether shows himself to be incapable of love and commitment precisely because he is so perceptive.

17. See Nussbaum, *Love's Knowledge*, p. 52, for a brief discussion of the tension between erotic love and a moral point of view.

18. There is a tendency to confuse two senses of "qualitative distinctness." One sense refers to the recognition that a thing has properties not shared with something else. The other involves recognition of a difference in quality or value. Nussbaum's account of perceptiveness is inherently normative in that

moral perception recognizes a difference in value. The difficulty with theoretical reduction is that something of value, which the virtue of perceptiveness is capable of preserving, is lost.

19. Of course, I do not mean "objectively" higher. I am arguing that part of what it means to hold such a belief is that one believes in its superiority to competing beliefs or judgments.

20. Judgments of qualitative contrast are discussed by Charles Taylor, "The Diversity of Goods," in Sen and Williams (eds.) *Utilitarianism and Beyond* (Cambridge: Cambridge University Press, 1982). For a more recent discussion, see Charles Taylor, *Sources of the Self: The Making of the Modern Identity* (Cambridge: Harvard University Press, 1989).

21. Taylor, *Diversity*, p. 136.

22. Nussbaum, *Love's Knowledge*, p. 52.

Chapter Four

1. Martha Nussbaum, *Love's Knowledge: Essays on Philosophy and Literature* (New York: Oxford University Press, 1990), p. 28.

2. Nussbaum, *Love's Knowledge*, p. 26.

3. Nussbaum, *Love's Knowledge*, p. 173.

4. For a comprehensive account and defense of internal realism, see Hilary Putnam, *Reason, Truth, and History* (Cambridge: Cambridge University Press, 1981).

5. Nussbaum, *Fragility*, p. 312.

6. Nussbaum, *Love's Knowledge*, p. 181.

7. Nussbaum, *Love's Knowledge*, p. 174.

8. Nussbaum, *Love's Knowledge*, pp. 66–75.

9. Martha Nussbaum, "Non-Relative Virtues: An Aristotelian Approach" in French, Uehling, Wettstein (eds.) *Midwest Studies in Philosophy* 13 (Notre Dame: University of Notre Dame Press, 1988), p. 33.

10. Nussbaum, *Virtues*, p. 37.

11. Nussbaum, *Virtues*, p. 43.

12. Nussbaum, *Virtues*, p. 46.

Chapter Five

1. Richard Rorty, *Contingency, Irony, and Solidarity* (Cambridge: Cambridge University Press, 1989), p. 73.

2. Rorty, *Contingency*, p. 77.

3. This obviously does not refer to all inquiry but only that involving significant revisions of belief. Rorty does not deny there is such a thing as normal discourse in which the meaning and reference of theoretical terms are relatively stable.

4. Rorty, *Contingency*, p. 80.

5. Rorty, *Contingency*, p. 94.

6. Rorty, *Contingency*, p. 190.

7. There are differences between the contrast judgments discussed in Chapter Three and Rorty's account of these contrastive we-intentions, especially regarding the notion of intrinsic value. Rorty will not explain the obstacles to "trading-off" one good for another in terms of the intrinsic value of the goods in question, but rather in terms of the role they play in one's "final vocabulary."

8. For versions of this criticism, of particular interest is "Solidarity or Singularity? Richard Rorty between Romanticism and Technocracy," in Nancy Fraser, *Unruly Practices* (Minneapolis: University of Minnesota Press, 1989). Also see "Private Irony and Public Decency: Richard Rorty's New Pragmatism," Thomas McCarthy in *Critical Inquiry* vol. 16, Winter 1990. Subsequent issues of this journal contain Rorty's response and an additional reply by McCarthy.

9. For a discussion see Chapter One, pp. 21–28.

10. See especially Walter Benjamin, "The Work of Art in the Era of Mechanical Reproduction," in *Illuminations*, trans. Harry Zohn (New York: Harcourt, Brace, and World, 1968). For a historical account of this thesis, see Bill Kinser and Neil Kleinman, *The Dream That Was No More a Dream: A Search for Aesthetic Reality in Germany, 1890–1945* (New York: Harper and Row, 1969).

11. Rorty, *Contingency*, p. 89.

12. Rorty, *Contingency*, p. 99.

13. Rorty, *Contingency*, p. 60.

14. For a discussion of this point, see Chapter Two.

15. I have in mind the section "On Free Death" in Friedrich Nietzsche, *Thus Spoke Zarathustra*.

16. There are versions of expressivism involving substantial commitments to an objective account of human capacities. See Sabina Lovibond, *Realism and Imagination in Ethics* (Minneapolis: University of Minnesota Press, 1983). Also see Marx and Engels, *The German Ideology*, ed. C. J. Arthur (New York: International Publishers, 1970), p. 50–51; and Charles Taylor, *Hegel* (Cambridge: Cambridge University Press, 1975), p. 16.

17. Rorty, *Contingency*, p. 87.

18. Rorty, *Contingency*, p. 12.

19. Rorty, *Contingency*, p. 55.

20. Rorty, *Contingency*, p. 196.

21. Rorty, *Contingency*, p. 60.

22. Richard Rorty, "Pragmatism and Feminism" in *Michigan Quarterly Review*, Spring 1991.

23. Rorty, "Feminism and Pragmatism," p. 236.

24. Rorty, "Feminism and Pragmatism," p. 247.

25. Nancy Fraser, "From Irony to Prophecy to Politics: A Response to Richard Rorty" in *Michigan Quarterly Review,* Spring 1991, p. 266.

26. Rorty, *Contingency,* p. 17.

27. Rorty, *Contingency,* p. 17.

28. Rorty, *Contingency,* p. 19.

29. See the study entitled "Ethnic Images," Tom W. Smith, National Opinion Research Center, University of Chicago, December 1990. This study measures the persistence of negative ethnic stereotypes despite advances in integration and racial equality.

30. Rorty, *Contingency,* pp. 181–83.

31. Rorty, *Papers* 2: 184.

32. Rorty, *Contingency,* p. 32.

33. Rorty, *Contingency,* p. 37.

34. Judith Shklar, "Giving Justice its Due," *Yale Law Journal,* vol. 98, April 1989, p. 1135.

35. *Contingency,* p. 74

36. Rorty, "Pragmatism and Feminism," pp. 233–34.

37. Commentators such as Nancy Fraser miss this dimension of Rorty.

38. Solidarity understood in terms of contrastive we-intentions also embroils Rorty in a dilemma on this question of accounting for transcendence. He must assert the initial intelligibility of "our" moral practices because the notion of solidarity and ethnocentrism demand it. Happily, the aspiration to transcend is central to "our" moral practice, thereby obviating the need to account for it. Yet Rorty believes the imposition of inappropriate ideals on others is a source of cruelty. The difficulty is a very fine line between "extending the reference of we" and imposing these ideals on others. This is especially true if "our" moral practice requires the public/private distinction—this suggests others should be restricted from allowing their deepest beliefs to be expressed in their public lives.

39. Rorty, *Contingency,* p. 198.

Chapter Six

1. Emmanuel Levinas, in *The Provocation of Levinas: Rethinking the Other*, eds Bernasconi and Wood (New York: Routledge, 1988), p. 156.

2. Levinas, "Substitution," in *The Levinas Reader*, ed. Sean Hand (Cambridge: Basil Blackwell, 1989), p. 91.

3. Martin Heidegger, *Being and Time* (New York: Harper and Row, 1962), p. 32.

4. Heidegger, *Being and Time*, p. 68.

5. Emmanuel Levinas, *Totality and Infinity* (Pittsburgh: Duquesne University, 1969), p. 304.

6. Levinas, *Time and the Other* (Pittsburgh: Duquesne University Press, 1987), p. 86.

7. Levinas, *Totality*, p. 266.

8. This is an important point for the connection between time and ethics, for it means the good need not be defined by the present. The peculiar character of "ought" statements is that they refer to a state of affairs not yet present. It is the fecundity of time, its capacity for infinite renewal, that enables us to make sense of ethics as a project, and that in part explains the claim the possibility of a better world has on us. Morality is what it is, in part, because fecundity and *eros* give to time the structure of infinity.

9. Levinas, *Time and the Other*, p. 74.

10. Levinas's thesis is not simply concerned with the fallibility of memory nor that any retention will leave out features of the context in which the remembered event was originally experienced. He argues that there is an important dimension of time that is not a function of history or memory at all. This questions Heidegger's claim that intelligibility is dependent on our always being caught up in a fundamental understanding of what we are trying to understand. In being bound up in a past prior to taking hold of that past explicitly, we have already suffered a loss of understanding. The effects of the past can never be fully recuperated or reiterated, thus calling into question the legitimacy of any attempt to thematize our preunderstanding.

11. Emmanuel Levinas, "Ethics as First Philosophy," in *The Levinas Reader*, ed. Sean Hand, (Cambridge: Basil Blackwell, 1989), pp. 80–81.

12. By a trace, Levinas seems to mean evidence of an event, but also something very subtle such as a suggestion, hint, or intimation. Something is deposited in experience but not clearly denotated.

13. Levinas, *Reader*, pp. 82–83.

14. I return to this notion of obligation and its relationship to diachronic time in the following chapter.

15. Levinas, *Reader*, p. 92.

16. Levinas, *Reader*, p. 83.

17. Levinas, *Totality and Infinity*, p. 33.

18. Levinas, *Totality and Infinity*, pp. 33–34.

19. Levinas, *Reader*, p. 117.

20. Levinas, *Reader*, p. 82.

21. Levinas, *Reader*, p. 84.

22. Levinas, in Bernasconi and Wood, *Provocation*, p. 175.

23. Levinas, in Bernasconi and Wood, *Provocation*, p. 176.

24. Levinas, in Bernasconi and Wood, *Provocation*, p. 169.

25. Levinas, *Totality and Infinity*, p. 35.

26. Steven Smith, *The Argument to the Other: Reason Beyond Reason in the Thought of Karl Barth and Emmanuel Levinas* (Chico: Scholars Press, 1983), p. 190.

Chapter Seven

1. By "self-representation" I mean the formation of a social identity, not a fully individuated autonomous self.

2. Jean-Francois Lyotard, *The Postmodern Condition: A Report on Knowledge* (Minneapolis: University of Minnesota Press, 1984).

3. Lyotard, *Condition*, p. xxiii.

4. Lyotard, *Condition*, p. xxiv.

5. Lyotard, *Condition*, p. 14.

6. I have provided an appendix at the end of this chapter that attempts to explain in more detail Lyotard's conception of pragmatics. Readers unfamiliar with Lyotard's conception of language might benefit from reading it. See p. 195.

7. Lyotard sometimes expresses reservations about this term "language game," arguing that it presupposes too much intentionality on the part of language users. It is, nevertheless, a convenient way of referring to Lyotard's position, and I will continue to employ it here. See Jean-Francois Lyotard, *The Differend: Phrases in Dispute* (Minneapolis: University of Minnesota Press, 1988), p. 188.

8. Lyotard, *The Differend*, p. 130.

9. Lyotard, *The Differend*, p. xi.

10. The purpose (or stakes) of the descriptive language game is to establish the reality of something. Science and history are genres made up primarily of descriptive phrase regimes.

11. For Kant, "transcendental illusion" refers to the tendency of reason to assign reality to concepts beyond the limits of possible experience as defined by time and space. For example, notions such as world, soul, freedom, and God are not phenomena, although reason treats them as such. See *The Critique of Pure Reason*, trans. Norman Kemp Smith (New York: St. Martin's Press, 1965), p. 297ff.

12. Lyotard, *The Differend*, p. 108.

13. Lyotard, Jean-Francois, "Levinas' Logic," in *The Lyotard Reader*, ed. Andrew Benjamin, (Cambridge: Basil Blackwell, 1989).

14. Lyotard, "Levinas' Logic," p. 283.

15. Lyotard, "Levinas' Logic," p. 283.

16. Lyotard, "Levinas' Logic," p. 286.

17. Lyotard, "Levinas' Logic," p. 287.

18. Lyotard's objections to the priority of descriptions are more extensive than this. He identifies the loss of the specificity of prescription with (at least) lin-

guistic terrorism and perhaps political terrorism by means of the totalization of language. This is taken up next.

19. I will take up next the question of whether this account of language games attempts to do what it claims on its own grounds cannot be done—generate a conception of justice. See "The Postmodern Sublime," upcoming.

20. In fact, one of the deep questions about Lyotard's work is the extent to which ethics is a genre. It is not obvious that there is a rule-governed discourse at all here except as a prohibition against its assimilation to description.

21. Lyotard, *The Differend*, p. 117.

22. Lyotard, *The Differend*, p. 109.

23. Lyotard, *The Differend*, p. 13.

24. Lyotard, *The Differend*, p. 143.

25. Lyotard, *The Differend*, p. 143.

26. Lyotard, *The Differend*, p. 144.

27. Lyotard, *The Differend*, p. 98.

28. Lyotard, *The Differend*, p. 97.

29. Lyotard, *The Differend*, p. 144.

30. Lyotard, *The Differend*, p. 155.

31. For a detailed account of how this form of narrative works, see the discussion of MacIntyre in Chapter Two.

32. Lyotard, *The Differend*, p. 151.

33. The Cashinahua are Indians of the upper Amazon. Lyotard's understanding of their myths is drawn from D'Ans, Marcel, *Dit des vrais hommes* (Paris: Editions 1018, 1978).

34. Lyotard, *The Differend*, p. 150.

35. Lyotard, *The Differend*, p. 147.

36. Lyotard, *The Differend*, p. 157. The contrast between these two narrative types maps rather neatly onto the dilemma contemporary society confronts with respect to multiculturalism. Either deny the particularity of cultures in the name of universalist claims, or assert the importance of particularity and risk the fragmentation of community. Each option yields its own form of injustice.

37. Lyotard, *The Differend*, p. 5.

38. There are differences between contrast judgments and differends. In the case of contrast judgments, moral blindness is the result of judgments of quality that dialectically produce an "other." The intelligibility of the judgment of quality is, in part, dependent on this "other." In Lyotard's case, differends are not dialectically produced but result from the contingent play of language games.

39. This is a version of Samuel Weber's "Great Prescriber" objection, which is understood as the principle objection to Lyotard's work. If justice is a matter of preserving the integrity of language games, by what authority are these language games deserving of such protection? See Sam Weber, "Afterward:

Literature—Just Making it," in Jean-Francois Lyotard, *Just Gaming* (Minneapolis: University of Minnesota Press, 1985).

40. Lyotard, *The Differend*, p. 179.

41. It should be clear from this that Lyotard's objections to grand synthesizing conceptions of history are not directed only at Hegel and Marx, but at any attempt to explain the contingency and complexity of history by appeal to general concepts. Although Lyotard clearly rejects dialectical necessity, there is more at stake.

42. In Lyotard's terminology, notions lack referents that can figure in the network of ostensive phrases required for the establishment of reality, and thus fail to satisfy the conditions genuine cognitive statements must satisfy. See the appendix for a more detailed account of the cognitive phrase regime.

43. Lyotard, *The Differend*, p. 131.

44. Lyotard argues that freedom cannot be deduced from the moral law, as in Kant's second critique, without falling victim to the transcendental illusion. He claims Kant recognized this in his later work. See Lyotard, *The Differend*, p. 123.

45. The Idea of freedom is, in Lyotard's reading of Kant, a regulative ideal that also purchases its intelligibility from laws governing nature. It reverses the direction of causality because it is an unconditioned cause (i.e. an agent's moral actions issue undetermined from the will of the agent). Nevertheless, it is a causal relationship analogous to the laws of nature that govern fully conditioned causal relationships. See Lyotard, *The Differend*, pp. 118–27.

46. Kant does not intend this notion of history as the recognition of a sign of moral progress to supplant ordinary historical accounts. See "Idea for a Universal History with a Cosmopolitan Intent" in Immanuel Kant, *Perpetual Peace and Other Essays*, trans. Ted Humphrey (Indianapolis: Hackett, 1983), p. 39.

47. Kant, *The Critique of Judgment*, pp. 114–15.

48. This is, of course, the basis for Kant's claim that aesthetic judgments regarding the pleasure one receives from experiencing the beauty of nature are universal and disinterested. See Immanuel Kant, *The Critique of Judgment*, trans. Werner S. Pluhar (Indianapolis: Hackett, 1987), pp. 53–56.

49. Lyotard, *Condition*, p. 81.

50. Lyotard is not conceptualizing postmodernism as a period in history that occurs after the modern period. Although the prefix "post" suggests otherwise, Lyotard considers postmodernism an aspect of modernism, as his writings on art make clear. Modernist avant-garde art, in Lyotard's view, continually questions the basis of art and the notion of what an aesthetic object is, thus employing the kind of judgment Lyotard thinks of as postmodern. See Lyotard, *Condition*, p. 79.

51. Jean-Francois Lyotard, "Judiciousness in Dispute or Kant after Marx," in Andrew Benjamin, *Lyotard Reader*, p. 351.

52. Lyotard, *The Differend*, p. 131.

53. This attempt to place Levinas's work at the heart of postmodernism can be accomplished without endorsing his claim that the ethical relation provides the transcendental conditions for self-identity. See Chapter Six.

54. Emmanuel Levinas, "Useless Suffering," in *The Provocation of Levinas: Rethinking the Other*, ed. Bernasconi and Wood (New York: Routledge, 1988), p. 156.

55. Levinas, *Time and the Other* (Pittsburgh: Duquesne University Press, 1987), p. 69.

56. Levinas, *Time and the Other*, p. 69.

57. Levinas's conception of death is a marked departure from that of Heidegger. In contrast to Heidegger's understanding of death as uniquely one's own, as the possibility for *Dasein* that conditions all other possibilities, Levinas argues that death cannot be one's own at all. "It is not just that there exist ventures impossible for the subject, that its powers are in some way finite. . . . What is important about the approach of death is that at a certain moment we are no longer *able to be able*. . . . This end of mastery indicates that we have assumed existing in such a way that an *event* can happen to us that we no longer assume. . . . This approach of death indicates that we are in relation with something that is absolutely other. . . . My solitude is thus not confirmed by death but broken by it." Levinas, *Time and the Other*, p. 74.

58. Primo Levi, *The Drowned and the Saved* (New York: Summit Books, 1988), pp. 83–84.

59. See Jean-Francois Lyotard, *Just Gaming* (Minneapolis: University of Minnesota Press, 1985), p. 9.

Appendix

1. Jean-Francois Lyotard, *The Differend: Phrases in Dispute* (Minneapolis: University of Minnesota Press, 1988).

2. Lyotard, *The Differend*, p. 11.

3. Lyotard, *The Differend*, p. 140.

4. See Lyotard, *The Differend*, p. xii. Lyotard does not say what he means by a rule, but I see no reason why it cannot be assimilated to Wittgenstein's notion, perhaps best described as a pattern of behavior.

5. Lyotard, *The Differend*, p. xii.

6. Lyotard, *The Differend*, p. 136.

7. Lyotard, *The Differend*, p. 40.

8. This, of course, does not guarantee the reality of the referent. There is no certainty with respect to reality.

9. Jean-Francois Lyotard, *The Postmodern Condition: A Report on Knowledge* (Minneapolis: University of Minnesota Press, 1984), p. 9.

Bibliography

Baier, Annette. *Postures of the Mind*. Minneapolis: University of Minnesota Press, 1985.

Benjamin, Walter. "The Work of Art in the Era of Mechanical Reproduction." In *Illumininations*. Trans. Harry Zohn. New York, 1968.

Bernstein, Richard. *Beyond Objectivism and Relativism*. Philadelphia: University of Pennsylvania Press, 1983.

Brandt, R.B. "The Science of Man and Wide Reflective Equilibrium." *Ethics*. January 1990.

Caws, Mary Ann. "Moral-Reading, or Self-Containment with a Flaw." *New Literary History*. vol. 15, no. 1.

Clarke, Stanley G., and Evan Simpson, (eds.). *Anti-Theory in Ethics and Moral Conservativism*. Albany: State University of New York Press, 1989.

Daniels, Norman. "Wide Reflective Equilibrium and Theory Acceptance in Ethics." *Journal of Philosophy*. vol. 76, 1979.

——. "Reflective Equilibrium and Archimedean Points." *Canadian Journal of Philosophy*. vol. 10, no. 1, March 1980.

D'Ans, Marcel. *Dit des vrais hommes*. Paris: Editions 1018, 1978.

Danto, Arthur. *Narration and Knowledge*. New York: Columbia University Press, 1985.

Davidson, Donald. "On the Very Idea of a Conceptual Scheme." *Proceedings and Addresses of the APA*. vol. 47, 1974.

Derrida, Jacques. *Of Grammatology*. Trans. Gayatri Spivak. Baltimore: Johns Hopkins University Press, 1976.

Dray, William. "On the Nature and Role of Narrative in Historiography." *History and Theory*. vol. 8, no. 1, 1971.

Foucault, Michel. *The Order of Things*. New York: Vintage Books, 1973.

Fraser, Nancy. *Unruly Practices*. Minneapolis: University of Minnesota Press, 1989.

———. "From Irony to Prophecy to Politics: A Response to Richard Rorty." *Michigan Quarterly Review*. Spring 1991, p. 266.

Gallie, W.B. *Philosophy and the Historical Understanding*. New York: Shocken Books, 1964.

Kant, Immanuel. *The Critique of Pure Reason*. Trans. Norman Kemp Smith. New York: St. Martin's Press, 1965.

———. *Perpetual Peace and Other Essays*. Trans. Ted Humphrey. Indianapolis: Hackett, 1983.

———. *The Critique of Judgment*. Trans. Werner S. Pluhar. Indianapolis: Hackett, 1987.

Kinser, Bill and Neil Kleinman, *The Dream That Was No More a Dream: A Search for Aesthetic Reality in Germany, 1890-1945*. New York, 1969.

Korsgaard, Christine M. "Two Distinctions In Goodness." *The Philosophical Review*. vol. 92, no. 2, April 1983.

Levi, Primo. *The Drowned and the Saved*. New York: Summit Books, 1988.

Levinas, Emmanuel. *The Levinas Reader*. Ed. Sean Hand. Cambridge: Basil Blackwell, 1989.

———. "Useless Suffering." In *The Provocation of Levinas: Rethinking the Other*. Edited by Bernasconi and Wood. New York: Routledge, 1988.

———. *Otherwise Than Being or Beyond Essence*. Trans. Alphonso Lingis. The Hague: Martinus Nijhoff, 1981.

———. *Time and the Other*. Pittsburgh: Duquesne University Press, 1987.

Louden, Robert B. *Morality and Moral Theory*. New York: Oxford University Press, 1992

Lovibond, Sabina. *Realism and Imagination in Ethics*. Minneapolis: University of Minnesota Press, 1983.

Lyotard, Jean-Francois. *The Postmodern Condition: A Report on Knowledge*. Minneapolis: University of Minnesota Press, 1984.

———. *The Differend*. Minneapolis: University of Minnesota Press, 1988.

———. *The Lyotard Reader*. Ed. Benjamin, Andrew. Cambridge: Basil Blackwell, 1989.

———. *Just Gaming*. Minneapolis: University of Minnesota Press, 1985.

MacIntyre, Alasdair. "Relativism, Power, and Philosophy." In *After Philosophy: End or Transformation*. Edited by Baynes, Bohman, and McCarthy. Cambridge: MIT Press, 1987.

——. *After Virtue.* 2nd ed. Notre Dame: Notre Dame Press, 1984.

——. *Whose Justice? Which Rationality?* Notre Dame: University of Notre Dame Press, 1988.

——. "The Relationship of Philosophy to its Past." In *Philosophy in History.* Edited by R. Rorty, J. B. Schneewind, and Q. Skinner. New York: Cambridge University Press, 1984.

Marx, Karl and Friedrich Engels. *The German Ideology.* Ed. by C. J. Arthur. New York: International Publishers, 1970.

McCarthy, Thomas. "Private Irony and Public Decency: Richard Rorty's New Pragmatism." *Critical Inquiry.* vol. 16, Winter 1990.

McDowell, John. "Virtue and Reason." *Monist.* vol. 62, 1979.

Mink, Louis. "History and Fiction as Modes of Comprehension." *New Literary History.* vol. 1, 1970.

Nagel, Thomas. "Moral Luck." In his *Mortal Questions.* Cambridge: Cambridge University Press, 1979.

Nussbaum, Martha. *The Fragility of Goodness: Luck and Ethics in Greek Tragedy and Philosophy.* Cambridge: Cambridge University Press, 1986.

——. *Love's Knowledge: Essays on Philosophy and Literature.* New York: Oxford University Press, 1990.

——. "Non-Relative Virtues: An Aristotelian Approach," *Midwest Studies in Philosophy.* 8. Edited by French, Uehling, Wettstein. Notre Dame: University of Notre Dame Press, 1988.

Putnam, Hilary. "Taking Rules Seriously: A Response to Martha Nussbaum." *New Literary History.* vol. 15, no. 4, 1983.

——. *Reason, Truth, and History.* Cambridge: Cambridge University Press, 1981.

Ramberg, Bjorn. *Donald Davidson's Philosophy of Language.* New York: Basil Blackwell, 1989.

Rawls, John. "Justice as Fairness: Political not Metaphysical." *Philosophy and Public Affairs.* vol. 14, no. 3, 1985.

——. "The Independence of Moral Theory." *Proceedings and Addresses of the American Philosophical Association.* vol. 48, 1974–75.

——. *A Theory of Justice.* Cambridge: Harvard University Press, 1971.

Rorty, Richard. *Contingency, Irony, and Solidarity.* Cambridge: Cambridge University Press, 1989.

——. "Method, Social Science, and Social Hope." *Consequences of Pragmatism.* Minneapolis: University of Minnesota Press, 1982.

——. *Objectivity, Relativism, and Truth: Philosophical Papers* 1. Cambridge: Cambridge University Press, 1991.

——. *Essays on Heidegger and Others: Philosophical Papers* 2. Cambridge: Cambridge University Press, 1991.

——. "Thugs and Theorists: A Reply to Bernstein." *Political Theory*. vol. 15, no. 4, November 1987.

——. "Pragmatism and Feminism." *Michigan Quarterly Review*. Spring 1991.

Shklar, Judith. "Giving Justice its Due." *Yale Law Journal*. vol. 98, April 1989.

Smith, Steven. *The Argument to the Other: Reason Beyond Reason in the Thought of Karl Barth and Emmanuel Levinas*. Chico: Scholars Press, 1983.

Smith, Tom W. "Ethnic Images." National Opinion Research Center, University of Chicago, December 1990.

Taylor, Charles. "Rationality." In Hollis and Lukes, *Rationality and Relativism*. Cambridge: MIT Press, 1982.

——. "The Diversity of Goods." *Utilitarianism and Beyond*. Edited by Sen and Williams. Cambridge: Cambridge University Press, 1982.

——. *Hegel*. Cambridge: Cambridge University Press, 1975.

White, Stephen. *Political Theory and Postmodernism*. New York: Cambridge University Press, 1991.

Williams, Bernard. *Ethics and the Limits of Philosophy*. Cambridge: Harvard University Press, 1985.

——. *Moral Luck: Philosophical Papers 1973-1980*. Cambridge: Cambridge University Press, 1981.

——. "Auto-da-fe: Consequences of Pragmatism." *Reading Rorty*. Edited by Alan Malachowski. Oxford: Basil Blackwell, 1990.

Wollheim, Richard. "Flawed Crystals: James' *The Golden Bowl* and the Plausibility of Literature as Moral Philosophy." *New Literary History*. vol. XV, Autumn, 1983.

Wong, David. "Three Kinds of Incommensurability." *Relativism: Interpretation and Confrontation*. Edited by Michael Krausz. Notre Dame: University of Notre Dame Press, 1989.

Index